IN A
HEARTBEAT....

Brian Zelmer

ISBN 978-1-66789-254-2
eBook ISBN 978-1-66789-255-9

TABLE OF CONTENTS

ABOUT THE AUTHOR

Brian Zelmer was born in Everett, Washington, on March 20, 1958. He has been married to his wonderful and beautiful wife, Barb, for 43 years. He has four wonderful kids, Nichole (Jason), Stephen (Jenna), Kyle (Kacie), and Jennifer (Jacob). He has two wonderful grandsons, Garren and Edison. Brian was an EMT, firefighter/paramedic and captain for 35 years. After retirement, Barb and Brian became franchisees with Jersey Mike's Subs for eight years. After living in the State of Washington for 60 years, Barb and Brian decided to take their webbed feet and moved to Arizona to enjoy the warm, sunny weather. With the writing of this book, Brian has scratched another goal off his "bucket list." Brian has only two goals left: scale Mount Everest and become a Chippendales dancer.

DEDICATION

This book is dedicated to my wife, Barb, for always being there and pointing me in the right direction.

To my kids, Nichole, Stephen, Kyle, and Jennifer for being the lights of my life and putting up with my absences from your important events and understanding that what I did was always for you.

To my "baddest boys," grandsons Garren and Edison: You will never know how much I love and miss you. Stay on the path that you're on. You'll be great.

To the Linnell and Wetstein families: Thank you for always being there for me. You are an inspiration.

To all my fellow firefighters: Thank you for getting me home safe after every shift.

To the dispatchers, doctors, nurses, ER techs, and police: You are all teeth in the cog of this crazy machine. Without any one of you, the machine doesn't run.

INTRODUCTION

This is my first time writing a book. I am not a literary person by any means so please bear with me. If you're reading this, I want to wholeheartedly thank you for taking the time and spending your hard-earned money to take a journey with me through my life as a first responder. I have read several books during my 35+ years about my occupation. These books have been well written and have shone a light on our profession, but I have not read the incidents that I have experienced in any of these books so I thought I would share them with you.

Hopefully, this book will inspire at least one person to gain interest and pursue their passion to enter this rewarding field. Unfortunately, unlike the "good old days," numbers are dwindling, and departments are having difficulty finding volunteers and members to fill vacancies in paid departments. Some say it's because of COVID; I think it's just a new generation that is not community-driven or would rather do high-tech. Who knows?

There are millions of fire/rescue, EMS, nurses, doctors, and law enforcement professionals (although the lowest amount since 1991) who put their lives on the line every day. I know in the back of their minds they have all thought, "I should write a book" about all the chaotic, bizarre, tragic, and at times, heartwarming events that have impacted their lives. Just like me, it was probably always "Yeah, maybe someday I'll do it," but for some reason they haven't followed through. Perhaps they (like me) decided that no one would be interested in their story, or perhaps they want to leave those memories deep in the vault of forgetfulness and not dig them up again. I procrastinated on this adventure for the past 20 years. It was only until recently when I moved to Arizona and, while unpacking, found all these boxes full of memories and memorabilia (from the Vault of Forgetfulness) that inspired me to finally "do it." Plus, you can only work so much on your tan and golf game in Arizona. Tan is good; golf is bad.

I worked in very rural, rural, suburban, and urban settings. Some responders may have only experienced one or two of these settings so they may not have been exposed to the different types of incidents that can occur. In the very rural areas, people have the "old west mentality" of rub some dirt on it and get back to work. I recall an incident where a farmer got his arm detached from his body when it got caught in an auger attached to a tractor. He extracted the bloody extremity from the auger and walked a quarter mile to his house (his wife then drove him to the hospital). On the other hand, in an urban setting you can get a different definition of emergency: I have a build-up of earwax, and I can't hear. (I responded to that.)

A fair warning: My descriptions, profanity, quotes, graphic detail, etc., will be nothing new to first responders but the layperson may find what they read to be rather offensive, unbelievable, or plain disgusting. The environment that we work in is neither rated "G" nor utopian. There are a lot of ugly, tragic events in our profession that we see 24/7/365 that ordinary citizens don't even know exist. Every story I'm about to tell is true. For the most part, the names mentioned are real people. Some names have been changed to protect the innocent (as well as the guilty). I tried to keep this story in chronological order, but sometimes events may have gotten in a little earlier (or later) than they occurred. Sometimes events tie in with others. I have included a glossary of words, terms, and quotes at the back of the book to help you navigate our lingo.

Finally, I would like to give a shout-out to all the great first responders, law enforcement, and fire departments out there like New York, Boston, Seattle, Los Angeles City, Los Angeles County, Washington D.C., Miami/Dade, and the smaller ones in the USA. Lastly, I want to give a thank you and "job well done" to all the nurses, doctors, and dispatchers who are the backbone of what we do. Without you, our job means nothing.

EARLY YEARS

When I was five (back in the early 60s), I wanted to be a fireman (today termed firefighter). When I was eight, I wanted to be an Everett fireman. When "Emergency" aired in the early 70s, I wanted to be a fireman/paramedic. This ambition was clinched when I read the book *Report From Engine Company 82* (my all-time favorite book). The book was written by the great author Dennis Smith, a New York fireman who chronicled his life and career in the New York Fire Department. Sadly, Mr. Smith recently passed away.

I was like most other kids in my early years, building forts, playing with the neighbors, and playing in the mud. One strange thing that set me apart was I chased ambulances and fire trucks. I lived in Everett, Washington (located approximately 30 miles north of Seattle). In Everett, there was only one ambulance company, named "Barker's Ambulance," and they responded all over Snohomish County. In the old days, "Barker's Ambulance" looked just like a hearse but was painted differently and with a lot of red lights. They had electronic sirens but also a windup siren "growler" (also known as a Q2, used by many fire departments today).

They would push a button until the siren would wind up from a low growl until it maxed out with a high shrill. These sirens had what was called a "siren brake" so the ambulance crew could slow down and then stop the siren as they approached the scene. If not used, the siren would wind down over several minutes. This siren could be heard from miles around so every time I heard it, I would jump on my bike and peddle as fast as I could to the end of the road to watch them go by. My friends just shook their heads.

Back in the 60s, 70s, and early 80s, 90 percent of rural/county fire departments were made up of volunteer firefighters. Most departments didn't have the luxury of pagers, so they were issued plectrons. Plectrons were medium-sized radios that the volunteers plugged into the wall (they also contained a chargeable battery so they could be portable) and this was how they were notified of a call. Before the advent of 9-1-1, people would have to dial a seven-digit number for emergencies. As a backup, fire stations would have large civil defense sirens attached to the roof of their station that would go off simultaneously with the plectron to notify volunteers who were outside working in the garden, shopping, or when they weren't in hearing range of their plectron that a call was being dispatched. These dedicated, non-paid people would drop what they were doing and make a mad dash for the fire station to work the apparatus required and respond to the call. Late-arriving volunteers would either respond with requested equipment or "standby" in the event another call came in. If the call was between the volunteer's house and the fire station, they would just drive to the scene. In today's world, volunteer fire departments are being shut down and being replaced with paid, professional fire departments from neighboring towns because they cannot recruit new volunteers, (referred to as part-paid firefighters). I remember at an early age, a real estate office at the end of our road caught fire. A volunteer fire department (Silver Lake Fire Dist. #11) showed up and put it out. Unfortunately, the building rekindled and this time the Everett Fire Department responded, all that was left was a large burn pile.

I remember when I was six and in the first grade, my mom took me up the road to Lowell Elementary School, where they were having a combination cub scout and boy scout (I joined both) jamboree. There were all types of demonstrations, ranging from building a fire, putting up a tent (there were probably 50 tents up as they were spending the whole weekend there), and how to make a rope bridge, but my favorite was a staged car accident with victims. I remember victims on the ground with moulage props for broken bones, cuts, burns, and an avulsed eye sticking out of one of the victims' heads.

One victim that particularly caught my eye was a person that had been thrown through the windshield and had a wound on her neck that spurted blood every couple of seconds (controlled by a bulb in her hand that you couldn't see). It was gory and scary at the same time, but it didn't affect me. Apparently, it was all I could talk about, and I couldn't wait until Monday morning to tell my teacher and all of my classmates. On Monday morning I ran into the classroom and told my teacher how "cool" the demonstration was. She grabbed me by the arms and got about two inches from my face and started shaking me and screaming, "That is not cool, and I don't ever want to hear you speak of this again." She went on to lecture me about not telling any of my classmates and that if she heard that I did, I would be in "big trouble."

Naturally, on the way home, I told everyone. I couldn't believe the scolding that I got, after all, I didn't know what all this meant. To me, it all seemed like a cool Halloween costume. I didn't know what injury or death was. I was only six years old. I had two classmates the same year that had been killed after each being hit by a car four months apart. We were told by the same teacher that they wouldn't be coming to school anymore. Again, death did not register with me. I just thought they moved away without saying goodbye.

When I was eight, I played little league baseball at the old Roosevelt Elementary School (now the 4 Square Church) up the street from Everett

Fire Station 5. My mom worked at the local K-mart and started work at 4 p.m., but my practice didn't start until 5 p.m., so three times a week I would walk down to the fire station and visit the firemen. I remember them being so nice and showing me around and letting me sit at the table while they smoked, read the paper, or ate dinner. I'm sure those firemen have long passed but if they are still with us, "Thank you" for making a huge impact on my life. You were why I wanted to become an Everett fireman.

I remember starting school at Mariner High School in September 1972. On our first day, the big event was the Olympic hostage situation that led to the killing of several Olympic athletes. I turned out for the freshman football program and had the pleasure of meeting Coach Tag Christianson, Coach Bill Hill (who became a mentor), Coach Ken Sather, and Coach Reg Nelson. My dad had just died six months earlier and I had no structured male adult interaction in my life and these gentlemen stepped up nicely.

After the first airing of "Emergency," that I started concentrating on subjects that could prepare me for that type of profession. I excelled in science, anatomy, and physiology. During one of the classes, we had to go to the commons area and learn how to do CPR. Everyone in the class was moaning and groaning about having to learn this technique and how they would never use it (except me). Pat Lorbiecki (ironically, I would work with Pat 20 years later), was an Everett fireman who taught our class. I listened intently to his every word and aced the written test and got my first American Heart Association CPR card.

As I mentioned earlier, my father died six months before I started high school. He went into the hospital on my 13th birthday and died the next day. He died of complications from alcoholism. It wasn't pretty. In 1973, mom met a man at an event, and they started dating and they eventually married. I despised this man (for lack of a better term) more than anyone I've ever known. We relocated to Edmonds, Washington, and I left all my friends behind. Living with my mom and this guy was a living hell. He verbally and physically abused me, and I just took it. It all came to a head one day when I hadn't emptied the garbage in a timely matter, and I came home and found it in my bed. Coffee grounds, potato peels, stale beer…you name it, it was probably in my bed. I ran away from home.

At this point, I had just enrolled at Meadowdale High School (my junior year) in Lynnwood and didn't know anyone. I remember my first day was during football homecoming week and I was watching people walk by. The hallways were all decked out in paper banners, crepe paper, confetti, etc. After the hallway cleared, I noticed one of the students close his locker and pull out a lighter. He ignited some of the crepe paper and the flames started traveling down the hallway. The fire alarm went off and everyone started running. Teachers came out of classrooms and when they saw flames, they grabbed fire extinguishers. The fire was out by the time Lynnwood Fire Department arrived, but the hallways were still full of smoke, so everyone had to wait outside until they were given the clear. At that point I thought, *This school is going to be interesting,* and I made friends easily. As it turned out, transferring to Meadowdale High School was a blessing. Heck, I even met my future wife there. Also, to this day, there are only two people who know who lit that fire. Him and me. I haven't told anyone, Ray.

After running away from home, I came back several days later and found all my belongings in the backyard. "Dickhead" had kicked me out of the house, and they arranged for me to "live" with a woman who was renting out a room in Lynnwood, but I wouldn't be able to attend Meadowdale. I would have to attend Lynnwood High School. It was the summer of 1975, and the beginning of my senior year, and I was expected to start as running back for Meadowdale's varsity football team and this didn't sit well with me or my teammates. The lady who was renting out the room was very specific about where I could and could not do or go in the house and that she worked evenings and would entertain "clients" in her home. If she was home, I wasn't allowed to come out of my room. The lady was a hooker. One of my teammates went home and told his parents about what was going on and his dad said "bullshit, he's moving in with us."

I had never met this man before, but he was opening his house for me to live in. The family that was my salvation was the Linnell family. My teammate (and great friend), Steve Linnell, had told his parents about my situation and without hesitation (I'd like to think), they graciously opened their home to me, and I quickly became their favorite. Thank you and God bless you Dad (Larry Linnell, RIP), Mom (Mary Linnell), (Tom, RIP), Steve, and Diane (also a big kiss and hug to Kay and Charlie). You will never know how much your kindness and acceptance meant to me. I had such great respect and love for Mr. and Mrs. Linnell that I have never called them by their first name. I would jokingly call them mom and dad just to piss Steve off. Even though Steve and I have not talked in years because of political differences, you know I still love you.

FIRE DISTRICT
NUMBER 1

In the Spring of my senior year of high school (1976), I heard that Snohomish County Fire District 1 (referred to as Fire Dist. #1) was recruiting for volunteer firefighters. The only prerequisite was to be 18 years of age and to have a vehicle. Bingo, I fit the bill. I went to their headquarter station and filled out an application. They told me that recruit school started in two weeks and that I would have to take a physical agility test before recruit school, so I made an appointment for the end of the week. On a sunny Friday afternoon, I arrived 30 minutes early, sat in my car, and took in the fact that I was finally going to become a volunteer fireman (if I passed the physical agility test and recruit school). I was beyond excited. At my scheduled time, I was met by firefighter Larry Keller, who explained to me how the agility test would be administered and told me if I failed any station, I would be disqualified and would have to go through the process again in six months. I had no problem passing the test. Larry congratulated me and told me to go to Station #3 on Monday to get my bunker gear (coat, pants, gloves, and helmet). I reported to Station #3 as directed and was issued my gear by Lt. Dave Mullins (it's amazing to remember all these names after 47 years). As it turned out, Station #3 became my responding station, as I lived only two miles away.

Saturday morning, the first day of recruit school had finally arrived, and I was out the door early. Unfortunately, my car wouldn't start. I thought, *Great, the first day of recruit school and I'm going to be late.* Mr. Linnell, who was a sergeant with the Washington State Patrol, was just leaving for work and gave me a ride. I'm sure I made a great first impression when I pulled up to the station in a WSP vehicle. The recruits (probably 12 of us) were met by Captain Larry Farrar (Capt. Farrar was a big man with no sense of humor. He was a volunteer fire captain, but his professional occupation was sergeant of the narcotics division for the Seattle Police Department). Our other instructor was Volunteer Captain Len Champion (Capt. Champion was a fit individual with a calm demeanor and a southern drawl. He was the Ying to Capt. Farrar's yang.) One of the first recruits that I became friends with was Brent Chomos. Brent was a very energetic and outgoing individual who was always encouraging others. Brent went on to become a paid firefighter for Dist. #1 and just recently retired at the rank of captain.

We started class at 0800 hrs. and went until 1700 hrs. (with a 30-minute break for lunch). We were taught the basics of hose handling, how water went into the engine from a supply (hydrant, another engine), and how it came out at the end of the hose. We proceeded to pull every foot of the hose off the engine, spray water, then pick it up and load it. We did this probably eight times on that hot first day of training. It was hot, sweaty work and I lost probably 10 pounds, but it was rewarding, and I thoroughly loved it. We figured we deployed and loaded 8,000 feet of hose that day.

Recruit school lasted eight weeks (eight full Saturdays and four hours a night, twice a week). Over the next eight weeks, we learned about proper loading of hoses (yes, there is a way, so the hose comes out easily and doesn't get hung up). Different ways to deliver water to extinguish the fire, (Forward Lay, Reverse Lay, Blind Alley, Water Shuttle, Drafting, and

Tagging Tight to a hydrant), (just the basics to get you to the front door of the fire). We learned breathing apparatus (BA), buddy breathing, what to do if you run out of air while in a fire, refilling bottles, forcible entry, searching for victims, ladders, ventilation, salvage, and overhaul. This training just scratched the surface of all the knowledge and technical skill of the fire service. Paid fire departments train every day to keep their skills sharp. Like the old saying, "Train Like You Fight."

After eight weeks we finished off our training with a drill fire. Note: There is no realism simulating putting out a fire; you need fire. Departments will go out and look for old abandoned or soon to be torn down structures that benefit the department as well as the owner of the building. First, the department gains valuable experience by fighting a real fire, which can include forcible entry, ventilation, fire behavior, and search and rescue. The owner wins because they don't need to demolish and haul away the building. There are several hoops that must be jumped through before you can legally burn a building. You must get a permit from air pollution control, the EPA (if there is potential environmental impact), and maybe the FFA, if the building is in a direct path of flight activity. All asbestos must be removed, asphalt roofing must be removed, windows boarded up (to retain heat) and vent holes in the roof need to be cut in case of emergency (these holes are usually covered with plywood and pulled off if needed). Once everything is in order, you need to load the house with combustibles (fire load) to get good heat production.

Our drill fire was held on Sunday morning so volunteers who had to work Saturdays could attend. Safety was paramount. Backup lines, exposure lines, and every conceivable piece of equipment were in place. Captain Farrar took us, eight recruits (four had dropped out), into the living room of this fairly good-sized house. It was probably 2500 square feet. It was one story but had four bedrooms so there would be a lot of "fire attacks" so everyone would get great hands-on experience. Captain Farrar lit some combustibles on fire in a corner of the living room and started to talk about fire behavior. We were in full protective clothing but did not have a breathing apparatus on. We watched the flames climb up the wall and it started getting smoky and hot. Captain Farrar got on his knees and probably was wondering if we were smart enough to do the same. Soon the heat and smoke were halfway to the ground, and we had to get on our stomachs to breathe. A couple of recruits immediately exited the house, but stubbornness, pride, ego, or lack of common sense kept the rest of us in the room. Finally, when the smoke and heat were so unbearable, we all exited coughing and hacking up black stuff. We learned the first rule in firefighting, stay low and never stand up in a fire.

We were split up into groups and told to don our breathing apparatus. Each group had several attacks on bedrooms, the garage, and the recreation room. We all got opportunities to be on the nozzle as well as backup man. We were instructed to "knock down" the fire but not put it out. Finally, towards the end, the living room was lit to the point that it was "fully involved" and flames were coming out of every crack in the house. We were allowed to go to the front door, advance five feet and use a fog pattern (a wide spray) versus a "Straight Stream" (narrower pattern under more pressure). All recruits got their final time on the nozzle and then the instructors let it burn. It was very impressive to see how hot and smoke-filled a house could get from a relatively small fire, not to mention, the destruction of letting it get out of control. It was a great memory for an inexperienced 18-year-old volunteer fireman.

Afterward, we threw any existing wood found on the ground onto the fire, pushed the chimney over, picked up all the dirty equipment and hose, and went back to the station where we spent the next three hours cleaning, hanging, and reloading hose. We then made sure that all breathing apparatus had full bottles and washed all of the rigs. (You'll find that firefighters take great pride in their equipment and apparatus. No one wants to be seen with a dirty rig or disheveled looking hose beds.) A second valuable lesson was learned: Fighting fire is usually 30 minutes of excitement followed by hours of tedious clean-up. We all passed recruit school. We were issued new bunker gear, given a Plectron, and allowed to respond to calls.

After recruit school, the next step to becoming a firefighter was to become trained in first aid. State law required that anyone tending to a patient and transporting them was required to have a minimum of Washington State Fire Service First Aid & Rescue, a long title that meant you had to attend 45 hours of first aid training. Being Emergency Medical Technician (EMT) certified was the highest training level at that time. A couple of years later paramedics would be established in South Snohomish County. It was a big deal at the time to become an EMT (it was 40 hours of more advanced training than basic first aid, plus you got this cool blue and gold patch that said EMT to put on your uniform). There weren't many at the time and classes were not as readily available as they are today.

Captain Steve Gibler was our First Aid instructor. Captain Gibler was a well-spoken, highly knowledgeable guy with several years of experience. Like recruit school, classes were all day Saturday and three hours, two nights a week. We learned the basics of first aid, CPR, administering oxygen, controlling bleeding, treating for shock, burn care, obstetrics, splinting and bandaging, triage, and how to make a traction splint (femur fracture). We had a final written test and then a practical test.

The practical test was a simulated explosion with multiple casualties. Casualties ranged from hysteria, walking wounded, severe burns, severe bleeding, airway obstruction, impaled objects, amputated extremities, and dead victims. It was our job to assess the situation, call for help, triage (sort out the patients who will live with treatment and those who are dead or soon will be), treat, and then transport. A triage leader was chosen (a big ex-Marine) and it was his job to decide who got treated first. I was instructed by him to climb up into a big metal container (like a boxcar without a roof) and search for any victims. I found one who was unconscious from an airway obstruction. Simple. Tilt the head back and open the airway. At this point, there was no spontaneous respiration so I attempted mouth-to-mouth resuscitation (something you wouldn't dream about doing today), and the victim spit a half-chewed sandwich into my mouth. Being unphased and gung-ho, I spit the food out my mouth and continued mouth-to-mouth. The victim opened his eyes and said, "What in the hell are you doing?" Meet Kevin Hayes, my victim. Kevin was a volunteer firefighter with a couple of years of experience, but his main job was as a photographer for the *Everett Herald*. Kevin was impressed with my aggressiveness even if it was only a drill. I passed the class and was now ready to ride on the aid car.

My very first aid call (which happened 46 years ago, but I remember it as if it occurred yesterday) was for an unknown type of medical call. A woman from out of state had managed to contact SNOCOM (dispatch center for South Snohomish County) and asked if someone could go to her elderly parents' house to check on her mom. The woman stated that every time she called her mom, her dad would answer and say, "Oh your mom is sleeping, and I don't want to wake her up." SCSO (Snohomish County Sheriff Office) was also dispatched and arrived before we did. SCSO advised dispatch that the county coroner would be needed and advised us that "you need breathing apparatus."

Upon our arrival, we were met outside near the front door and advised of the situation. Apparently, the elderly woman had fallen asleep on the couch in the front room. Every time the elderly father tried to wake her up to eat, she didn't respond. He would make her something to eat throughout the day and the food never got eaten, so he threw it away. This had gone on for three days and on the fourth day, the daughter became worried because her mom was sleeping "way too much." Apparently, the husband had been diagnosed with organic brain syndrome (known today as Alzheimer's disease) and he had lost all track of time and didn't realize what had happened. The elderly woman had died four days earlier, but the husband didn't notice the stench or the unresponsiveness of the patient. "She was just sleeping." The front door was ajar, but you could smell the putrid odor of death (it didn't help the fact that it was very warm in the trailer).

We waited outside for the arrival of the coroner, who went inside and immediately exited. This coroner was relatively new and apparently hadn't adjusted to the smell of a decaying body (this was my first experience, too, which would set the foundation for hundreds more). We were asked to take the stretcher in and place the body in a "body bag." We donned our breathing apparatus and went in. The first thing I noticed was how hot it was in the living room. With the heavy bunker gear and the heavy tanks on our backs, we started sweating immediately. The plan was to lift her by the shoulders, middle, and legs and swing her body over to the stretcher next to the couch. I positioned myself behind the couch and bent over and ran my hands under her back. On three, we all lifted and put her on the stretcher. After I removed my hands from her back, I noticed skin, fluids, and what looked like rice on my gloves. Maggots. We looked down at the couch and it was infested with maggots. I vomited in my mask and had to leave. Outside, I took off my mask and the smell made me puke again. There's an old saying, "Eat only as much as your mask can hold." Another lesson learned.

There are certain smells and sights you can't appreciate unless you see and smell them first hand. Alcohol, vomit, blood, gas, oil, brake and hydraulic fluid, battery acid, feces, urine, and death are smells prevalent in our profession. Sometimes you'll be lucky and only smell one or two. Other times you may get the whole bouquet. I went through a lot of Vicks VapoRub under my nose during my career.

My first trauma (and death) occurred at 164th and Ash Way (considered Alderwood Manor). A biker had been drinking at the Martha Lake Tavern (now a county park), and after several hours, decided to go home. While traveling west on 164th, a woman in a station wagon at Ash Way pulled out in front of the motorcyclist and he plowed into her broadside (estimated speed 60 mph from measurements) and was ejected over the hood. Witnesses state that he flew approximately 100 feet before landing on his front side. His motorcycle skidded the entire length and ran over him.

I was at a training class at headquarters, so the aid car (Aid One) went first with the paid crew, and I jumped on the engine. District #1 had recently received two brand new aid cars, but the new Aid One had some mechanical issues, so it was sent back to the manufacturer for repair. The manufacturer provided Dist. #1 with a "loaner ambulance." This ambulance was probably 10 years old and was the old-style hearse look-alike with a very long profile but a small low patient compartment. The engine arrived about the same time as the aid car, and we all converged on the motorcyclist.

The first thing I noticed was his eyes looked like they were going to pop out of his head and that his chinstrap was cutting into his neck. He was purple from the nipple line to his head and had clam strips, French fries, blood, and beer coming out of his mouth and nose. Blood and vomit were running down the hill. This patient had classic traumatic asphyxia as well as multiple broken bones and angulations. We attempted to suction the patient but due to all the chunky vomit he had, it just plugged up the machine. While other firefighters brought a backboard and gurney, I used scissors to cut the chinstrap so we could get his helmet off. We used our fingers to get the vomit out of his mouth the best we could and inserted an oropharyngeal airway. The patient had agonal respirations, so we took over his ventilations with a Bag Valve Mask, (BVM), and oxygen. We knew this guy was "circling the drain" and probably wouldn't make it to the hospital, so we provided cervical stabilization, put him on a backboard, and attempted to put him in the back of the "loaner ambulance." We had a problem: one of the patient's leg was so badly fractured and angulated that we couldn't get him in the back of the rig. One of the firefighters grabbed the angulated extremity and straightened it as best he could so we could get him in the back of the rig. Straightening an angulated fracture at a joint is frowned upon, but in his situation, it was the least of his problems. Just as we were leaving the scene, the patient lost his pulse. The two people who arrived on the aid car had jumped in the back to work on the patient but there was no one to drive. The Battalion Chief looked at me and said, "Do you think you can drive that thing without killing anyone?" I had never driven something this big, but I assured him I could. Someone at the scene knew the motorcyclist and had contacted a family member who started a phone tree and when we arrived at the hospital, many family members were there standing at the emergency entrance and hallway. We unloaded the patient and continued CPR. While we were wheeling him in, one of his arms had fallen from his side and we ran over his fingers with the gurney. Add broken fingers to his list of injuries. Unfortunately (and without surprise), the patient was pronounced dead on arrival (DOA).

During the times before paramedics, we did a lot of CPR on the way to the hospital but in my experience, we never resuscitated anyone. Zip, zero, zilch. It became very frustrating and depressing knowing the outcome before you ever reached the hospital. A couple of years later, that would change (TCL). I started my EMT training in October 1976. The classes ran for three hours, two evenings a week and eight hours every Saturday. The classes were held at the headquarters of Mountlake Fire Department. Terrace Fire Department was a smaller department than Fire Dist. #1 and they had a few paid personnel but relied heavily on volunteers.

Dr. Michael Copass, who at the time was the medical director for the highly prestigious Seattle Medic One Program out of Harborview Trauma Center in Seattle was our EMT Lecturer/Coordinator. Dr. Copass is a highly respected (and loved) doctor known throughout the United States. On day one, the first words out of his mouth to the class were, "Do not assume anything. To assume makes an ass out of you (u) and me." Words I lived by throughout my entire career. It was an honor and a privilege to have had Dr. Copass as a lecturer. I would interact with Dr. Copass later in my career on several occasions.

I spent a lot of my free time at Fire Station #3. Even though I had a job (greens crew for Everett Golf and Country Club), I loved hanging around the station waiting for calls and being one of "the guys." While working at EG&CC, I would frequently see Everett Fire running "code" (lights and sirens) down Colby Avenue and just hoped someday I would be one of them. The city of Everett required that you be 21 years old just to test (due to insurance regulations), and since I was only 18, I had to wait. At Fire Station #3, I met some great people: Mike Crosby, Don Redford, Gary Summers, Steve Lindsay, Rick Wirtz, Jeff Larmore, Jim McGaughey, Wes Miller, Warren Aspden, Bill Thompson, Bruce Krause, Tom Delisle, Steve Mace (who taught me how to drive a manual 1968 Crown fire engine) to name a few. But my favorite person was Lt. Tom Foster.

Tom Foster was a great instructor, a great officer, a great listener, and a great mentor. You could talk to Tom about anything, and he was always there to help. Tom had an outstanding career and retired from Dist. #1 as a chief officer. Tom went on to become an investigator for the Snohomish County Fire Marshall's office. Tom is completely retired and enjoying his grandkids. Thank you, Tom, for everything. One of Tom's philosophies was to make training fun. Several times he incorporated breathing apparatus with basketball, or "BA Basketball." Depending on how many people were at the station, we would make two teams, don our bunker gear and BAs, and go out in the back parking lot and play a game. At the time, breathing apparatus were heavy with steel bottles that were rated for 30 minutes. The harder you worked, the harder you would breathe, "sucking" the air out at a pretty good pace. Generally, one of these "30-minute bottles" would only last 10 minutes. We would record the pressure in the bottle (full was 3000 psi) and proceed to play. It probably looked ridiculous to the public seeing these grown men awkwardly trying to make a basket dressed the way we were. We would constantly bang into each other, causing this "clanking" sound of the bottles hitting each other. Soon you would start hearing the alarm bell on the bottle ring. When your air level was down below 800 psi, every time you took a breath, a bell would ring indicating you were getting low on air. When the alarm bell rang constantly, it meant you were below 500 psi, and it was time to get out of the hazardous environment that you were in. We would continue to play until the air was gone and you were sucking your mask in. The team that was ahead and or had the most players still breathing air was declared the winner. Dave Moses always seemed to win because he was a long-distance runner. I once sat on the couch with a full bottle and tried to conserve my air and stay as still as I could. I lasted 25 minutes. Breathing apparatus bottles of today are made with a composite material that makes them lighter and can hold more pressure. Most bottles today are rated at 4500 psi and there are newer 60-minute rated bottles.

We were called for mutual aid to Paine Field airport one early evening for a hangar fire. The paid crew had already left the station so when two other volunteers and I arrived, we jumped in the aid car to proceeded to the scene. I was the driver, the second was in the right seat (officer), and the third was in the patient compartment. One volunteer was a lieutenant and had more experience than I did so he jumped in the officer's seat. As we were responding, you could see a large column of black smoke coming from the area. I asked the officer which way he wanted to go, and he told me, "See that gate up there? Take a left." The officer must have been fixated on the large column of smoke because he told me to go "that way," which was across an active runway. I don't know whose eyes were bigger, the officer's or the pilot of the Cessna that was landing on the active runway we were crossing. I swear he left tire tracks on the top of the aid car. It was a big fire, and we were there for several hours. The pilot filed a complaint and the battalion chief absorbed most of the ass-chewing. We got a throttled down talking to by the chief. Do not cross active runways without permission or a pilot car. Another valuable lesson learned.

On a nice sunny morning, we were dispatched to a burn victim with breathing problems. The aid crew had already gone to the scene, and we followed in the engine a couple of minutes later. A company had been doing a "hot tar roof" down towards Picnic Point. While a crew was on the roof, another worker was down on the ground chopping bricks of tar and placing them into the burner to liquefy. They had a large bucket tied to a rope and would pull up the full bucket of hot liquified tar and mop it onto the roof. While pulling the bucket up, it got hung up on the facia of the building and wouldn't budge. One of the workers yanked on the rope and broke either the rope or the handle. Either way, the whole bucket of tar rained down on the worker and covered him with scalding tar. The patient started screaming and luckily for him, a doctor had been out working in his yard when he heard the screams. The doctor ran over and found the patient covered in tar, screaming and saying he couldn't breathe. By the time the aid car arrived, the tar had begun to harden, and the patient's airway was cut off. The doctor took out a pocket knife and began cutting and chipping away tar from the patient's nose and mouth. The tar had hardened on the patient's chest and was preventing the chest from expanding. We started pouring cold water on the tar for pain relief as well as to make it easier to pull the tar off the chest. Unfortunately, the skin under the tar had developed second – and third-degree burns and just peeled off along with the tar. Since this was before the establishment of paramedics, there was nothing more the aid crew could do but assist respirations with BVM and rapid transport. This patient had critical burns and would require more advanced care at Harborview Trauma and Burn Center in Seattle. The patient was loaded and transported via I-5. It was requested that Medic One from the Seattle Fire Department meet them en route. Both units rendezvoused at NE 45th and I-5 and the patient was transported to Harborview. Unfortunately, due to his critical burns, he succumbed to his injuries two weeks later.

After several months as a volunteer, one day I was approached by a battalion chief and asked if I wanted to work part-time. This entailed working as a paid firefighter without benefits, job security, or pension. The wage was $5 an hour (a very good rate in 1976 as the minimum wage was $2 an hour and I was single with only rent and a car payment). There were a couple of us throughout the fire district that filled in for vacationing, injured or ill firefighters.

The fire district had four stations and covered much of South Snohomish County. The fire district employed (at the time) roughly 36 full-time personnel (firefighters, lieutenants, and battalion chiefs), and utilized a 48-hour work week (four 12-hour shifts for four days in a row, then four days off). Work hours were from either 0600–1800 or 0900–2100. At 0600, two personnel would start work and at 0900, another would report for duty. The firefighter (or lieutenant) that came on duty at 0900 worked until 1800 hrs. the next day as he had to sleep one shift while the other two went home. After 1800 hrs., a volunteer firefighter would come in for a 12-hour shift known as sleeper duty. The pay was $20/night and was good pay for sleeping all night (or maybe getting up once or twice for a call). During the day, if an aid call was dispatched, a firefighter (assigned to the aid car) and the lieutenant would respond, leaving the firefighter assigned to drive the engine behind and wait for volunteers. If the call was dispatched as a fire, all three of the on-duty crew would respond and leave the aid car and reserve engine behind and let the volunteers respond with those rigs. Every station had a reserve engine that was used if the first out engine had a mechanical issue but was used exclusively by the volunteers.

Every Monday night was volunteer drill night, and it was up to the volunteer officer to organize and put on the drill. The Dist. #1 Professional Firefighters were represented by the International Association of Firefighters (IAFF) and abided by a contract agreed upon between the fire district and the Professional Firefighters of Fire Dist. #1. The union fought for working conditions, salaries, and working hours. At the time there had not been any stipulations in the contract stating that the fire district could not hire part-time labor. The firefighter's union strongly discouraged the fire district from hiring scab labor but had no recourse until they negotiated a new contract a year later. In January 1977, scabs were out. I was 18 years old, fresh out of high school, and earning $5 an hour doing something that I had wanted to do since I was five. I knew nothing about unions. The terms collective bargaining, negotiations, and mediation were concepts I was not familiar with. I didn't realize that I was taking money out of these guys' pockets or food off their table. I have been a union paying member of IAFF for over 30 years. I know about unions now, so to all the firefighters, for my actions back in 1976, I'm sorry. Today I truly regret my decision.

I was working a day shift at headquarters station (Sta. #1) with Lt. Jim McGaughey, and I was assigned to Aid 1. We received a call for a neck laceration from a chainsaw. I was more nervous going on the call with Jim than the nature of the call. Jim epitomized the fire service. Jim was well respected in the department for his knowledge, experience, and calm demeanor. Jim always had a smile on his face and laughed easily. Jim was heavily involved in training and organizing fundraisers and events for the department. I'm sure going out the bay door, Jim had 50 percent of his mindset on the call and 50 percent on how the guy to his left would perform.

Upon arrival, we found a male patient who had a large laceration to his neck from his ear to the bottom of his chin. Witnesses stated that the patient had attempted to cut a limb while on a ladder and the saw "kicked back" and struck him in the neck. Even though the patient sustained this large laceration, there was minimal blood loss. You could peer into the wound and see all his anatomy; he missed every vital vessel. The patient said he had just put on a new chain, so the sharpness of the blade gave him a nice clean cut. We dressed his wounds and transported him to Stevens Hospital in Edmonds. He was sewn up and released several hours later. Sometimes the most serious sounding calls turn out to be minor and the minor turn out to be serious.

Over the years, Jim and I became good friends. Jim climbed the advancement ladder and retired as a battalion chief. Ironically, Jim's daughter (Brie) became good friends with my oldest daughter, Nichole. Tragically, Brie was involved in a vehicle accident near their home and was killed. Jim was working as the battalion chief that day and was the first one to arrive on the scene. Unfortunately, the experience affected Jim dramatically and he retired soon after.

It was Easter Sunday, March 27, 1977, and Kevin Hayes and I were at Sta. #3 watching "The Wizard of Oz" when we got a report of a house fire approximately three miles away. Kevin got in the jump seat behind the driver and was the "nozzleman" and I got in the jump seat behind the officer and was the "Hydrant man." Kevin's job was to don his breathing apparatus and extend a houseline to the front door. My job was to stay at the hydrant and make the connections to the hydrant, wait for the driver's signal with a horn blast, and then open the hydrant. In this case, though, the house fire was down a long driveway, so I jumped off the engine and pulled off the manifold and a couple of sections, (known as "flakes), of 4"supply line and told the driver to proceed while holding the hose so it didn't get pulled down the driveway. Also, since this was at night, we left at the end of the driveway a flare or flashlight so the incoming engine can see the hose and have enough illumination to visualize connecting the hose together.

This technique, called a "blind alley," is used a lot in rural areas where the fire is down long narrow driveways or gravel roads where there is no room for the incoming engine (water supply) to perform its task. Instead, the incoming engine (water supply) hooks to the manifold (or directly to the supply line, depending on their hose bed configuration), and will either stay at the end of the driveway waiting for another incoming engine to lay a water supply line to them (known as a water shuttle) or continue down the road until they find a hydrant. In rural areas, hydrants may be scarce or non-existent. This presents a logistics problem (the use of water tankers known as tenders), and how you're going to tactically attack a fire. Ideally, it's best to have an engine at a hydrant, if possible, to boost the pressure, especially if it's a long distance between engines or due to elevation (known as hydraulics). Sometimes you'll find a "dry hydrant" (won't flow water because of an underground pipe issue or malfunctioning components of the hydrant, a broken operating stem, for example). These are all sorts of concerns the first arriving company officer must contend with. The bottom line, establishing a water supply is priority number one.

The engine we responded on had breathing apparatus secured to the jump seats, so we were able to put them on while in route to the fire. At the time, the officer's breathing apparatus was located in an outside compartment so he would have to get out of the engine, open up a compartment to don his (engines of today have a breathing apparatus attached to the officer's seat so he can put his on in route). After securing the hose at the end of the driveway, I jogged the 100 yards or so straightening out the hose as I went.

Finally, I went to back up Kevin on the hose line and as I was putting on my mask someone behind me said "get your ass in there" and pushed me through the front door opening. Flames were rolling over our heads and I was trying to get my mask on, and it was so hot I was on my stomach sucking the air out of the carpet. Kevin had knocked down the flames overhead and now I had to deal with smoke and hot steam. I pulled the hose as I was trying to get my mask on. Kevin took a turn to the left down a hallway and again we were met by flames rolling over our heads. After about two minutes, I was able to get my mask on but didn't have a good seal so every time I took a breath, heat and smoke made their way between the mask and my face. Suddenly, as Kevin was putting water on the fire, there was a bright flash and a large "boom." Kevin had sprayed right into the electrical panel and was thrown backward. Kevin received an electrical jolt but not strong enough to kill him. I pulled Kevin back the same way we came and out the door. By this time, I couldn't control my coughing and was hacking up black shit. Kevin was loaded up into the aid car and when the battalion chief saw me coughing with trouble breathing, he told me to go to the hospital also. Fortunately for Kevin, he did not sustain any electrical burns but there was a concern for his heart. I was treated for elevated CO levels (carbon monoxide) and possible respiratory burns. Both Kevin and I were admitted to the hospital and spent a day and a half there. I have been involved in many large fires since that night. I was fortunate to have had a relatively injury-free (except for two incidents) (TCL) career.

We received a call to Picnic Point Park (a beautiful area approximately four miles west of Sta. #3, which is located on Puget Sound, halfway between the cities of Edmonds and Everett) for a brush fire on the railroad tracks. At the same time, Edmonds and Lynnwood Fire Department were dispatched for a brush fire. A northbound train with a "hot brake" was emitting sparks that caused multiple brush fires that were traveling up the hills and endangering homes. When we arrived, we noticed fires about every quarter to half a mile along the railroad tracks. We broke up into teams and grabbed shovels and picks and started the arduous task of putting out the fires. (Note: I have the greatest respect for wildland fire-fighters. In structural fires, you go in and put them out. In wildland fires, you must chase the fire up hills, dodge falling trees, and dig firebreaks. Wildland fires also tend to come up behind and overrun you. You must also be in great shape. Thank you, wildland firefighters, for representing us as you do). Some engines were located on top of the hills to protect the homes, and others were directed to the areas where the fire could be accessed. There was a set of train tracks (one north, one south) and they were both shut down during the extinguishment and overhaul of the fires. After the fires were extinguished, one track was opened (as there were sev-eral trains held up) but the trains from Everett (going south) were rerouted to the northbound lanes.

A young girl near the park was riding her horse and was familiar with the route of travel that the trains used. While riding on the tracks, the girl heard a train approaching from the north and saw the lights (early eve-ning by this time) coming around a blind bend. Knowing she was on the proper track for a train going that direction, she didn't move. Suddenly the train came around the corner on the track she was on. The girl had barely enough time to jump off the horse and get off the tracks. The horse stood on the tracks and like a "deer in the headlights" didn't move. The horse was hit at probably 30+ miles per hour and was reduced to "many pieces." There were remnants of the horse everywhere. It took the train almost a mile to stop and when it did, we were able to walk on both sides of the track and see more pieces. The girl had a few minor cuts and scrapes but was obvi-ously emotionally traumatized. She was taken by the aid car to the hospital for observation and probably sedation. The area where this happened is heavily occupied by families during the day and there was no way we could leave this poor horse laying around. Thankfully a boater had witnessed the incident and offered to dispose of the horse in the water of Puget Sound several hundred feet from the railroad tracks. We tied ropes around the large pieces, and he dragged them out to deeper water. We shoveled up the guts and gore the best we could, and they were disposed of properly. The area where the horse's final resting place ended up is a very popular spot for catching Dungeness crab. I'm sure the horse didn't go to waste.

At the time, Fire Dist. #1 was the only department that had a Hurst tool (aka the jaws of life). This was an expensive piece of equipment, and it couldn't be justified to be carried by neighboring fire departments so Fire Dist. #1's battalion chief carried it in the back of his station wagon, and he would respond to any request for the "jaws" in Edmonds, Lynnwood or Mountlake Terrace. Due to the work schedule at the time, after 1800 hrs. on the fourth night of shift, the battalion chief would drive the duty car to the oncoming battalion chief and that battalion chief would drive the other home. Battalion Chief Jim Shoenthrup was the oncoming battalion chief and was driving the "duty car" and his designated call sign was "12."

At the same time as the battalion chiefs were exchanging the car, a couple of miles from headquarters there was an underaged drinking party going on. Several of the partygoers were drunk and apparently, two males got into a fight. One of the males had gotten pretty beat up and was pissed so he told everyone who had ridden with him to "get in the car, we're fucking out of here." Witnesses stated they observed the car "burn rubber and fishtail out of there" at a high rate of speed. Other witnesses stated they observed the car traveling west on 164th St. SE like a "bat out of hell." At the top of the hill on 164th and 35th Ave SW, there was a four-way stop (traffic light now). Witnesses stated that the car ran the stop sign at an estimated speed of 80 miles per hour and proceeded west about a quarter of a mile where there was a bend in the road. It was reported that the car was airborne when it collided head-on into another vehicle. 9-1-1 reports started pouring into the emergency call center about a head-on vehicle accident with serious injuries and people trapped. Because of the serious nature and multiple calls, E-3, A-3, E-1, A-1, and "12" were dispatched (because of entrapment and the need for the "jaws"). All units went responding but

"12" had not come on the air yet. Dispatch tried several times to raise "12" on the radio. No answer. "12" was paged a second time and in an almost inaudible voice "12" told dispatch, "I'm involved in the accident." After being interviewed at the hospital days later, Chief Schoenthrup (who suffered a broken femur, broken jaw, and permanent injury to his hand) stated that he saw headlights "coming down on him" and immediately laid flat on his side. The "jaws" (which were damaged) had been thrown forward and broke the back seat and traveled through the front seat with the tips embedded into the horn of the steering wheel. While one crew worked to extricate the battalion chief, other crews worked to get the five victims out of the other car.

The driver and front passenger were obviously DOA as was the middle passenger in the back seat. One patient had a severe head injury with agonal respirations, a fractured arm, and an obvious fractured lower extremity. The crew I was with extricated the head injury patient (a 14-year-old girl) onto a backboard and was waiting for the gurney to be brought over. Our intention was for rapid transport and to try to stabilize the fractures (the least of her worries), en route to the hospital. While wheeling the patient to the aid car (several hundred feet away), the patient stopped breathing. Without a BVM available, I started mouth-to-mouth resuscitation on her, and she proceeded to projectile vomit in my mouth with enough force to shoot her stomach contents (somewhat filtered by my nose) back onto her face. I had what I guessed to be stew and beer vomit in my mouth, so I quickly spit it out, gagged a few times, and continued. By this time my eyes were burning from the vomit that had splashed in my eyes and I could barely see. We got the patient in the back of the aid car and I suctioned her the best I could, wiped the vomit off her face (and mine), and performed CPR on the way to the hospital. She was DOA. The lone survivor was a young male who was seated behind the driver. He sustained major injuries and took years to recover. Chief Schoenthrup recovered from his injuries and returned to work several months later. He walked with a limp and eventually had to retire due to his disabled hand. Two more serious vehicle accidents were spawned from that underaged drinking party. I never heard if any legal action was ever taken.

I was working a day shift at Sta. #2. with Lt. Wes Miller (a brilliant officer and great guy), when the front doorbell rang. We had just sat down to lunch, and I was starving. Lieutenant Miller looked at me and said, "Your turn." It was not unusual to have visitors during the day, (blood pressure checks, kids wanting to see the engine, people wanting directions), but Lt. Miller knew who it was. There was a guy who would come into the station regularly at lunchtime and "shoot the shit" with whoever would answer the door. This was my first-time meeting "Squeaky."

"Squeaky" was an old-timer who was very opinionated. I said hello and how could I help him. Squeaky had had his larynx (voice box) removed several years earlier and talked with the help of a little instrument that he held to his throat. "Squeaky" had a stoma (a permanent opening in his neck so he could breathe), and he was wearing a turtleneck so you couldn't see the stoma. A lot of people with stomas wear a turtleneck or bandana to prevent the inhalation of foreign objects like bugs or dust. People with stomas are also prone to respiratory infections due to the fact they can't clear phlegm out of their mouth like normal people. The passage from the lungs to the mouth is cut off. Squeaky had talked almost non-stop for 30 minutes when he said, "You're probably missing lunch, so I'll get out of your hair." Before "Squeaky" left, he coughed several times after pulling his turtleneck down; he pulled a handkerchief out of his pocket and tried to expel the phlegm buildup in his airway. He didn't do a very good job, as a portion of the green stuff flew past his handkerchief and landed on the back of my hand. "Oops, sorry about that," he said as he walked out the door. I went into the kitchen and threw my lunch in the trash.

A lot of modern fire stations today have drive-through bays, meaning you pull around to the back of the station, open the rear bay door and drive through to the front bay door. No backing into the station. However, some stations have the old "back-in stations." A large percentage of accidents are backing accidents. Sure, getting T-boned at an intersection or driving too fast for the conditions and hitting a tree or power pole occur, but a majority are backup accidents. Most departments have the motto "Do not back up without a backup man." In rare occurrences when you don't have a backup man, the driver is required to exit the vehicle and do a "walk around" to ensure pedestrians, equipment, and other objects are not in the way.

I had just arrived at Station #3 probably a minute after a backing accident occurred. The driver was doing some minor work in the cab and when he was finished, without a backup man, backed the engine into the station. Since it was an all-glass bay door, he didn't notice that the door was only three-quarters of the way open. He backed the engine into the bay door and the ladder rack, destroying several rows of metal, track, and glass. At that time the engines carried 1000 feet of rubber-coated four-inch supply hose. All the glass shattered and covered the supply hose. The lieutenant who shall remain nameless), knew the driver was in a predicament and decided to cook up a story that in the long run, and after an investigation, didn't fly. The priority (after calling the battalion chief) was to get all the supply hose unloaded and get all the glass out of the hose bed to prevent further damage to the hose. The lieutenant told the driver of the aid car to pull it out of the bay and park it out in front of the station. For some reason, the lieutenant told the engineer to drive the engine into the aid car bay, cab first, which he did. We began carefully pulling the supply line off the engine (removing the glass as we went) until all the hose was in a heap behind the engine. We then swept and vacuumed the hose bed clean of any more glass.

We were just ready to reload the hose bed when we were dispatched to a house fire with the possibility of trapped children. The fire reported was roughly a mile and a half from the station. We all donned our protective gear and were just mounting the engine when we realized there was a 1000 feet of wadded-up supply line behind the engine and we couldn't get out of the station. Luckily, there were four of us, so we were able to throw the hose out of the way. We were responding to a house fire without a supply line with the next arriving engine probably eight minutes away. We had 500 gallons of water in the tank so hopefully, we would be able to perform a rescue, if needed, with tank water. Fortunately, the call ended up being a malfunctioning furnace and all occupants were out of the house upon arrival. Again, something sounding serious turned out to be nothing.

Upon returning to the station, we were met by the battalion chief, the chief, and the assistant chief. Everyone had to fill out an accident report (except me, as I wasn't at the station when this occurred). While the paid crew filled out their reports and were interviewed by "the brass," we volunteers were reloading the supply bed. After the interview process, we went out and laid all 1000 feet of the hose bed and pressure-tested it. No leaks were found. After an investigation, the administration found inconsistencies in the stories and measurements didn't line up. The two firefighters were given four shifts off without pay and the lieutenant was demoted.

I was working a day shift at Sta. #4 and the task for the day was to go out and do hydrant maintenance. I was assigned to the aid car, so I followed the engine wherever it went. Hydrant maintenance was done annually. We would cut down any tall grass that had grown around the hydrant, so they were visible. (Most departments today use little blue reflectors placed near the centerline of the road on the side the hydrant is on to indicate where the hydrant is. The reflectors usually only last until the first snow, then the snowplows scrape them off the road.) Next, we'd take off all the caps and open the hydrant fully until the water was running out of all the ports (water flowed until the water was clean). This was done to make sure the operating stem worked properly and that when the hydrant was shut down, it would drain properly. Finally, we'd clean all the port threads then spray graphite on the threads, replace the caps, and move to the next one. Any discrepancies found would be reported to the water company having jurisdiction and they were responsible to repair it.

One of the major drawbacks of testing hydrants this way was the damage caused to landscaping, erosion, or flooding of a street. Also, water sitting idle in the underground pipes would cause rust. This rust was stirred up anytime the hydrant was opened, and rust-colored water would flow from the pipes in to houses. Rusty water would flow from kitchen faucets and cause rust stains to laundry. This practice has been scaled down to turning the hydrants on with all the caps still attached then turning the hydrant off, removing the caps, cleaning, lubing, and replacing the caps. Same concept, fewer complaints.

I was finishing up the last hydrant for the day when I noticed a large plant growing near the hydrant. It had funny leaves on it and it didn't look like any other plants we had knocked down. Upon conferring with the rest of the crew we decided it was a marijuana plant. Warren Aspend, one of the other firefighters, started laughing and said, "I got a plan." That night was volunteer drill night, and he knew Capt. Farrar (Seattle narcotics sergeant) would be there. We dug up the plant (again, a very impressive size) and took it back to the station. That evening, while training was being done, I (I was "elected" because I was the low man on the pole, plus I had the least to lose) placed the plant on the hood of Capt. Farrar's truck. When drill night wrapped up, we watched Farrar walk to his truck and get in. At first, he didn't notice the plant but then realized it was there. He got out of the truck and examined it and looked back at us doubled over in laughter. By the look on his face, it was obvious that it wasn't as humorous to him as it was to us. He snatched the plant and drove off. Thankfully nothing was ever said.

Early in 1977, the "scab" employees were no longer being utilized and except for sleeper duty (which I still had my fair share of), I didn't have a job. I got hired by a cable company to lay undergrown cable. It was hard work, but it paid the bills. There was talk of a paramedic system being started up that would be based out of Stevens Hospital in Edmonds, Washington. Throughout the rest of 1977 and into 1978 things had become stagnant for me. I didn't like my job; all I did was party all the time (my philosophy was "why worry about tomorrow when I can get drunk tonight?"). I was immature and irresponsible, and I was going nowhere fast.

On the way home from work one night, I was tired, but I knew that there was a party nearby. I pondered driving straight home or taking the next right. I chose the latter, and as it turned out it was one of the best decisions I ever made. At this party, I met a very good-looking girl by the name of Barb. I had never seen her before and found out she was a junior from the same high school (Meadowdale) that I had graduated from. At first, she didn't want to have anything to do with me. Finally, we played some pool, and she started talking to me. We dated for about a year and then got married. This January will be our 43rd wedding anniversary (TCL).

In 1979, the only paramedic program outside of Snohomish County was the Seattle Fire Department. Seattle Fire Department was nationally (and internationally) recognized for its outstanding program. Medic 7 (based out of Stevens Hospital and designed to work on the same premise as Seattle's) went into service and made an immediate impact on EMS in South Snohomish County. Cardiac arrest patients were being saved and the new age of Advanced Life Support, (medication administration, defibrillation, airway control, etc.) was here. As I had mentioned earlier, my goal was to become a firefighter/paramedic, but unfortunately, there was no training around and you had to be the age of 21 to be hired by Seattle. I went down to Barkers Ambulance and applied for a job, but they weren't hiring. I went out to my car and thought long and hard. *Join the military,* I decided.

I proceeded down to the recruiter's office and enlisted in the Air Force. I enlisted under "guaranteed enlistment," meaning I was guaranteed a specialty, Medical Specialist. I was told by the recruiter that I would leave for basic training in one month, so I got my affairs all in order and prepared for basic training. I had said all my goodbyes, turned in my bunker gear, and was ready to go. Unfortunately, on the day I was scheduled to leave, I was told that there was a problem with my technical school (where I would be sent for medical training after basic training) and that since I was "guaranteed enlistment," basic training would overlap with the upcoming technical school. I would have to go on "delayed enlistment" for four months. I had just moved out of my apartment, had no car, and no job. I couch-surfed for the next four months, spent a lot of time hanging out at the station (I got my bunker gear back), and lived at my sister's house. It was a long four months. Finally, the day arrived that I would leave for basic training. I said my goodbyes and boarded the plane for San Antonio, Texas.

AIR FORCE

I had never flown before. Heck, I'd never really been out of the State of Washington in my life. Now I was headed to Lackland Air Force Base in San Antonio, Texas, a foreign land I had only read about in a brochure that my recruiter had given me. I was flying Braniff Airlines and we made several stops along the way. I had been up most of the previous night packing and unable to sleep so I was tired. I cat-napped during the flight and was awoken by a flight attendant when we arrived in San Antonio.

We (me and probably 15 other recruits) were ushered to a blue bus that had "United States Air Force" written in white letters on both sides. We were bussed to Lackland AFB, and I remember it being a very quiet ride. As we were nearing the front gate, the bus driver announced, "Welcome to Lackland Air Force Base, your home for the next eight weeks." He then chuckled. None of us knew what to expect, but once the door opened, we were met by three screaming T. I's. (Training Instructors) who yelled, "Line up, short in the front, tall in the back!"

All of us had luggage in our hands and were scrambling to find a spot and checking out the guy in front of you and adjusting according to height.

I'm 6'4" so it was easy to find my spot. When everyone was in their proper spot (or so they thought), the T.I.s continued to yell at people until finally, we were in order. I've never seen a human being scream so much without taking a breath, except maybe a woman in labor. "Drop it!" was then yelled, referring to our luggage. Some laid their luggage down, and others "dropped it." "Can't follow a simple command?" he said, and we proceeded to "drop and pick up" our luggage for the next 15 minutes. The T.I.s yelled for another 30 minutes then told us to get upstairs and find a bunk. There must have been 45 bunks and only 15 of us. We woke up six hours later and the barracks were full. I never did hear the other 30 recruits come in.

That day (Day 1 of training), we fell out for formation and since we had 30 new bodies added to the picture, we had to scramble again to find our position. We were quite a sight: guys with long hair, afros, high and tight haircuts, and even two bald guys. We were called "rainbows," as everyone had different colored shirts, pants, and shoes. Our T.I. for the day was Sergeant Smoak, an ex-Marine who re-enlisted to become a T.I. He was close to 6'6" and probably weighed 250 pounds. With his "Smokey the Bear hat" (known as a campaign hat) while always peering down on you, he made for a real intimidating sight.

The first week's schedule we were with Sgt. Smoak for the day (0500–1800), and Staff Sergeant Berger would be our mother hen from 1800–0500. Every week they would rotate shifts. On the weekends, they were around but you never knew where they were. Sgt. Smoak told us the first thing we were going to do was go to the chow hall. "Look straight ahead and don't make eye contact with anyone."

There was an area off to one side called "The Pit." This area was where the T.I.s would eat, BS, and smoke. You avoided this area at all costs. If by chance you had to walk past "The Pit," you never looked over in their direction. I saw a couple of recruits look in their direction while walking by and I've never seen someone get so verbally abused in my life. There was a recruit in week 3 of training who was trying to get out on "psych medical."

He threatened to shoot all of us at marksmanship training (week 5), but no one batted an eye. One morning during breakfast, the recruit got up on a chair, pulled down his fly, and attempted to urinate on a couple of instructors. All we saw were lions attacking a rabbit. Threatening to shoot someone won't get you kicked out but pissing on an instructor definitely will.

After 10 minutes the T.I. would yell, "Up and out!" You immediately stop eating (don't try to sneak in an extra bite), and you walk over (no talking or eye contact) to the garbage can and throw all that delicious food into the garbage. U.S. citizens would be up in arms if they saw all the waste that happened many times a day, every day.

We then lined up in formation and attempted to march to our next destination: the barber shop. We were lined up five across and when five recruits came out, five more entered. You walked to the chair and handed the barber a one-dollar bill (as a tip) and sat in the chair. Thirty seconds later you looked like a scrotum. You thanked the barber and went back into formation. Our next stop was the issuance of uniforms (known as fatigues). Here we were measured for uniforms (green) as well as our dress uniforms, T-shirts, underwear, socks, belt, boots and dress shoes, coats, hats (both green and dress), plastic name tags for your dress shirts, rain gear, and name tapes. It was impressive how the fatigue coats and shirts were done. You would take them over to a window where they were taken back to several seamstresses who embroidered your name and sewed it onto your fatigue's shirts and coat (initially, all the insignias were blue and silver). A week later we had to return to the seamstresses and get green and dark blue insignias (known as subdued insignias), as the Air Force had just switched over to this style. Since all but three of us were Airman Basics (E-1), we had no stripes. The three who had college degrees or who had enlisted for six years were automatically Airman (E-2) and had one stripe on their shirts.

We marched (or tried to) back to our barracks. There we were taught how to make a bed, (not your normal at-home bed making), how to stow away all our personal hygiene belongings, how to prepare our locker for inspection, how to shine our boots, and how to properly wear the uniform. All these things may seem obvious, but the Air Force has their own way. We were allowed to make one phone call to a loved one. There was a sign over the phone that read, "Hello, this is (your name). I have made it safely to basic training and this is my squadron number as well as my flight number. I will be writing to you soon. Goodbye." Then hang up. That's it, no conversation. There were a lot of teary-eyed recruits walking away from the phone.

We went back to the chow hall for dinner then returned to the barracks for perhaps one of the most important training classes we had, dorm guard duty. We were told earlier in the day that training day 1was "dumb shit day." You know nothing and cannot be held responsible for any of your actions because you don't know the rules or laws when it comes to ignorance. Training day 2 changes all that. You are taught military bearing, policies and procedures, and the big one, the Uniformed Military Code of Justice (UCMJ), which is the "bible" when it comes to what you can and can't do while in uniform (or out of uniform and off duty). After day 2 of training, you must sign a contract stating you understand the law of military justice. Once signed, you are basically at the will of the Air Force. You can now go to jail, receive an Article 15 (punishment short of discharge), be charged with absent without official leave (AWOL), and after 30 days of being AWOL, you can be charged with desertion. Time to walk the straight and narrow.

One of the threats always held over our heads was being "sent back." Every day of training a new subject was taught. If you "screwed up" on one of these subjects, you could be "sent back" to that day of training, meaning you must make up every day of training from that point. As I said earlier, dorm guard duty was probably the most important, because it was taught on day 2, and because the T.I.s would do any and everything in their power to make you "screw up." Dorm guard duty is this: Every evening from 1800–0500 there is a dorm guard on duty. It was his job to walk around inside the barracks while everyone is asleep and watch for any fire or anyone trying to leave the barracks or enter without proper authorization. Our T.I.s (Sgt. Smoak and SSgt. Berger), were allowed entry on "facial recognition". The squadron commander (the sergeant's boss) is admitted by proper name and special colored card. Through basic training, I never saw the squadron commander once. Any other T.I. had to have a special-colored card, a current picture, and other current credentials, and the dorm guard must look at the person, compare the picture to the card, and ask them their name and reason for entry. Other platoon T.I.s would screw with the dorm guard and try to slip him up. I did dorm guard duty three times during basic training and never had a problem, but a couple of my fellow recruits did and were almost tricked.

One time a T.I. (not ours) was banging on the door and screaming that the barracks were on fire and for everyone to evacuate. The recruit kept his cool and asked for proper identification. The T.I. refused to show identification and kept banging on the door. The T.I. threatened to have him thrown in jail but the dorm guard stood firm and relied on his training. The T.I. eventually became frustrated and left. The lesson to be learned was, if unsure, never let anyone through the door. They can't hurt you if they can't get to you. I had heard stories of recruits on their 28th day (two days from graduation) being sent back to training day 2 because they didn't follow their training and allowed an unauthorized person into the barracks.

On day 2 of training, we were up at 0500 (and given two minutes to get our physical training (PT) gear on) and told to fall into formation. We exercised, then ran. At 0545, we were given until 0600 to shower, dress, and be back in formation to go to breakfast. When we lined back up, we all looked the same. Green fatigues and black boots. Every time you entered the chow hall there was a full-sized mirror that you had to salute and say "Airman (your last name), reporting as ordered." This prepared you for when you got called into the T.I.s office to get your butt chewed. Every recruit was required to carry a "351" in their right shirt pocket. A 351 was a slip of paper with your name, squadron number as well as your flight number that you carried in case you screwed up. The piece of paper had to be perfectly folded in half with the top folded over so it would hang out of your pocket (hidden by the flap of your pocket) and be able to be easily "plucked" from the pocket. T.I.s, (as well as officers) on the base could at any time pull this paper from your pocket if they saw you screwing around, misrepresenting the Air Force, or a million other things. They would write a comment on the slip and keep it and put it in the recruit's T.I.'s mailbox. Big Brother was always watching. You always carried two 351s in your right front pocket because you were required to always have one on your person. If one was taken, you always had a backup. If two were taken and you didn't have anymore, God help you. Recruit T.I.s did not take kindly to receiving these slips and the recruit undoubtedly would suffer their wrath.

After breakfast and UMCJ training, we marched, and marched, and then marched. While in basic training, you had no contact with the outside world, so you never knew what was going on. As we fell into formation for dinner, our T.I informed us that a man named Jim Jones and about a thousand of his followers had committed suicide in a place in Guyana called Jonestown. There had been talk up the chain of command of sending several flights (including us), down to help with body retrieval. The next morning, we were told that there was a change in plans and that other bases around the U.S. would be sending personnel down.

Weeks 1, 2, and 3 went by and everything was a blur. Physical Training, marching, more marching, classroom, more marching, you get the picture. During Week 4, recruits were offered the chance to take a "bypass test." If a recruit could score higher than 40 percent of the exam related to the specialty they were pursuing, then they could "bypass" going to technical school and upon graduation from basic training, be assigned immediately to a base and have on-the-job training. I took the test and scored a 60 percent so I would be going directly to my permanent base, (even though nothing's permanent). Weeks 4, 5, and 6 were a blur also. We marched, learned to fire an M-16 rifle, ran an obstacle course (known as the Confidence Course), and lastly prepared for graduation. The last week was focused on parade marching, flag etiquette, uniform preparedness, etc.

Graduation went off without a hitch and we prepared to leave the base in two days. Since I had taken the bypass test, my orders were not to go into effect for two weeks, so I was able to fly home for two weeks. I remember flying home from a warm San Antonio to a bone-chilling Seattle. On the flight home, the pilot was kind enough to put the airplane on its side somewhere over Oregon so we could all see the area where a fatal commercial airplane crash had occurred the day before.

My orders stated to report to McClellan AFB in Sacramento on or before January 15, 1979. McClellan AFB was an Air Force logistics command base (AFLC) on the outskirts of Sacramento near North Highlands. The base had a ratio of four civilians to one soldier and it was almost like working at Boeing. The base's main function was to repair and paint fighter jets (F-4, A-4, F-5, F-111) and cargo planes (C-130, C-141, C-5). There was the constant sound of planes in the air, and when an F-111 took off, all the buildings would shake (quite an impressive jet). When a C-5 took off, it seemed to stand still in the air (there was more than one time I caught myself saying "come on baby you can do it, fly, fly"). They always got off the ground.

I was assigned to the emergency room. In the same building, we had a clinic, pharmacy, X-ray, and records. Downstairs was Optical and Hearing. Upstairs was the flight surgeon's office. Next door (roughly 10 yards away) was the immunizations and pediatric clinic. We had two van-type of ambulances and a crash truck that was operated by the flight surgeon's office during the day and by the emergency room crew at night. The clinic and E/R were open Monday to Friday from 0700–1700. At 1700 hrs., when all the doctors went home, the E/R shut down and any on-base emergencies were handled by the E/R crew. If military personnel or a dependent were ill or injured, (and non-emergent), the patient would be transported to Mather AFB. If civilian, the patient was transported to American River Hospital by military ambulance.

I rode a train from Edmonds, Washington, to Davis, California. I was to be met by a sponsor from the base, but he never showed up. After an hour of waiting and standing in the rain, I took a cab to the base. I checked in at the administration office and was assigned a room in the barracks. I grabbed all my gear and walked the two blocks to the barracks. I unlocked the door and lo and behold, I had a roommate. Meet Sgt. Pete McAuliffe. Pete was surprised (and a little miffed) that he had a new roomie. Normally, sergeants did not share a room (rank and privilege). Unfortunately for Pete, there was no room available in the barracks. Pete and I became good friends. Pete was honorably discharged about six months later, and I had a room to myself (until I got married and had to move off base). Pete had his room set up like an apartment. Stereo equipment covered one wall, bookshelves, a microwave area, etc. I told Pete I wouldn't need much space and we made it work.

The next morning at 0700, I reported to the noncommissioned officer in charge (NCOIC), SSgt. Pete Pidlypchack, who showed me around and introduced me to everyone. The first thing I had to do was get measured for uniforms. I arrived wearing a light blue uniform shirt with dark blue pants and uniform shoes. The uniform of the day for medical personnel was a white shirt, white pants, squadron baseball cap, and black boots. The rest of the day was base orientation, paperwork, and policy/procedure manuals. I picked up my new ice cream uniforms and I was finished for the day. I had just gotten promoted from airman basic to airman and now had a stripe on my uniform and a little more cash per month.

On day 2, I reported for duty as the new "pecker checker" (as we were fondly referred to because we did physical exams) and started shadowing the other personnel and learning as we went. I observed the others perform minor surgery, give injections, start IVs, debride wounds, and dress wounds, (to name a few duties). I became proficient at all the care that was provided and soon, I was on my own. My specialties were suturing and toenail removal. I became so good at suturing that the doctors would refer their patients to me. Facial suturing was by far the most challenging (especially on kids) because of the fine suture material as well as the goal of leaving no scar. Toenail removal wasn't glorious, but it was rewarding. Patients would come into the E/R walking on their heels because of the pain and walking out normally. I would see patients "flinch" when someone came within five feet of them because of the fear that they would step on their toes. If I was a doctor with my own private practice, I could make $800 per toenail. I saw some very gnarly toes with the nail so far into the skin that the toe looked like a plumb. As I said, it wasn't glamorous but heartwarming to see the relief on their face.

There is an unwritten rule in the military that you don't mess with two organizations (three, if you want to include chow hall personnel). These two organizations are medical and military. There is a very high likelihood that you will cross paths with either medical personnel or military police during your enlistment. Every active-duty personnel must be up to date on vaccinations as well as physical exams. Military police are there to intervene when you get drunk and do something stupid. One of the services we provided in the clinic were "4.8s." Personnel would come in with painful urination, pus discharge from the penis, and generally feeling "like crap." Diagnosis: "The Clap" (sexually transmitted disease). After diagnosis, the patient would have to attend a class on S.T.D.s in environmental health and then was given a medication called Benemid, (to "potentiate", or increase the strength of the antibiotic, they were about to receive). STD patients fell in one of two categories. Category One: 99 percent of the patients we gave these injections to were ashamed, remorseful, and swore they would never do it again. Category Two: 1 percent of the patients were arrogant assholes and would flip us shit or come in multiple times because they didn't learn their lesson.

Category One patients were treated specially. They would come back to the exam room with the script in hand and confirm to us they had taken their Benemid then be sent to the waiting room for 30 minutes while the Benemid started acting. While the patient waited, we would take two syringes full of Penicillin out of the refrigerator and let them get to room temperature. Each syringe looked like mayonnaise and contained

2.4 million units (X 2, thus 4.8) of penicillin and was so thick it had to be given by deep intramuscular injection (IM), which meant it had to be given in each buttock. Since the medication had to be given deep within the muscle, it had a 2-inch needle on it. Just before the patient was due to receive his injection, we would hold it in our hands and roll it back in forth to help warm it up. The patient came back to the treatment room and dropped his pants (and underwear) and would lean over the exam table (or sink) and prepare for the shot. It seemed every patient's bare ass was like snowflakes: no two looked the same. We had to visualize a "plus sign" on the buttock and inject it in the upper right (or left, depending on which cheek) region to avoid the sciatic nerve. We would confirm they were not allergic to penicillin, tell them to "hold on," and give the injection. The patient would instantaneously tense up, let out a scream, and grab for the injection site and try to rub away the pain. We would give the patient the choice of waiting a few minutes for the next one or giving it right away. A majority of the patients wanted to get it over so they would request "now." After the second injection and the same results, the patient would have to sit out in the waiting room for 30 more minutes to ensure no reaction, then they were free to go. I never gave a "4.8" to a female.

Category Two patients were handled differently. (Trust me, I did not invent this barbaric way, but I was told it taught a lesson.) The patient would report back to the treatment room and instead of going back to the waiting room, he would be placed in an exam room immediately. The medic would take the syringes out of the refrigerator, pull the caps off the needles and tap them on the metal desk to dull the needle (known as the Square Needle). We would clean the tips with alcohol (to prevent infection) and quickly give the injections. Cold Penicillin and dull needles made for a more painful experience. As I said, I did not come up with this idea but did as I was ordered.

There was one medic in the E/R who was fantastic: well trained, great skills, and just a good guy. His name was Senior Airman (SRA) Jim Harvey. Jim was openly gay and when he "came out," he was unable to re-enlist (he didn't want to). Jim and I responded to calls together and things always went smoothly. When it came time for discharge from the military, and you got your discharge papers, you would write "FIGMO" (Fuck I Got My Orders) in black pen and tack it to the bulletin board for everyone to see. Jim, in his last act of defiance, wrote "FAGMO." I had just gotten promoted to Airman First Class (two stripes, more pay), and things were going uneventfully until one morning my partner, and I were ordered to the squadron commander's office for an unknown reason.

In the military, you are never outside without a hat (known as "cover") and you never walk into a building with your cover on.) We hastily made our way for the commander's office when I couldn't find my hat (it was in the ambulance, which was out on a call) so one of the captains tossed me his hat and said, "Take mine." I was in my fatigue coat with two stripes as we walked and all these enlisted soldiers with stripes were saluting me. Enlisted personnel do not salute other enlisted personnel. Enlisted personnel only salute officers. It dawned on me that the hat I was wearing had captain's bars on it and the enlisters thought I was an officer. I could have been arrested on the spot for impersonating an officer (a serious offense). I turned the hat around, so the captain's bars were not obviously visible and bee-lined it to the commander's office.

We were escorted into his office, saluted him, and stated, "Reporting as ordered." The commander held up a plastic bag filled with plastic objects and asked me, "What in the hell are these?" "Vaginal speculums," I replied. "I know, dammit/ I'm a doctor." Apparently, his kids had been dumpster diving near the clinic and found all these "cool space guns" and brought them home to play Martians. The commander's wife saw and confiscated them and gave them to her husband. My partner and I were wrongly accused of throwing them away when in fact it was the night crew (whom we had relieved that morning) that had thrown them in the dumpster. They had cleaned and stocked all the exam rooms the night before. We took the verbal abuse, saluted, then hightailed it out and back to the clinic (we took a path less traveled). We reported our interaction to the NCOIC. Cleaning protocols were changed and as far as I know, never happened again.

We had a diverse group working in the clinic/emergency room and all got along like family. One impressive thing I learned was how the members of color on the team kept their hair "regulation." At night, they would put nylon stockings on their heads and the static electricity kept their hair compressed down to acceptable standards. After getting off duty, they would use their pick combs and re-style their hair back into an afro.

We worked three 12-hour shifts on, then three days off, so every other weekend, we worked Friday, Saturday, and Sunday. We worked days for three months, then switched to nights for three months. One Saturday, I was tasked with tearing out the old linoleum in the patient compartment of our frontline ambulance and replacing it with new linoleum flooring. This meant responding in our backup rig, an old Pontiac that looked like a hearse. Luckily, we only had one on-base call that day, so I was able to remove all the trim and hardware (and linoleum) and replace it with new before I got off duty for the day. It turned out well (if I say so myself), but couldn't be used until the next day, giving time for the smell of the adhesive to dissipate and the glue to adhere. Bad news for the night crew.

About 1100 hrs. the next day (Sunday), we were dispatched to the base golf course (about five miles from the base), for a possible heart attack. Myself and my new partner, (a small female airman, (females were called "airman"), (who had just gotten out of technical school), responded in our newly refurbished ambulance. I drove as she had never driven an ambulance before and didn't know the area. We made the eight-minute trip without incident. Upon arrival, we were directed to the ninth green and were met with several golfers, two of whom were doing CPR.

The story was that a 60-year-old male who had just been released from the hospital for congestive heart failure (CHF) had been in the golf course bar having several beers while waiting for his tee time. The patient had just finished breakfast and complained of a "little chest tightness" and was a little diaphoretic (sweaty), when he teed off. Members of his foursome had tried to discourage him from playing, but he shrugged it off. The patient had a couple of more beers as they walked the course and he even lit up a cigar. By the ninth hole, the patient was pale and was short of breath. The ninth hole was up a gradual incline, and the patient was just about to putt when he "just collapsed." CPR was initiated by his buddies, but typical of cardiac arrests, the patient began vomiting and no one was willing to do mouth-to-mouth.

Upon our arrival, the patient was blue (cyanosis). I got out of the rig and ran to the aid kit compartment, grabbed what I needed, and told "Jane" to grab the oxygen. We rolled the patient on his side and using towels and my fingers was able to get the big chunks out. I then suctioned more beer and hashbrowns out of his throat and ventilated him several times with the BVM. I expected Jane to connect the BVM to the oxygen, but she wasn't there. I looked between the golfers and saw Jane standing next to the ambulance in a catatonic stare. I called over to her, but she didn't move. I inserted an esophageal obturator airway (EOA), inflated the cuff, and we began better ventilations. (An EOA is a tube that runs down the esophagus with a bulb near the end near the stomach and an inflation cuff located on the other end that extends out of the mouth. You fill the cuff with approximately 35 ccs of air from an empty syringe that inflates the bulb and prevents vomit from traveling up the airway out of the mouth. There are little holes in the tube located right about where it sits in the throat that allows oxygen to be delivered to the lungs. The EOA comes with a mask that attaches to the tube that allows you to hold the mask firmly against the face for a better seal and better oxygenation.) We were having difficulty getting a good seal because a bystander had pulled out the patient's dentures and his mouth "caved in." The vomit on the face was also making it difficult. (Suggestion to anyone who may have to do CPR: If the dentures are in place and don't pose an airway problem, leave them in.)

By this time, I realized I was on my own. The base fire department didn't respond to aid calls (off base), so I relied on bystanders to help. I showed one citizen how to ventilate and the others were performing good chest compressions, so I went to the ambulance to get the gurney and a backboard, and we loaded up the patient. (You want to have something rigid under a cardiac arrest patient, so the heart has something to compress against when being pressed on. Without rigidity, you're just pushing the patient, and not the heart, into a soft surface.) It had been raining and the ground was soft and slippery as we made our way to the ambulance.

By this time, Jane had moved from her spot but still had a bewildered look on her face. After we loaded the patient in the back of the ambulance, the first thing the citizen who was performing chest compress did was to dig his golf shoes into my brand-new floor and put slices in it. I asked the two golfers if they could assist us to the hospital as I couldn't treat the patient by myself. They agreed to, but I had another problem. Who was going to drive? Jane was in no condition to drive—let alone code (run the lights and sirens)—to a hospital she had never been to. I quickly told her the route to the hospital and told her to drive as carefully as she could (this guy was dead, no use in killing four more). Jane replied, "I'm pretty sure I can do it." I switched the siren to "manual," which allowed her to press on the horn for the siren to work instead of taking her eyes off the road looking for buttons. We had parked on the cart path/service road and began transport to the hospital. First thing Jane did was cut the cart path too early and the next thing I know, we're stuck in the mud. Jane's accelerating just got us in deeper. I told her to stop. I got out and recruited some golfers to push us out. I jumped in the driver's seat and after several attempts, we became unstuck.

Jane began crying and said, "I can't do this, I'm going to be sick." I attempted to reassure her that she was doing great, and this would soon be over. She hesitated, then got back in the driver's seat and away we went. We got thrown around quite a bit on the way to the hospital, (slamming breaks, hard acceleration, turning corners on two wheels will do that), so the golfers dug into the floor even more. Soon the golfers were sweating, and you could see the fear in their eyes. I mouthed "she's new" to them and I assured them we would be at the hospital soon. Wrong. When you're transporting a patient who is dying (and in this case, dead), time stands still. It seemed like it was taking a very long time to get to the hospital (should have been a 15-minute ride), but we were approaching 30 minutes. I asked Jane how much longer and she said, "I don't know." I looked out the front and noticed we were going away from the hospital. In her flustered state, she had turned right at a street that I had told her to turn left onto. We had to back track our route and finally made it to the hospital. The hospital staff worked on this poor guy for 15 minutes then pronounced him dead. Friends at the golf course had beaten us to the hospital and taken my two rescuers home (thank you, gentlemen, for your hard work).

Needless to say, it was a quiet trip back to the base. I tried to make small talk, but all Jane did was sniffle and stare out the window. It was almost 1400 hrs. when we got back to the clinic. Jane went home sick, and I got stuck cleaning the mess in the ambulance. Monday morning, Jane was transferred to Records, and discharged from the Air Force a couple of months later. Moral of the story: If you just got out of the hospital for CHF, don't go golfing.

Roughly two to three times per month, we would receive reports that there was an in-fight emergency known as a "corker." F-111s were constructed with a material that when ignited, would give off a residue that could damage electrical equipment. Every time an alarm was sounded (a red phone that would continuously ring until answered, known as a "ring down phone" from the air traffic control tower), the flight surgeons office would respond out to the flight line, and we would cover all the electrical equipment in the E/R.

During my time at McClellan, we never had a serious incident on base, but we did have a private plane with engine trouble attempt to land. The plane went down about half a mile from the runway and everyone on board was killed. One day, after another corker false alarm, one of the people from the flight surgeon's office (Sgt. Randall Pitts) was walking through the E/R and we got to talking. Randall worked part time for an ambulance company in Roseville (roughly 10 miles northeast of the base) and told me I should apply.

I went to Roseville and was interviewed by the owners (a nice married couple) and was hired on the spot, (I was still full-time military and worked part time for the ambulance company on my days off). There were two ambulance companies in Roseville at the time and they didn't get along, akin to the movie "Mother, Jugs, and Speed." (I'll refer to them as Company A and Company B.) They serviced Roseville, Rocklin, and a portion of Placer County. Both companies worked on a "rotation" basis for the fire departments but also responded to private calls. Both companies' "bread and butter" were interhospital transports and long transports (Roseville to San Francisco, for example). One of my first calls was for an "1180" (CHP code for "Accident, major injuries") on I-80. It was dark and the report was vague on exact location. We arrived but no other agencies were on scene.

We shone our spotlights and found a single vehicle that had gone off the road and hit a railing. As my partner got the kits, I went up to the driver's side and noticed the railing had entered the front windshield and exited out the back. The spotlights illuminated just enough to where I could see the driver but no one else. The driver's window was shattered, so I shouted, "Hey, are you ok?" No response. I then shook the driver's arm. Again, no response. I went to check for a pulse and put my fingers on his neck, but I couldn't find his head. I pulled out my penlight and shone it on the driver and noticed a lot of blood but no head. It was in the back seat. I'll never forget the expression on his face as he saw that railing coming at him.

I was working a night shift on base, and around 0630 hrs. the next morning, we were dispatched to an industrial accident at the paint shop building. When we arrived, we were directed to drive into the building. As we pulled in, I noticed a guy smoking a cigarette, being propped up in a sitting position with the help of a co-worker. The co-worker was helping the guy smoke. The first thing that caught my eye was the skin on the man sitting was as white as the white coveralls he was wearing. I walked up to the patient and noticed that the man's two hands were flopped over with bones protruding from the wrists. Also, both legs seemed to be shortened by almost a foot (he reminded me of Tim Conway's "Dorf").

The paint crew had been attempting to unload the fuselage of an F-5 when it shifted and began to fall. The patient's first instinct was to stop it from falling. The fuselage broke both of his wrists and landed on his legs, breaking both femurs. I called for a second ambulance as we only had one Hare traction splint on our rig, and we were going to need two. We laid the patient on his back and started high flow oxygen via a non-rebreathing mask. We placed a blanket under and over him to keep him warm and splinted his two wrists. By this time, the second ambulance arrived with two great physician's assistants (Lt. Jones and Lt. McMillan). While Jones and McMillian started two large bore I.V.s, my partner and I applied the traction splints. After a fluid challenge, (a large amount of IV fluid infused into the patient), he was given morphine for pain and loaded up for transport. The destination was UC Davis Trauma Center. Going out the gate, my partner and I were relieved by the oncoming day crew. Amazingly, the patient came into the clinic about nine months later. With the help of canes, he was getting his mobility back. His wrists were repaired, and he looked a million times better than the morning I first met him. No amount of money could replace the joy and accomplishment we felt that day.

As I mentioned earlier, the two ambulance companies did not get along. Company A was having an employee appreciation party and had invited Company B to attend. Much to everyone's surprise, Company B arrived in their one and only ambulance. The date was November 4, 1979 (I remember, because it was the day the Iranian hostage situation began). Everyone was having a great time getting along, when Company B received a call to respond (they were "up for rotation"), with Roseville Fire Department. The crew got into their ambulance to respond and found that they had a flat tire (slashed to be precise) and couldn't respond. Company

A ended up taking the call. This incident put a further wedge between the two companies that was never resolved (at least in my time there).

On April 7, 1979, my fiancé, Barb, gave birth to our first daughter, Nichole (did I fail to mention I was going to be a dad?), and it was one of the happiest days of my life. It also changed me as a person. Now I had responsibilities that I was going to have to live up to. Barb and I were married on January 4, 1980, and I had to move off base. We rented an apartment a couple miles from the base in North Highlands, and I liked the freedom of not living on base.

In August of 1980, Company A had reduced my hours and since I got along with Company B, they hired me as a part-time employee. One evening I was working with the owner of Company B, when a full-time employee, Kesner "Jay" Flores, came in and told the owner that he was giving his four-month notice, as he had just got accepted to paramedic school starting in January 1981. Envious (and a little jealous), I asked where he was going, how he got accepted, and the cost. Jay had taken a written test and interview to get into Daniel Freeman School for Paramedics in Inglewood, California.

The next morning, I contacted Daniel Freeman and talked to an administrator (Winnie Hobbs), and she told me about the curriculum and answered all my questions. She told me the class was filling fast and that I would have to come down as soon as possible if I wanted to attend the next class. The only opening was two days later at 1300 hrs. and the whole process (test taking and interview) would last approximately three hours. I knew I had to work the night shift on base that day, but felt I could make it back before 1900 hrs.

I flew from Sacramento to Los Angeles and arrived two hours early for my appointment. My appointment ended up getting delayed for 90 minutes and now I was worried I wouldn't get back in time for duty on base. I started my test around 1430 and was finished with the first three parts quickly. The final part was reading comprehension and had roughly

20 short stories (each about a half page long), then questions about the content of the stories. By this time, my test time was nearing its end and I still had five stories to read. Knowing I still had the interview, and fearing I wouldn't get back in time, I guessed on the final five questions.

I went into the interview right after the test. Winnie Hobbs went over my test results, and I had only missed one answer on the first three parts. However, I missed the last five answers on the reading comprehension. She told me that reading comprehension was critical in learning such a complex training course. She told me she had great concerns that I wouldn't be able to keep up with the class. I assured her I would be able to excel in class (I didn't mention that I guessed on the last five questions), and she told me she would have to think about it.

Disappointed, I caught a cab and flew back to Sacramento. I walked through the E/R doors with five minutes to spare. It was a weekend, and I hadn't heard a word about acceptance into the school. First thing Monday morning, I received word that I had been accepted and they would be sending me some prerequisite materials to study and return. I was honorably discharged in November. We packed up and moved back to Washington. Since I had two months before starting school, I worked with a high school buddy of mine (Ron Steele) doing repairs and roofing at many of the nursing homes his parents owned. One night, we were playing cards and watching Monday Night Football, when Howard Cosell announced that John Lennon had been killed (December 8, 1980). I was a big Beatles fan and my prediction of a Beatles reunion faded along with him. On December 30, I packed my bags, kissed the family, and flew to Sacramento.

PARAMEDIC SCHOOL

Jay and I were to leave Sacramento and drive down to Los Angeles on January 1, 1980. Didn't happen. Jay's car engine threw a valve as we were leaving, so we had to find a used car. Jay was a Native American as well as a military veteran, and as soon as he started paramedic school, he would be receiving benefits. I had two thousand dollars in my wallet that was to hold me until my wife could send me some money (she had just gotten a full time Job at Flukes Manufacturing). Jay made a deal with me. If I purchased a used car, I would never have to worry about money during school again. We purchased a reliable looking used car that day and we were on the road that night.

We pulled into Los Angeles the next morning, and our first objective was to find a place to live. The school had suggested that students arrive a week before class to find housing. We didn't. We ended up living in a motel in Compton for the first month. On January 4, 1981, (my one-year wedding anniversary), we arrived for the first day of class. We were required to wear a shirt and tie, along with a white lab coat that had our name tag.

Picture day. As we walked in the door, we noticed desks with two rows of three books stacked two high. One of the students moaned "Are we going to have to learn all this?" Carol Hagberg (one of our great instructors) replied, "There's more." Sure enough, when we came back from lunch, there were just as many more new books. Classroom, ("Didactic"), ran from 0800–1700, Monday through Friday for eight weeks. We took a written test every morning covering the material we were taught the day before. We had lectures and practical exams every day. One of my favorite lecturers was Dr. Walter Graf (Dr. P-Wave).

Dr. Graf was a well-respected cardiologist and a big part of the Los Angeles County Paramedic Program. What Dr. Michael Copass was to Seattle Medic One and King County EMS, Dr. Walter Graf was the equivalent In Los Angeles County. Dr. Graf had a wonderful ability to get his point across and make it understandable. I took a great interest in cardiology because of Dr. Graf. (Dr. Graf was also the only cardiologist I knew who smoked.)

In the early 70's, there was such a need to get paramedics on the road, they were given a crash course on how to start IVs and secure the airway with EOAs. EKGs were sent by way of telemetry and the doctor would interpret what type of cardiac arrythmia the patient was in. The doctor would order the paramedic to give a medication by the color of the box. "Give three-quarters of the red box" (lidocaine). "Give two of the gold boxes" (sodium bicarbonate). "Give one of the gray boxes" (1:10,000 Epinephrine). Or "give one of the blue box" (D50W). Color-coded boxes eventually went by way of the dinosaur. Paramedic students of today are taught how to analyze and interpret twelve lead EKGs, endotracheal intubation, and drug dosages for the myriad of illnesses and injuries confronted in the field.

Jay had gone to the administration office to get enrolled for benefits but was told that there was a glitch, and he wouldn't start receiving anything for three weeks. We were getting low on cash and resorted to eating hot dogs and nacho cheese Doritos every night for dinner (Friday and Saturday night we ate leftover pizza and chicken from the "all you could eat pizza" joint we went to on Fridays).

We learned about the circulatory, respiratory, and nervous systems and all the medications given in the field for each. We were taught medications that counteract the medication given. We learned how to start IVs, intubation, pediatric emergencies and treatment, IM and IV medications, and how to read EKGs in the field. We were taught invasive procedures like central lines (subclavian, internal jugular, femoral), emergency cricothyrotomy, chest darts, nasogastric tubes and activated charcoal, defibrillation, and cardioversion. We learned OB with complications as well as overdoses and psychological problems.

As we finished up the classroom portion of our training, it was now time for hospital internship; time to apply what we had learned. By this time, Jay and I had moved out of Compton and rented two rooms from fellow student Terry Quella. Also renting a room was a great guy from Idaho by the name of John Meade (known as "Tater"). Jay and I had not ventured out for the nightlife while in Didactic, every night our noses were in the books, asking each other questions until the wee hours of the night. As soon as hospital internship started, we were putting in 12-hour days at the hospitals. The hospital where I spent most of my time was Martin Luther King Jr. Community Hospital in Watts. A fellow student and I were paired up and he would drive us to the hospital on his motorcycle.

Watts, California, is a predominately Black community. Since we were white, there was concern by the administrators for our safety. We were told to wear black-visored helmets along with black gloves and to look straight ahead when at stop lights and never make eye contact with anyone. I wasn't concerned (however, we were escorted in and out of the hospital by security on several occasions because of threats on our life).

The training I received at MLK was priceless. The E/R was always understaffed and always overloaded with patients. From trauma to medical,

I saw hundreds of patients. Even though we were told by the school that we were there to learn and apply our knowledge, we weren't there to be janitors or gofers. I was happy to help the staff with anything they wanted. They treated me so well that I wanted to pay it back. I did my fair share of cleaning poop, vomit, and blood, but I was rewarded 10-fold by the knowledge, training, kindness, and patience of the nurses and doctors. Although I had experience in starting IVs, a Korean nurse who went by the name Monty made me better. Monty probably started 30 IVs in a shift, and I never saw him miss. He could get lines where no vein was visible or palpable. I was probably starting 15–20 IVs a shift, giving meds both through IV and injection. I got to intubate cadavers. I put in NG tubes. A majority of the IVs I started were for "banana bags" or "Drunk Cocktails." These were liter-size bags of either normal saline or Ringer's lactate that had a combination of thiamine, folate, magnesium sulfate, multi-vitamins, and potassium.

A lot of the patients that came in would be highly intoxicated so they would be given this concoction in their IV. It turned the fluid yellow, thus the term banana bag. Any patient that came into the emergency room got an IV. There were a lot of "regulars" and "returners" who would come in when the weather turned wet and cold. You would see a patient come in from the night before with their wrist band and band aid from a previous IV still on. I don't think I ever went a shift without a shooting or stabbing. We had a young girl (14 years old) brought in for combativeness and hallucinations. She had smoked a "Sherm" (a Sherman cigarette dipped in PCP (phencyclidine), known as "angel dust"). This girl could not have weighed more than 80 pounds, but she was strong enough to throw me (6'4" and 215 pounds) off the gurney after I was directed to sit on her while an IV was being started.

We had a lot of patients come through the E/R doors because of this drug. One of my more memorable calls was a patient brought in by the LA City Fire Department. Their patient had attempted to commit suicide by drinking a bottle of DDT. Organophosphate poisonings are unique because they stimulate the parasympathetic system (opposite of the sympathetic system), and cause a drop in hear rate, drop in blood pressure, and an increase body secretion (salivation, diarrhea, and vomiting). The paramedics in the field had given the patient several milligrams of atropine (a parasympathetic blocker) to reverse the effects, but it did little good. The patient left a trail of vomit and diarrhea from the E/R entrance to the treatment room. We ended up giving the patient more atropine to the point that we ran out. I had to run to the pharmacy to get more. Finally, the patient began to respond to the atropine (all the previous abnormalities mentioned reversed). The patient was transferred to the ICU. I never heard of his outcome.

In between patients I would have my nose in the "Bible" (the LA County drug book), studying for the upcoming LA County paramedic test. After several weeks in the E/R, it was my time to spend a week in pediatrics and labor and delivery (upstairs at MLK). They were more understaffed than down in the E/R. Again, the staff was great. At the time, if someone cut the umbilical cord, California law stated that person had to sign the birth certificate. I ended up signing five. Labor and delivery was so busy, the doctors would concentrate on high-risk deliveries and allow the students to perform "routine deliveries." I also was allowed to be "up close and personal" on several Cesarean sections.

I finished up my hospital internship at a couple of hospitals in Van Nuys and Torrance. Soon, it was time to take the LA County paramedic written test (I passed with a score of 98%). You had to pass this test to be allowed to go onto the final step in school, paramedic evaluations. Los Angeles City, Los Angeles County, Pasadena, and Beverly Hills were the fire departments that participated in the paramedic evaluations. I was assigned to Los Angeles City Fire Department Station #53 in San Pedro. At the time, LA city paramedics were not firefighters. They were "certified paramedics" that responded out of the stations for medical emergencies but did not get involved with firefighting. (This changed in the 1990s when paramedics were trained to be firefighters.) LA City referred to their paramedic units as "rescues."

Station #53 housed an Engine #53 (manned by an engineer, a captain and two firefighters) and Rescue #53 (manned by a Paramedic I and a Paramedic II). Paramedic I's drove the rescues and oversaw getting the vehicle to the scene and hospital safely. Paramedic I's were also responsible for starting IVs and airway control. Paramedic IIs had more seniority and experience (and made more money), and normally rode in the officer seat (right seat) and directed the driver where to go, oversaw patient care, and rode in the back on the way to the hospital. Paramedic II's were responsible for all the paperwork and reports getting done properly. LA City Fire Department worked a "modified Detroit schedule" (24 hours on/24 hours off, 24 on/24 off, 24 on/96 hours off).

Since I was assigned to a certain shift, I only rode along when they were "on shift." My first shift was the day after President Reagan's assassination attempt. On my first day, I walked into Sta. #53 and was met by Paramedic I Rex Roth and Paramedic II Van Berquist. (These two guys were great mentors and made a huge impact on my training.) Rex was showing me the Rescue and where all the equipment was stored. I hadn't been there ten minutes, when we got a call for a possible stabbing at the Federal Correctional Institution on Terminal Island. We were also advised to await police escort, as this sounded like a potential prison escape. Reportedly, the patient was a "bad ass" who had attempted to escape on several occasions. We were escorted through the gate and met by prison guards who wheeled the patient out on their gurney. The patient had suffered multiple minor lacerations to the arms and chest that police (and the E/R doctor) classified as self-inflicted. We walked the patient to a SWAT vehicle that looked like an armored car and transported him to the hospital. The patient had all his minor wounds cleansed and then was transported back to the prison via the SWAT vehicle without incident.

During the day, when the Rescue got dispatched, OCD (the dispatching agency for LA city) would make an announcement of "Rescue" (followed by a tone) and give the nature of the call and the address. There was a ring down phone on the wall, a direct line from OCD to the station that rang continuously until someone pushed a button on the wall to silence it. Pushing the button would signify that the Rescue was responding. Since there was so much voice traffic over the station's speaker, a lot of radio transmissions were sent by MODAT (mobile data) that sounded like a robot whenever a button was pushed. At night, the radio was placed on "alert" so the firefighters would not get woken up every time the Rescue was dispatched to a call (which I found out was several times a night).

My job as the "probie" was to immediately get dressed and run out to the bay and silence the ring down phone while the Paramedic II (who slept next to the phone) wrote down all the information. If an alarm came in for the firefighters, the station lights would come on, a horn (klaxon) would sound, and out the door they went. If it was a working fire, the Rescue would sometimes tag along to watch and standby in case someone got hurt. Every shift had its own cook. He would prepare lunch and dinner but did not partake in the clean-up. Every shift morning, everyone on duty had to pitch in $5. One dollar went to the "grapevine phone," a private line everyone used for non-business calls, and one dollar to the TP (toilet paper) fund. For some reason the city did not provide toilet paper. Any money left over at the end of the shift would be put in a jar for future expenses. These station cooks could prepare a feast on very little money (although they used a lot of coupons).

We were dispatched one night for a stabbing roughly two miles from the station. When we arrived, we found a "homeless wino" (according to friends) sprawled out on the sidewalk with his throat slit ear to ear. Apparently, the victim and two "friends" were sharing a bottle of Thunderbird. One of the of the "friends" accused the victim of taking a "double gulp" and finishing the bottle. A fight ensued and the "friend" broke the bottle on a light pole and cut the victim's throat. There was nothing that could be done for him. He was DRT ("dead right there").

Occasionally, on Friday nights during the cruise season, the crews from Sta. #53 would go down to the Port of San Pedro and spray water on the "Love Boat" (Pacific Princess), to the delight of all the passengers. By departure time, a lot of alcohol and champagne had been consumed.

Rescue 53 was dispatched to a reported gunshot wound to the chest. When we arrived, we were met by several police officer smoking and joking with each other. When asked about the patient, a sergeant replied, "Oh he's dead alright, you can go in and check for yourself." The patient had suffered a shotgun blast at close range to the chest and he was obviously dead. Suddenly, we heard a "KK" sound (the sound of a shotgun shell being put in the chamber). We turned around to find the wife of the victim standing behind us. Her exact words were, "I wanted the fucker dead, now get out." Apparently, the police had cleared the immediate area of the shooting but not a shed in the backyard. The wife had hidden in the shed and when she saw us through the widow, she came back in the house. We slowly collected our kits and backed out of the house. The police, shocked and embarrassed, ran into the house and disarmed and arrested her. I heard that the sergeant got demoted. Now, every time I hear a shotgun being cocked, the hair on the back of my neck stands up and this fond memory comes rushing back.

That same day, we were dispatched to "someone sleeping" near a tree at a local golf course. We were advised the patient was on the back nine (usually where all medical emergencies occur), and an employee in a golf cart led us to the patient. When we finally got to the patient, he was propped up against the base of a tree with his chin to his chest. Witnesses stated that the patient had been on the ground at the tee box when a foursome picked up the patient and propped him up next to the tree and "played through." No one had bothered to check the breathing status of the patient (they were probably running late for the 19th hole). We worked the cardiac arrest, but the patient had been down too long. We waited for the police to show up (a couple of them had been at the shotgun incident); they didn't make eye contact.

I finished my paramedic internship soon after and then it was time for graduation. I had responded to so many great calls and gained an enormous amount of experience and self-confidence. I finished in the top five in my class (thank you, Winnie, for taking the chance on me). Barb, my daughter, Nichole, and several friends and relatives flew down from Washington. It was a nice ceremony. I have nothing but great respect and appreciation to all my instructors, the doctors and nurses, my classmates, and especially to all the personnel at Station #53. You will never know how much I learned from both the fire personnel and the paramedics. Thank you, Van and Rex, you were the greatest. It's no wonder the Los Angeles City Fire Department is rated a Class 1 department. You may ask, what did you do after graduating from Daniel Freeman School for Paramedics? We went to Disneyland.

FIRST JOB AS
A PARAMEDIC

I returned to Washington, and it was time to find a job. I had been encouraged to apply to the Los Angeles City Fire Department, but as mentioned earlier, they were not firefighters. If I were in my younger years (and the fact that LA City now has firefighter/paramedics), I would do it in a second. Unfortunately, when I returned to Washington in June 1981, there were no firefighter/paramedics (except for the Seattle Fire Department), and the only paramedic system in Snohomish County was Medic 7 out of Stevens Hospital. I applied at Medic 7 but was turned down because I did not have the two years of experience that they required.

I traveled south looking for a job until I hit Longview, Washington. I walked in and was met by a short man (reminded me of Louie DePalma from the show "Taxi," but minus the crazy hair) by the name of Lou Castillo. Lou was the manager for EMA/Longview Ambulance (Emergency Medical Ambulance) and we talked for over two hours. Lou explained their program: A paramedic and an EMT/ALS (trained to start IVs and intubation) were teamed together and would respond on BLS (basic life support) and ALS (advanced life support). Starting pay was $800/month working up to 17–24-hour shifts (which worked out to $1.96/hr., but heck, you must start out somewhere). The work schedule was 72 hours on and 72 hours off (every other weekend was a three-day work weekend). Lou asked me if I could start the next day, I said "Yes, I can." (I had to drive 150 miles back to Lynnwood and drive 150 miles back down again the next day.)

Lou took me over to St. John's Hospital to meet Dr. Gary Penner (Cowlitz County EMS medical director), who oversaw the hiring of all paramedics and approved me to start the next day, but I would have to take the Washington State Paramedic Test within the next 30 days. Even though I was a certified Los Angeles County paramedic and nationally registered, Washington State did not recognize these certifications. I was required to gain reciprocity. I passed the test and now I was officially a Washington State paramedic.

My first day on the job was July 3, 1981. I walked in and was greeted by the owners, June and Gene Summers. They owned the ambulance company as well as several rentals and a souvenir store (TCL) in Castle Rock. Gene was in his early 70s, (as was June) and still worked part-time on the ambulance. EMA had two frontline paramedic ambulances and two back up BLS ambulances (one of which Lou would take home every night). If anyone called in sick, Gene would cover that opening.

After introductions, June told me that they had to get me "equipped" before I could start responding on calls. I was a little confused by her comment as I thought I had just put on a uniform shirt and was ready to go. Wrong. Getting "equipped" meant purchasing my own equipment. June took me into a room that had all types of equipment I would need. First, a Plano 747 medical kit; second, a set of curved and straight laryngeal scopes (for intubation); third, a blood pressure cuff and Rapaport stethoscope; fourth, IV fluids (D5W, normal saline and Ringer's lactate); and finally, IV infusion kits and all the medications we were authorized to administer in

Cowlitz County (controlled substances like morphine, Demerol, Valium, and phenobarbital that were dispensed by the hospital). Total: $800. I had not even run a call yet and my first paycheck was spent. I was responsible for all my own equipment and if anything got lost or stolen, it came out of my pocket (I ended up losing three stethoscopes during my tenure at EMA).

All the paramedics took their "med kits" home with them when not on duty. All other supplies (nasal cannulas, O2, gauze, bandages, etc.) were supplied by the ambulance company. Every item used (even a Band-aid) was itemized on a charge sheet and sent to the patient. Charges were ridiculous. The company inflated every item used by 400 percent. Taking a typical call (for example, breathing difficulty), here were the standard charges, if treated and transported by EMA: base rate (just to show up at the door): $125; running code (lights and siren), $50; mileage: $5/mile; after 1800 hours (night charge), $25; oxygen therapy (not including nasal cannula), $65; nasal cannula, $25; IV therapy (just to start the IV, not including IV fluid, IV tubing, or IV catheter), $65; IV equipment, $50; medication (isoetharine, terbutaline, atrovent, aminophylline), $75; nebulizer, $35. I ran cardiac arrests where the final bill was well over $1300. I used to supply my own Band-aids so the patient would not get charged $4.

My partner was an EMT/ALS by the name of Mike Nelson. Mike was a nice guy who had perfect black hair. If we had a call, he had to stop by the mirror and make sure not one hair was out of place. We ran several BLS and ALS calls on day one but the most serious was early the next morning. At the time, there had been road construction near the Longview/ Kelso area. There were temporary (and confusing) on and off-ramps to I-5. A motorcyclist somehow had gotten onto I-5 Southbound in the Northbound lanes and went head on with a car. The patient looked like an unconscious ragdoll, with broken extremities, chest injuries, and closed head trauma. The only agency on the scene was Washington State Patrol. Since the fire department did not respond to accidents on I-5 (they would only respond with the "jaws" if requested), we called for the other crew on duty. The second crew (Paramedic Mike White and EMT/ALS Louie Stewart) arrived approximately 10 minutes later. We had the patient on a backboard (had WSP stabilize the patient's head) and secured the fractures the best we could. We ventilated the patient with a BVM and oxygen. We got the patient in the back and put him on the EKG monitor, which showed an idioventricular rhythm with a rate of 40 with no palpable carotid pulse. The patient was in electrical mechanical dissociation (EMD) (a grave sign). With EMD, the electrical portion of the heart is still (or barely working), but the heart is not pumping blood, which could be caused by several things (exsanguination, cardiac tamponade, tension pneumothorax, to name a few). The term EMD has been changed to pulseless electrical activity (PEA).

While I and the other crew were intubating and starting IVs, Mike started chest compressions and we all heard the crepitus as he pressed on the sternum. "Pretty spongy," Mike said, so I felt the chest and told him that it felt like a flail chest (when three or more ribs are broken in two or more places). Once intubated, we noticed the paradoxical respiration (when the broken side of the rib cage moves opposite of the other rib cage). We notified the hospital that we were coming in with a "trauma code" with an ETA of 15 minutes. The term trauma code sends an announcement throughout the hospital notifying respiratory therapy, X-ray, lab personnel, and the blood bank (with six units of O+ blood) to report to the E/R.

Dr. Penner met us at the E/R entrance, and since it was my patient, it was my responsibility to explain everything we found and did for this patient. When we went in the trauma room, there must have been 15 people waiting for us. Everyone was gowned up and ready to go. As soon as we transferred the patient over to the treatment bed, everyone pounced on the patient. A nurse started chest compressions, X-ray did their thing, respiratory hooked up a breathing machine to the endotracheal tube I had put in, blood was hung and being transfused, an orthopedic doctor was looking at the fractures (and shaking his head). Everything was being done, but the most important thing at that time was to get the heart started.

"Let's open the chest," Dr. Penner told the nurse next to him. She opened a large package full of surgical equipment as Dr. Penner was making his incision. A river of blood came pouring out of the incision. "Three liters," Dr. Penner estimated as the blood splattered all over the floor soaking everyone closest to the patient. "Rib spreader," Dr. Penner said as he held out his hand. The nurse handed him this unusual looking metal device with teeth and a handle. "Push in more blood," but as fast as they were pushing it in, the faster it was coming out. "Suction so I can see," Penner said. A nurse stuck a suction catheter in the man's chest and suctioned until a large container on the wall was full of blood. "I can feel two holes," Penner said while doing internal heart massage. About 30 seconds later, Dr. Penner said, "Forget it. His aorta is gone."

Slowly, everyone ceased their efforts and started disconnecting the equipment. The EKG monitor showed asystole (flat line). Housekeeping arrived and began the lengthy process of cleaning the room. There was blood everywhere, and these poor people were going to spend the next two hours sanitizing the place (just like a fire, 30 minutes of excitement and three hours of tedious cleanup). The back of our rig was a scaled-down version of the trauma room: blood everywhere, equipment strewn all over the place shelves, and cupboards trashed. Thankfully, with help from Mike and Louie, we got the rig back in shipshape after 30 minutes.

Since we had taken this call and because we worked on a call rotation, Mike and Louie were up for the next one, a chest pain. Off they went, emergency lights reflecting off the side of the building. I went into the nurse's lounge to write my report, and noticing ashtrays available, I lit up a cigarette (yes, I smoked, a habit I picked up in my early years at Fire Dist. #1). Dr. Penner came in the lounge and closed the door. He said that he had gotten the printout of the call and noticed we had been on scene for "25 minutes." Yes, I said, but before I could explain that we had had to wait for another crew to arrive to help, he said, "That's fucking unacceptable." I sat up in my chair, took notice, and proceeded to get a royal butt chewing. Explain to me, "the 'golden hour,'" he asked. I told him from the time the incident occurs to the time the patient gets to the E/R, the time should be less than one hour. "Wrong" he said. It is from the time the incident occurs to the time the patient gets to the operating room, "a big difference." I knew that a trauma patient who goes into cardiac arrest in the field has a less than 1 percent survival rate and if they arrested on the operating table, their chances of survival were a bit better.

"So now that you are familiar with the 'golden hour,' I want you to remember the 'Penner half hour.'" I had heard of the "platinum half hour" (when a patient is in the O/R within the first 30 minutes after trauma occurs), the patient's chances of survival are greater. Dr. Penner wanted to instill in me that since I had to deal with him, I would abide by his rules. "Medical emergencies are different," he said. "Transport when the patient is stable. You are going to do the same thing out there as we would in here." Dr. Penner went on to instruct me that from this point on, "Any trauma patient transported, you will do all procedures during transport." As he was leaving, Dr. Penner turned around and said, "Better quit those things, they'll kill you."

I was not sure if Dr. Penner was blaming us for the death of this bug that got squashed on a windshield, but I have remembered those wise words throughout my career. Thank you, Dr. Penner. I truly respected you as a doctor and as a good man. The next evening (remember, we worked 72 hours straight), we were dispatched to a restaurant about a mile from our quarters, for a subject who was choking. When we walked through the door, we could hear yelling, screaming, and crying in the back of the restaurant. We found a white male in his 50's laying on his back severely cyanotic and not breathing. Witnesses told us that the patient had been celebrating his birthday and I saw several wine bottles plus food on the table. The patient had been eating and laughing at someone's joke when he immediately stood up and put his hands to his throat (the universal sign of choking). Friends and family members started slapping the patient on the back in attempts to dislodge the foreign object but that did not work. Someone tried the Heimlich maneuver without any luck. I tried to ventilate the patient with the BVM, but the patient's cheeks just puffed up. I took the laryngeal scope and noticed a large piece of "something" in his throat. I took a pair of Magill forceps and was able to "latch on" to the obstruction and pull it out. Everyone gasped when I pulled out a chunk of steak that had to have been three to four inches long. As soon as I pulled out the chunk of meat, the rest of the meal came up with it. He began vomiting copious amounts of partially chewed steak, salad, scampi, and wine. We immediately turned him on his side and shoveled out as much as we could with a napkin, but the meal kept coming. Finally, he had emptied his stomach on the floor, and I noticed everyone who had earlier been "gawking" from their booths, had either left or pulled their heads back out of view.

I had just intubated the patient, when Mike said, "It looks like he is in V-fib" (ventricular fibrillation). I had Mike check for a pulse as I was charging the paddles, but he could not feel one. "No pulse," he said. I put some gel on the paddles, yelled "Clear!" (today they use gel pads: cleaner and better conductivity) and delivered a shock at 200-watt seconds (we always started low and worked our way up, no use "frying a heart" at 360 W/S when 200 might do). The patient gave a jerk, and I watched the screen return to the baseline but noticed a lot of "artifact," (electrical interference from an unknown source). We checked the leads and had found a lead that had come off due to the sweatiness of the patient, (yes there was V-fib, not artifact before I shocked). The patient had converted to a sinus rhythm with multi-focal PVCs (premature ventricular contractions), so we felt for a pulse (he had a weak one), and we attempted to get a blood pressure. Mike had already started an IV, so I gave the patient 75 milligrams of lidocaine, and I piggybacked a 3-mg per minute lidocaine drip. I looked at the monitor and the patient had gone back into V-fib. I shocked him one more time at 200 W/S and he converted to a sinus rhythm with occasional unifocal PVCs. By this time, the patient was trying to breathe on his own and his color had improved to light blue. By the time we got him to the hospital, the patient was breathing on his own, had a stable cardiac rhythm, and was pink. The patient was sedated in the E/R, sent up to the

ICU, and extubated the next day. The patient walked out on his own two days later. This patient was lucky. He had several things in his favor: a witnessed event, definitive care within three minutes, and the patient was otherwise in good health. This event was your "textbook call" and went very smoothly. A lot of patients do not do this well, and unfortunately a lot of them die. Happy birthday from Mike and Brian. Dr. Penner (whom I swore never went home) told us "Nice job." This type of incident happens around the United States every couple of minutes. Paramedics perform like this on a regular basis. Its why paramedic programs are invaluable.

Our quarters were in an old parking garage/repair shop on Commerce Avenue less than a mile from St. John's Hospital. On the other side of town was Monticello Hospital (I do not know if it still exists). Monticello was a laid-back hospital that usually catered to non-emergent type of care. I would estimate that we took 95 percent of our patients to St. John's Hospital. Our quarters were like a cave. It was so dark where we parked the ambulances that in the middle of the night you would bang into them when you got in to go on a call. There was a rule amongst the crews that if you received a call but got cancelled before you pulled out onto Commerce Avenue, you were still "up" for the next call. This was important, especially when there were transports to Children's Hospital in Seattle or a transport to Emmanuelle Hospital in Oregon.

We had just returned from a transport to Children's (a 240-mile round trip) and the other crew had just gone out on a call. Five minutes later, that same crew got cancelled, (and because they met the criteria for cancellation), we were "up" for the next call, and we had another transport to Children's Hospital.

After a couple of months driving 300 miles round trip in a beat-up Volkswagen, my family and I moved to Longview. At that time, Longview was a very depressed town with an unemployment rate of 15 percent. The only real businesses at the time were Weyerhaeuser and Reynolds Aluminum. We could not find a place to rent so June made me an offer

I could not refused. She told me, for no money down, and $450/month, I could buy one of her rentals and she would carry the deed of trust. Desperate, and with no place to live I accepted her offer (even though $450/month did not leave much from my $800/month paycheck). We stayed there for nine months before I headed back north (TCL).

Our ambulance quarters had no windows, so you never knew if it was day or night. However, like bats, we could sense when the sun went down and both crews would go out and do our favorite activity, play video games. Donkey Kong and Space Invaders had just made their way into convenience stores so we would spend time between calls playing these addictive games. During the night after returning from calls, we would play a game of "laser tag" with the streetlights. Most streetlights had a little sensor that when the sun came up, would shut off the light. Shining a spotlight on the sensor would trick the sensor into thinking it was daytime and shut off. After about a minute of being shut off, the sensor would detect that it was still dark and turn the streetlight back on. Whomever had the most "kills" by the time we pulled into quarters would win a Coke from the loser. You had to make your own fun.

Mount St. Helens had blown her top just a little over a year before I started at EMA. There was still noticeable damage, especially the log jams in the Cowlitz River. One day, we were responding to a call and the traffic was not moving (when driving down streets with buildings on both sides, the sound of the siren "bounces" off the buildings and you could not tell from which direction the siren was coming from), so I switched between the siren settings. There were three selections on the siren: wail, yelp, and hi-low. Wail is the traditional sound you hear; yelp sounds like a dog being kicked (used a lot when approaching an intersection); and hi-low sounded like the sirens used in London. I thought quickly switching through the tones of sirens would help the motorists know which way we were coming from. I switched to hi-lo and was immediately told by Mike, "Don't use that setting." Mike proceeded to lecture me how the hi-low siren was the universal signal that Mt. St Helens was erupting. Mount St Helens was still considered active and had "burped" several times during the year. Tensions were high for the townspeople, and I had increased it a little that day. Sure enough, people had called into the 911 center, asking if the mountain was blowing. I learned another lesson that day.

Speaking of Mt. St. Helens, I had mentioned that Gene and June owned a souvenir store in Castle Rock. This store was full of anything Mt. St. Helens, before and after she blew. They had just closed it down about the time I was hired. Hundreds of opened boxes were in this storeroom and June asked me if I wanted any souvenirs. She had said that she had so many boxes she had to get rid of that I could take as much as I wanted. Thinking I was helping June out, I filled three boxes with T-shirts, mugs, pictures, bags of ash, hats, pencils, shot glasses, banners, etc. The family and I were heading north (every other weekend, we would stay at Barb's parents' house in Lynnwood), for a family get together, so I thought I would give everyone a souvenir. Everyone took what they wanted, and soon the boxes were empty. At the end of the month, my paycheck was $400 dollars short. I asked June why and she said, "Oh, I just deducted what you took from your check." I was speechless.

We were dispatched to a woman in labor way up in the hills of Kelso. When we arrived, we were met by the patient and her sister (who made the call). The patient was full term and her water (amniotic sac) had ruptured. The crown of the head was presenting, so we prepared for a home delivery. Everything was progressing well until the head popped out. The newborn had meconium stain (fecal matter aspirated from the amniotic sac), so we used the bulb syringe from the OB kit and suctioned what we could.

Upon delivery (a boy), I estimated the APGAR score to be about a 4. At five minutes, and after a little intervention, his score had improved to 10. APGAR (appearance, pulse, grimace, activity, respirations) is a guide to tell how the newborn is doing on a scale from 0–2 for each category. We had a little chart in the pediatric kit and Mike called out the category and I gave an estimation. Most APGAR Scores on normal births at delivery are usually 7–10 and at five minutes, 10. Because of the meconium, our little guy needed a little help. This was my first delivery outside of the hospital and I had never intubated a child, let alone an infant. I cut the cord and then we wrapped the baby in a "silver swaddler" (an aluminum foil blanket) and worked on getting him to breathe. I must admit, I was shaking (hopefully I did not show it), so I took a deep breath and concentrated what to do next.

To deliver a baby in the field is usually an easy thing to do. The mother does all the work, and all we do is cut the cord, keep the baby warm, and transport. This was not the case. We tried stimulating the baby to breathe and he finally made attempts. There was still "gunk" coming out of his nose and mouth, so we suctioned more. I decided his breathing was not adequate, so I intubated him. I remembered that the size of the ET tube should be no larger in diameter than his pinky, so I grabbed one that was the right size and attempted intubation. I was completely surprised at how easy it was to intubate. It took only a couple of seconds on my first try to visualize the vocal cords and put the tube in. The only problem with infant intubation is there is not a cuff to inflate ("no hair on the pube, no cuff on the tube"), so the tube can be pulled out very easily. Plus, the area to secure (tape) the tube around the mouth is a lot smaller than the surface area of an adult. Mike ventilated the patient with a pediatric BVM with oxygen and the newborn started to pink up. Soon he was moving around, attempting to cry and rejecting the tube. I contacted the E/R doctor, and he told me if the newborn was stable and breathing on his own that we could extubate him, which we did. We continued oxygen by "blow by" and made the 30-minute drive to the hospital without incident. The newborn was evaluated, and it was felt that the patient needed to go to Children's Hospital in Seattle. With a pediatric nurse onboard, the other crew transported him north. The baby was discharged in "perfect health" a week later. One of the most rewarding calls of my career. While in Longview, I responded to three imminent births, the one just mentioned, a textbook delivery, and an unfortunate one where the female delivered a stillborn in the toilet.

Every Sunday, the on-duty crews were treated to a brunch at the Monticello Hotel by June and Gene. The Monticello Hotel was an old, beautiful building (with great food). While sitting around the table, June would ask the crews of any "unusual calls" during the week. Someone would pipe up and say, "Well we had a call for—" and June would immediately say, "I don't need to hear anymore, finish your brunch." She did this to write the whole meal off on her business expenses. One Sunday morning, Mike and I had arrived a little late for brunch. June asked why we were late. I explained that I had been in the E/R practicing central lines with Dr. Penner.

We had taken a patient to St. John's and while in the E/R, Dr Penner asked me if I would like to practice inserting a subclavian and intrajugular catheter. A patient had expired in the E/R, and they were waiting for the funeral home to come and pick up the body. I made several successful attempts on the body and thanked Dr. Penner for the great training. I had never attempted one of these procedures on a viable patient, so it was a priceless experience. June became extremely interested in our conversation. By the time I got back from the buffet line, June was gone.

The next day I was ordered by June to document everything I had told her about the central lines. June hated Dr. Penner and would do anything to get him fired. June had left the brunch and stopped by the E/R and was able to obtain all the cadaver's personal information, (many years before HIPAA), (Health Insurance Portability Accountability Act), and contacted the family and asked if they had given the hospital permission to perform experiments on their loved one. The family had not given permission, so June filled them in on what had occurred. After an internal investigation by the hospital and the family's attorney, an undisclosed settlement was reached out of court. Needless to say, any future procedures on cadavers were halted. After this incident, I despised June and made every attempt to avoid her.

Mike and I were called to the E/R for an "emergent transport" to a hospital in Vancouver, Washington. We had brought the patient in earlier after a motorcycle–car accident. The patient was a big man who had been riding his Harley without a helmet (at the time, the helmet law had been repealed in Washington) at a high rate of speed when he ran into a parked car. The patient was catapulted into the air, landing on his head. The patient was suffering Cushing's reflex (increase in blood pressure and slowing of the pulse due to increased intracranial pressure), but also decerebrate posturing and Cheyne-Stokes respirations. I intubated the patient; we secured him to a backboard and started the IVs en route to the hospital ("Penner half hour"). In the E/R, it was determined that the patient had an epidural hematoma and numerous cervical spine fractures. The patient was being kept alive on a ventilator. The E/R had drilled burr holes in the patient's skull to evacuate the blood that was causing intracranial pressure and had applied a "halo" (a medieval looking device that had prongs attached to a circular piece of metal and "screwed" into the skull to stabilize the neck). His long hair was in a pile on the floor from shaving his head. The patient had been taken off the ventilator and we were assisting his breathing with a BVM attached to high flow oxygen. The respiratory therapist (who had accompanied us) said, "Watch this." He quit ventilating the patient and the patient's brain began to swell out of the hole in his head. The R/T then started to hyperventilate the patient, and his brain "shrank" back into his skull. He told me, "Carbon Dioxide bad for brain, oxygen good." I had been taught how carbon dioxide was a potent vasodilator when it came to the brain and oxygen was a potent vasoconstrictor but seeing it in person was a real revelation.

The patient had a "chandelier" of IVs running (two peripheral, two piggyback medications running as well as a CVP (central venous pressure) line. There is a rule of thumb in EMS as well as in nursing that more than five tubes coming out of a body indicates a very poor chance of survival. This patient had a subdural bolt, endotracheal tube, two peripheral IVs, a central line, a Foley catheter, an abdominal tap, and a nasogastric tube: a total of eight tubes. As we were loading the patient up, the E/R doctor told me that he did not think the patient would make it to the hospital.

Fortunately, we had an uneventful trip, but he died a couple of hours later in the ICU.

Occasionally, we would respond in Rainier, Oregon. Our quarters were approximately two miles from the foot of the Rainier Bridge, which spanned the Columbia River. The area we responded to was covered by volunteer firefighters and had no paramedic service. Technically, since we were responding into another state, medical laws were different. Through a gentleman's agreement, we were allowed to perform some procedures but had to wait to get to "our side" of the bridge to do more technical procedures. One day I was working with Gene, and we got a call to Rainier for "chest pain." As I mentioned earlier, Gene was in his 70s and he drove like it. It took 15 minutes longer to get to the scene because Gene refused to go any faster than 40 mph. Gene's hearing was also non-existent. I would say, "Take a right at the next street," but he would keep going. The real entertainment with Gene was when he would start IVs. Gene always carried at least six pairs of glasses with him. When he attempted to start an IV, he would pull out all these glasses until he found the pair that he could "see" with (he reminded me of Fred Sanford of "Sanford and Son," digging through a drawer of glasses, looking for the right ones). Not a confidence builder for the patient. We had an unwritten rule: Three attempts and you are out. After the third unsuccessful attempt at an IV, your partner was to take over. I had several incidents with Gene regarding "three and out." Gene was a man of character with a good heart, but he saw the writing on the wall (it was glasses number 3) and retired (to the relief of us all).

With the retirement of Gene, the company had to hire a new part-time employee. I walked into work one morning and was introduced to Steve Dutton, a volunteer firefighter/EMT with Cowlitz County. Steve was also commuting to Portland to attend paramedic school. We hit it off great and had an enjoyable time (and interaction) on calls. One thing I immediately observed about Steve was he walked with a limp (not dramatic, but noticeable). One night, I got up to go to the bathroom (usually a premonition of an incoming call), and I noticed something next to Steve's bed: a fake leg. I later found out that Steve had been a volunteer firefighter in San Diego. He had stopped at an accident and was struck by a drunk driver. His lower leg was shattered, and it had to be amputated just below the knee. As I was headed to the bathroom, I nonchalantly picked up the leg and took it with me. I left the leg in the bathroom and went back to sleep. About an hour later, we get dispatched to a call and Steve stood up and attempted to put "his nub" into his prosthetic and fell flat on his face. Steve mumbled something under his breath as I flipped on the light. Steve's face was planted in the carpet, and I asked him, "Are you okay? What happened?" He asked, "What did you do with my leg?" I told him I had not done anything with it, but I think it might have walked to the bathroom and was sleeping in there. I offered to retrieve his leg, but he just started hopping one-legged to the bathroom. It was a real treat to watch him at night at the fire station. Jump into your leg, then jump into your boots. Steve would get his revenge years later.

We received a report of a fire on a large ship tied to a dock in Kalama. We were not requested to respond but as an FYI. Around 1500 hrs., Mike and I were transporting another "emergent patient" to Vancouver (WA), and on the way back we saw the heavy black smoke coming from the ship parked out in the middle of the Columbia River (originally, the boat was tied to pilings near shore, but a boater who feared the boat might catch other boats on fire, released the tethers and the boat drifted out). Naturally, this FUBAR decision ruined any chance of fighting the fire from the docks and all firefighting equipment and workforce had to be ferried out to the ship by small boats.

I told Mike as we drove by, "Mark my words, we will be down here for something before this shift is through." We listened to the scanner throughout the evening and heard how they were not having any luck getting to the seat of the fire. Around 0200 hrs., after returning from a call, we heard on the scanner that the Seattle Fire Department was offering to send down two "shipboard firefighting experts." Seattle's offer was immediately accepted, and the coast guard sent a helicopter to Seattle to fly them down. Around 0530 hrs., Mike and I were dispatched to respond to the ship fire for "an explosion with injuries." When we arrived, we were told that our patient was being brought to the dock by boat. Apparently the two "experts," who had just recently attended a class on shipboard firefighting, suggested to cut a hole in the bulkhead door leading to the seat of the fire and place a foam line through the hole and "suffocate" the fire. With everyone in position, a member of the coast guard used an acetylene torch and began to cut a hole in the door. Just as he was finishing, he heard the door making a noise and he jumped to the side. The introduction of fresh air into the hole caused a backdraft that was strong enough to send the bulkhead door flying, striking a coast guard firefighter in the head, and taking the top part of his head off. Killed instantly. Our patient was the one who had been cutting into the door. He received severe burns and was unconscious. Numerous bystanders (including the "two experts") received minor burns and lacerations and were treated at the scene.

The coast guard insisted on flying their injured companion to the hospital, which I happily agreed with. As we took off, the pilot asked me where I wanted to go. This patient was in need of a burn center, but I was more concerned with his head injury (which, if untreated, would kill him sooner than the burns). Knowing St. John's was closer, I told the pilot St. John's. From takeoff from the scene, to landing at St. John's heliport was approximately 15 minutes. Mike had to drive the ambulance back to Longview, so I had the crew members of the helicopter help me. While they applied burn sheets, I intubated the patient, drew bloods, and started two large-bore IVs with Ringer's lactate and infused the amount suggested using the Parkland Hospital formula.

While in flight to the hospital, the pilot jokingly asked me, "How do I get to this hospital?" I poked my head in and saw what I knew was the I-5 and told him, "At the next major interchange, go west." "Sounds good to me," he said, and soon I heard in my headset, "Hospital in sight." As we landed, the hospital staff were waiting with their gurney and wheeled the patient into the E/R. The patient was stabilized in the E/R and a couple of hours later was flown to Portland with a nurse in the same helicopter. After this incident, it was decided to abandon the ship and let it burn itself out. After several days, the ship (which was posing a major shipping lane hazard) was towed to Oregon and scrapped. Except for some disfiguring scars, the patient made a full recovery.

Dave Engebo, a great nurse as well as a prankster, was working a day shift in St. John's E/R. Dave had pulled so many pranks on us (more so on Mike) that the day of reckoning had arrived. I cleared it with Dr. Penner (who was working that day), who informed all the nurses except Dave. The scenario was that a bunch of us were out bird hunting when Mike was accidentally shot in the chest. There were five of us (Lou, Louie, Mike Nelson, Mike White, and me). We all donated about 50 ml of blood (we drew from each other using 50 cc syringes) and squirted it on Mike's t-shirt and covered his entire chest. We took an endotracheal tube and cut a portion off so only a little stuck out of Mikes mouth. We put Mike on a backboard and applied the uninflated MAST (Medical Antishock Trousers), (yes, they were still used back then), and taped IVs to both of Mike's arms.

We pulled up just short of the E/R doors and had our dispatcher call the E/R and tell them we were ready. One of the nurses (not Dave) announced that we were bringing a "gunshot wound to the chest and less than a minute out." We came through the E/R doors, and with Academy Award acting (after all, the patient was one of our own), we proceeded to inundate Dave with questions, pleading, and the "whole nine yards." Dr Penner got into the act by barking out orders: "Dave, do this"; "Dave, start another IV"; "Dave, we need to open the chest." By this time, Dr. Penner had Dave doing the OSRIC (Oh Shit, Run In Circles), and Dave probably couldn't remember his own name. One by one, we slowly exited the trauma room (nurses included), until Dave yelled out, "I need some help in here." We were all outside the room, when Mike sat up, spit out the tube and said, "Hi, Dave." Dave turned white as a sheet (and I think he may have even crapped himself) and started stuttering. At this point, we were all floored with laughter, but not Dave. For the rest of the day, when we brought in a patient, our first words were, "Hi Dave." He was still shaking.

It was March 5, 1982 (John Belushi had just died), and I needed a change. Although I loved my job, the guys I worked with, and gaining wonderful experience, I could not work for June anymore. There was talk of a company (Medix) out of Astoria planning to open shop in Longview. We had moved out of the old quarters and moved into a newer building at the foot of the Kelso Bridge. With the possibility of new competition, June had applied to incorporate three more ambulance names into her company. Since there would now be a "rotation of calls" between Medix and EMA, she had magnetic signs made that we would "slap on" the sides of the rig after every call. In theory, for every five calls, June would get four. Thankfully, I was gone before this happened. I had heard talk of Snohomish County starting their own system (separate from Medic 7 out of Stevens Hospital). There were three proposals of who would provide the service. Providence Hospital in Everett, "Barkers" Ambulance (both Paramedics only), and the Everett Fire Department (firefighter/paramedics). Everett Fire was the eventual selection. Everett's goal was to have the program up and running by July 1, 1982.

I went to apply at Everett, but they too required two years' experience as both a paramedic and paid firefighter. I was told that Snohomish County Fire District #7 (to be referred to Fire Dist. #7) in Clearview, Washington was also trying to develop a program. I went to Fire Dist. #7 and talked to Fire Chief Rick Eastman. He told me that the Snohomish EMS Council, (under the auspices of Dr. Steven Marks) had not yet voted on whether to approve Fire Dist. #7's request. Chief Eastman was confident that it would be approved. Chief Eastman told me if it was approved, his goal was to have it up and running by July 1, 1982. The request was unanimously approved three weeks later. Fire Dist. #7 planned to hire four certified paramedics and train them to be firefighters (one had already been selected to be the EMS Coordinator), Rick "Trauma" Rauma from M-23 out of Evergreen

Hospital in Kirkland). It was also rumored that a Fire Dist. #7 Volunteer (Bruce Young) was also "unofficially" hired, leaving two openings.

The testing process was going to be a "wham bam, thank you ma'am" process. Written and physical agility tests on one day, oral interview the next day. The written test was held in a little grange about two blocks from headquarters. There were 25–30 applicants taking the written test. I remember it was freezing in the grange even though the sun was shining through the windows. About three hours later, we took the agility test at the headquarters. The test consisted of advancing a charged 2½-inch line, "making and breaking" a hydrant, using a hose clamp to shut down a charged 4-foot supply line, lifting ladders, pushups, sit-ups, and finally a 1½-mile run. All the stations were timed events and if you did not finish in time, you failed and you were finished.

Between the written and agility tests, 50 percent did not score high enough to go to the oral interview. The next day, I woke up sicker than a dog. I could not keep anything down and I looked like "death warmed over" (according to my wife). The oral interviews were conducted in alphabetical order, and since my last name started with a Z, I was last. I arrived 30 minutes early and sat on a sofa next to the door. The interview panel consisted of the fire chief, two fire commissioners, and a retired Seattle paramedic. The fire district's secretary was also there, taking notes. Five minutes before my scheduled time, I ran to the bathroom and threw up one more time. I was now ready.

Bruce Young walked out of the interview, gave me a nod and a smile, then left. Two minutes later, I was walking through the interview room door. I walked up to each member of the committee and shook their hands. By the looks of me, they all probably thought I had typhoid. The interview lasted 30 minutes and they told me they would decide over the weekend and have a decision on Monday. I thanked them, shook their hands again and immediately went to the bathroom and threw up again, (thankfully none of them caught what I may have had), and went back to my in-law's house.

Ten minutes after walking through the door at my in-law's, the phone rang, and it was Chief Eastman. He wanted to congratulate me; on the "fine job" I did on the interview (I thought I had bombed), and offered me a job. The first words out of my mouth were, "Yes, sir, I want the job." He told me to report to Dist. #7 headquarters at 0800 hrs. to get fitted for new bunker gear and uniforms. Before he hung up, Chief Eastman said, "I hope you feel better" (they too could see that I didn't look well). After I got off the phone, I felt so much better that I went out and had Mexican Food (it must have been nerves). All four new hires were scheduled for medical check-ups later the next morning. We all passed our physicals, and we were to report for our first day of recruit school the following Monday. By this time, I had resigned from EMA, quit claimed my house back to June (my last dealings with her), and was ready to start my new career as a firefighter/paramedic.

FIRE DIST. #7

S nohomish County Fire District #7 is located south of the city of Snohomish and north of the city of Woodinville. It is bordered to the west by the city of Mill Creek and to the east by the city of Monroe. Fire Dist. #7 covers 55 square miles of unincorporated Snohomish County. Fire Dist. #7 has five stations (three that were strictly volunteer, and two stations manned by a crew of three (one lieutenant and two firefighters)). This information is based on my first day of duty, June 1, 1982. Since then, Fire Dist. #7 has merged with Monroe Fire Department as well as Lake Stevens Fire to form Snohomish County Fire and Rescue. At the time there were 28 fire districts in Snohomish County. Two were annexed by cities (there was no Fire Dist. #13), which brought the number down to 25. Twenty-five districts with 25 chiefs and 25 departments in their "own kingdom, doing their own thing." Each department had their own borders that they didn't cross, nor allow anyone to cross into. "Mutual aid" was virtually unheard of, and if used, the town must have been burning down. The emergency dispatching agency for fire and police was SNOPAC (located in the bowels of the Snohomish County court house, next to the coroner's office). Prior to the advent of Medic 71 (M-71), Dist. #7 relied on coverage from Medic 23 (M-23) out of Evergreen Hospital in Kirkland, Washington (King County). M-23 was usually unavailable (high call volume) or had an exceptionally long response time. Dist. #7 relied on "Barker's Ambulance" out of Everett, or Valley One out of Valley General Hospital in Monroe for BLS transports.

The major concern the Snohomish County EMS Council had when they approved the paramedic program was that there may not be enough advanced life support (ALS) calls in Fire Dist. #7 to keep four paramedics certified. Paramedics were required to have three endotracheal intubations and twelve IVs per quarter. M-71 would provide service to surrounding areas plus we were allowed to go to the operating rooms at Evergreen Hospital as well as Stevens Hospital to intubate surgical patients if need be. One cadaver intubation per quarter also counted. In my whole time at Fire Dist. #7, I had to go to the OR only once for an intubation, and that was because I was gone 12 weeks as an instructor at the state fire academy in 1987 (TCL).

Fire Dist. #7 had just passed a levy, (approved by the voters), to fund the paramedic program as well as to build two new "state of the art" stations, one in Clearview (Sta. 71, headquarters) and Sta. 72, (2.5 miles west of headquarters). The stations weren't expected to be completed for another 18 months so we ran out of an old "dome shaped" building that housed an engine, an aid car, and an old ladder truck. Dist. #7 had two major "death highways" that ran through their district: Highway 9, which ran from Snohomish to Woodinville, and Hwy. 522, which ran from Woodinville to Monroe. Occasionally, we would also respond to Hwy. 2, which ran from the city of Everett over the Cascade Mountains to eastern Washington. I saw more than my fair share of death and destruction on these roads.

The citizens of Clearview were still reeling from a horrific triple murder that had occurred on April 14, 1982 (just a month and a half before I was hired). Charles Rodman Campbell had been convicted of sexual assault on a female and sent to prison. One day, while on work release, Campbell escaped. Campbell got drunk and went to the home of his victim. Campbell murdered the victim, along with her eight-year-old daughter. A neighbor who lived across the street had gone to check on the victim (she hadn't been feeling well) and was also murdered. Campbell was tried and convicted of three counts of capital murder. He was sentenced to death. For the next 12 years, we had to watch this scum on TV strutting down the hallway of the courthouse, appealing his conviction, and later attempting to have his death sentence overturned. Justice was served on May 27, 1994. While kicking, whimpering, and pleading for his life, the "tough guy" had his neck elongated in the gallows of the Washington State penitentiary. One of my crew members was first on the scene and described the scene of the murders. Out of respect for the family, I won't.

June 1, 1982 was the first day of recruit school. The four of us reported to Sta.73 at 0800 hrs. In walked our instructor, Lt. Eric Andrews. Eric was a balding, grumpy-looking guy with no sense of humor. On first impression, I guessed he had to be 10 years older than me (later found out he was two years younger). I'm proud to say that Eric Andrews is perhaps one of the most intelligent people I have ever met. Eric knew a lot about everything (he even taught me how to disassemble a small engine and make it run again, along with teaching me how to wire my house). Eric retired from Fire Dist. #7 a couple of years ago but remains the chief of the Gold Bar Fire Department. Eric epitomizes the fire service and has trained hundreds, if not thousands of firefighters around the State of Washington.

Just like at a typical recruit school, we laid hose, carried and placed ladders, learned ventilation and overhaul, search and rescue, ropes and knots, pump theory, hydraulics, and how to drive and pump an engine. Fire Dist. #7 was unique in the fact that they were not civil service, and they did not have classifications for certain positions. From day one we were engine drivers as well as paramedics. Recruit school went by quickly and we all passed.

As we were participating in recruit school, we also had the responsibility of ordering and stalking supplies and equipment for the medic unit. A new 1982 Braun was on the way (but would not arrive for another month). Chief Eastman had told us, "I don't care what it costs, just have it ready to go by July 1." We purchased all the latest equipment, and except for a little haggling over where things should go (Rauma always had the last word), things went smoothly. Our medical control doctor was Dr. John Orozco out of Stevens Hospital (he was also the medical director for Medic 7).

Stevens Hospital was approximately 15 miles from our headquarters, and it was the E/R doctors at Stevens who would direct us. The main hospitals we transported to were Stevens, Evergreen, Overlake, Harborview, Everett General, and Providence in Everett. Firefighter Gary Meek and I were in an aid car that had been temporarily converted to a medic unit. We had all our equipment and were just waiting for July 1. Dist. #7 received a call for "difficulty breathing" off Paradise Lake Road. I looked at Gary and said, "Let's get the okay from the chief." The chief, without hesitation said, "Go ahead and respond." On June 28, 1982, I grabbed the mic and said "SNOPAC, Medic 71, (M-71), responding." The new dawn of paramedic service in Fire Dist. #7 had begun (not that we were trying, but we beat Everett Fire Department's paramedic program by three days).

Our first call was a routine shortness of breath (SOB). By the time we arrived, an engine with four volunteers was already on the scene with vitals taken and oxygen administered. Gary set up an IV. I started it and gave the patient a breathing treatment and she was "feeling much better" as we loaded her into the medic unit. The four volunteers were scratching their heads wondering where this guy (me), had come from. We transported the patient to Evergreen Hospital, and she was released several hours later. While at Evergreen, we were questioned by the nurses where we had come from. Since we weren't technically supposed to start for three more days, the word hadn't gotten to them who we were and where we were from. We also talked with the crew from M-23, who were relieved that they wouldn't have to respond into our area as much, plus we would be responding into King County to back them up.

Our new medic unit arrived around the middle of July, and it was beautiful. Large patient area, plenty of inside and outside compartments (including breathing apparatus storage), state of the art radios: the works. We switched all the equipment from the aid car we were using over to the new one, and that vehicle was moved to Sta. 72. By this time, all the paramedics had a partner that had been trained to be paramedic assistants, (PMA's). These were EMTs who were taught to be "the right-hand man" (or, as it turned out, women) for the paramedics. They were taught how to set up IVs, set for intubations, etc. Most paramedic programs run with two paramedics.

At the time, the fire district could not afford two paramedics per rig. (It's very costly to run a paramedic program.) Our system worked just fine, and I enjoyed it. I had come from a system that ran only one paramedic and I had enough confidence in my skills. There's an old saying "doctors save lives, but nurses save doctors." It's true in our profession, paramedics save lives, but EMTs save paramedics, (Emergency Medical Technicians have less training than a paramedic but focus on the basics that a paramedic may overlook). I had complete trust in my partners, and they saved me on more than one occasion.

Lt. Andrews had become my officer and my partner on the medic unit. If a fire was dispatched in our area, we both jumped on the engine and responded. If a medic call came in, we'd take the medic unit and leave the engine behind to be manned by the volunteers. Volunteer is kind of a misnomer, even though it's not their primary job, they get paid for coming to the station and so much per hour of call. I think they got a paycheck from the county once (maybe twice) a year. Ask a volunteer: they are not in it for the small amount of money. Volunteers do it because they are community driven and want to give back. Without volunteers, a lot of small departments wouldn't survive.

Eric and I were working one Saturday morning and the lettering for the new medic unit had arrived. Eric did all the wiring and design on the rigs, so I helped him put on the letters. We had put everything where it should go and had two large and two small "Star of Life" stickers. Rick Rauma hated the "Star of Life" as he thought it looked "cheesy" and resembled "a snake fucking a baseball bat." Eric asked me, "Do you think Rick will notice?" I said, "I'm sure he will." Eric put them on anyway, and sure enough, they were off five minutes after Rick walked in on Monday morning.

Up to this point, M-71 had not responded to anything memorable. We had our run-of-the-mill chest pains and respiratory distress calls but nothing challenging. On that Saturday afternoon, that would change. Eric and I had just finished washing the engine, when Fire Dist. #8 (Lake Stevens) was dispatched to a subject run over by a tractor. At the time, Dist. #8 was an all-volunteer department. District #8 had a lot of volunteer officers who had portable radios and when they received a call, all of them would come on the air asking questions, "What's the address? Nature of the call, etc. One of the officers arrived on the scene and immediately requested M-71. Depending on location, Lake Stevens could be 15–20 miles from Dist. #7. One thing we had in our favor was Highway 9. Hwy. 9 was a straight shot, and we could be there in 15 minutes.

Eric and I jumped in the medic unit and headed north. "Do you know where were going?" I asked Eric. "Nope," he said as he pulled out the Thomas Brothers map. I had a general idea where to go but Eric was going to have to fine tune the location. We came to a "T" in the road, and I asked, "left, or right?" "I'm pretty sure it's left," Eric said unconvincingly. Luckily it was the right way and we made it to the scene. When we arrived, there were several fire vehicles on the scene along with volunteer cars with all their green lights flashing. Along both sides of the road were more vehicles as well as a large field that was full of cars. When we couldn't get any closer, we parked, and grabbed as much equipment as we could both carry. We had not been given a "short report" while en route (status of the patient, vitals, what was being done for the patient, etc.). We were going in without an inkling of what was going on. When finally got to the patient, I estimated at least 100 people were in the backyard and pasture around the patient. The patient was celebrating his 50th birthday and his large family" had all chipped in and bought him a brand-new John Deere tractor. He had been driving it around (very intoxicated) and hit either a large rock or a log sticking out of the ground that threw him off the tractor and was promptly run over by it. I lifted the patient's shirt and saw a large bruising tire track that ran from his right pelvic crest to his left shoulder The volunteers had him on oxygen and had gotten a backboard ready. Eric was setting up IVs and I asked one of the volunteers to bring the MAST. There was a county deputy on the scene, and I asked him if he could do a "blood run" for us. (A blood run entails someone arriving with a tube of the patient's blood at the hospital before the medic unit arrives at the hospital. This advanced notice allows the blood bank to type and crossmatch the patient's blood and have it ready when the patient arrives. The red top blood tube is labeled with a sticker off the trauma wristband that is put on the patient. The rule of thumb is "one will get you six," meaning one red top should equal six units of blood.) The deputy took the blood and was on his way to Everett General Hospital. The patient was becoming combative (intoxication and shock were setting in). I had started two large-bore IVs of Ringer's lactate. Due to the patient's low BP and rapid pulse, Eric started inflating the leg compartments of the MAST (Medical Anti-Shock Trousers).

By this time, we were ready for transport. The volunteers had moved their vehicles and backed ours closer to the patient. Eric drove to the hospital and two Lake Steven volunteers assisted me in back. As we were crossing the Hewitt trestle, the patient went into respiratory arrest. As soon as I got the patient intubated, he went into cardiac arrest. CPR was started and we arrived at the hospital five minutes later. A renowned Everett thoracic surgeon (Dr. Jenkins) was just leaving the E/R to catch a plane for vacation. He noticed the deputy running towards the E/R with the blood tube and asked what was going on. The deputy told him the story, so Dr. Jenkins turned around and headed back into the emergency room.

When we arrived at the E/R, we were met by Dr. George Cossetto. We wheeled the patient into the treatment room (still doing CPR), and Dr. Jenkins said, "He won't make it to the O/R, we'll do it here." Dr. Jenkins proceeded to open the patient's chest and Dr. Cossetto performed internal cardiac massage. Dr. Jenkins located a couple of lacerations to the heart and repaired them. By this time, the units of blood were quickly dwindling, so Dr. Cossetto suggested using a filter and reusing the blood. Dr. Jenkins announced that he had a pulse. After suturing several other lacerations, Dr. Jenkins determined that the patient's liver was so badly damaged that there was nothing more that could be done. The patient soon went back into cardiac arrest, and that was it.

I went out to help Eric get the rig back in shape, then started writing my report. Soon, a large migration of family members started to arrive (a lot of them intoxicated) and asked me how the patient was doing. Perhaps the hardest thing to do in our profession is to tell someone their loved one has passed away. No matter how you say it, it still is received as "they're dead." I simply said, "I'm sorry, everything humanly possible was done, but he didn't make it." Several of the family members started cussing me out and accusing me of killing him. "You son of a bitch, he was talking when he left the house, what did you do to him?" I tried as best I could to explain what had happened, but they didn't want to hear any of it. "Fuck you, we'll see you in court," one family member said as he spit in my face. For years, that call weighed heavily on me.

Before I go any further, there are a few tidbits of advice I'd like to give to the newbies. One of the most important aspects of patient care is patient rapport. I estimate that 99 percent of all calls are initiated by the patient, a loved one, or a bystander. These people need care, and they want you to be there to help them in their time of need. The other 1 percent are incidents where the person doesn't want you there (the drunk who is being arrested, but needs evaluation before being carted off to jail, for example). First impressions are important. Before you walk through the door, take a deep breath, hold it for a couple of seconds, then exhale. Be confident (but not arrogant). As you approach the patient, make eye contact, (chances are, you'll see fear). These patients need reassurance now. The first thing I always did was get to the patient's eye level (being 6'4" and looking down at a little elderly lady could be intimidating for the patient). I would place my hand on the back of the patient's hand for two reasons: one, the feeling of a warm hand sometimes gave the patient a sense of relief and security, and second, it gave me a sense of the patient's skin vitals (warm and dry versus cold and sweaty). If the patient withdrew their hand, then I knew that made them uncomfortable and I would have to gain their confidence by talking. My first words were always, "Hi, my name is Brian, and we're here to help you." The second words were: "What's your name?" If the patient responded, "I'm Mrs. Anderson," or "I'm Mr. Johnson," that's what I referred to them as. If they responded, "I'm Jane" or "I'm "John," I would ask them if I could call them by their first name. If the patient answered yes, then so be it, if not, I would ask them how they would like to be referred to. Some patients may want to be referred to by a nickname or some other moniker. In the "old days," elderly people were brought up to be "proper." Never did you call an adult by their first name, only Mr., Mrs., or Ms. I made a mistake once and asked an elderly lady her name. She proudly announced, "I'm Betty Johnson." I said, "Hi Betty" and she flew into a rage. "How dare you call me by my first name? No one ever calls me by my first name," etc., etc. That generation has pretty much passed on, but beware, there are still some out there.

Another tidbit: Never sit down in a chair or on a couch without asking for permission. I was talking with a patient, and I sat down in a chair right next to her. She immediately started screaming at me at the top of her lungs, "How dare you sit there. That's my late husband's chair and no one has sat in it since he passed away." The last question I would ask would be, "How can we help you?" or "How may we help you"? I would finish my initial introduction with a pat on the back of the hand or a squeeze of the hand and look them right in the eye and tell them, "We're going to take good care of you." Sometimes you'll get sarcastic or uncooperative patient who'll just blurt out, "Fuck off, get the fuck out of my house." It happens. Don't take it personally. My little introduction would take no more than 15 seconds, but it set the tone for trust, reassurance, and a good foundation for patient care.

Speaking of trust, trust and honesty are two of the most important traits in our profession. I was always amazed how much trust most patients have in us You can't imagine the feeling when a crying mother blindly hands over her sick or injured child for you to care for. We are going into a stranger's home or business, and they don't know us from Adam. One of the most personal places in a home is the bedroom. Here we find patients in their most sacred haven, and we're allowed to "just walk in." I could have a patient in their night clothes who would willing lift their gown to allow me to listen to their chest or apply EKG patches. I could see that same person on the beach the next day, and they wouldn't even give me the time of day.

When I was promoted to captain, the paramedics would oversee the patient, but I would oversee the scene. Often it meant me going into someone's bathroom and looking for medications the patient was taking or looking in the refrigerator for insulin. Bottom line, I was trusted to walk unaccompanied through the home of a person I had never met. I have been in mansions, ritzy jewelry stores, and the like. I have had thousands of dollars and jewels sitting out in plain view and I'm proud to say, in my 35 years in this profession, I was never accused or questioned about any missing valuables. Not only is it wrong, but why risk your career and going to jail for taking something that doesn't belong to you? You will eventually get caught. Always be honest with patients, especially children. If the child asks "will it hurt" when starting an IV, tell them yes, you may feel some pain. If you say, "it's not going to hurt" and they start crying because of the pain, you've just lost the trust of that child. If you ever make a phone call from a patient's phone, always look at the mouthpiece before talking into it. I learned from Dr. Copass if a sick or injured child has a "fisted thumb," always beware. This is a bad sign. Always use your "gut feeling." If a patient ever makes the comment "I'm going to die" or "I feel like I'm not going to make it," heed these comments. They just might be right.

It was a beautiful August morning. Eric and I were responding to a "chest pain" in Lake Stevens, (Fire Dist. #8 had started requesting us on a regular basis). As we were approaching the Cathcart dump on Hwy. 9, a large two-trailered gravel truck was in the left turn lane to turn west. I was driving and we were probably doing 65 mph. As we approached the truck, I started to pass it on the left (state law stated emergency vehicles were required to pass on the left). I slowed down as we went into oncoming traffic (it was clear), and I mentioned to Eric, "I sure hope he sees us." He didn't. The truck started to turn, and if I had continued, we would have collided broadside with the cab of the truck. I slammed on the brakes and tried to avoid the truck by veering to the right. The medic unit hit the right side of the rear trailer. As we struck, the medic unit went on two wheels, almost rolling over. We then went on to the left two wheels, back and forth until the vehicle righted itself. Next, we were headed towards a 40-foot embankment. God must have been riding with us because we came to a screeching halt, inches before going over.

I looked out the broken driver's window and all I could see, and smell was black smoke and rubber from the 200-foot skid mark. The medic unit was just a month old, and it was already wrecked. My first thoughts were, *There goes my job*. I looked over at Eric and asked him if he was OK. "Holy shit," was all he could say. We got out to see if any other vehicles were involved and fortunately, none were. The damage was significant. Smashed left front end involving the motor, broken windshield, and left front quarter damage. Thousands of dollars damage and three months' downtime. Luckily for me, we had the windows rolled up and the air conditioning going. Pieces of glass were embedded in the molding above the door. If I had had the window partially down, those pieces of glass would have been embedded in my scalp. Fortunately, the WSP classified it as an "unavoid-able accident" and did not find me at fault. I kept my job and was given the wrecked hood as a souvenir.

On a Saturday evening, we were requested by Fire Dist. #8 to respond to a "possible heart attack" at the Boy's and Girl's club, right down the street from their headquarters. We walked into a wedding reception being attended by roughly 150 people. We had to maneuver our way through the dance floor to get to the patient. The patient was a big man (probably 350–400 lbs.), puffing on a cigar and short of breath. Family members had noticed he was sweating profusely, (the patient had just been sitting) and struggling to breathe. The patient had a history of heart problems and was on a long list of medications. The family had encouraged, then pleaded with the patient to let them take him to the hospital. He refused and argued that he wasn't going. Someone called 911. (This patient was one of the 1 percent I mentioned earlier.)

I went through my introduction and his first words were "Fuck you, leave me alone." I tried to develop a rapport with him but kept getting the "fuck you, get out of here." I talked with the patient's wife and told her I was concerned about his appearance and my "gut feeling." She pleaded, until she started to cry, then other family members chimed in. Finally, the patient agreed to be examined, but commented "Over my dead body am I going to the hospital" (a very prophetic statement). We placed the patient on oxygen (after having to wrestle his cigar away from him), obtained vital signs, and put him on the cardiac monitor. The patient's blood pressure was sky high, and his pulse was weak and irregular. The EKG showed multiple, multifocal PVCs and marked ST elevation (known as "tombstones), even though this was just a three-lead EKG (12-lead EGKs were years away).

I told the patient point blank that he needed to go to the hospital, and right now. "Fuck you," he said as he yanked the nasal cannula out of his nose. "Leave me the fuck alone," as he ripped off the EKG leads. I couldn't force the patient to the hospital because of his legal rights. I talked with the

E/R doctor who agreed with my assessment and told me to be sure to get a release form signed and have at least two witnesses also sign it. I asked him to sign a release form and he refused, saying something derogatory about me and my mom. I had the patient's wife sign the form as well as two police officers on the scene. As we walked out, I told the Dist. #8 volunteers, "Don't go home. We'll be back."

Sure enough, it wasn't 10 minutes later that we were dispatched to the same place for "male unconscious." "The King of Fuck You" was in cardiac arrest with Dist. #8 volunteer firefighters performing CPR. We intubated him, shocked him several times and threw everything in our drug kit at him. He was asystolic. I talked with the E/R doctor and told him everything we had done and the results. He told me to cease efforts. Normally, there are two avenues to deal with a dead body. Either the coroner comes out and takes the body or the funeral home. If there is an unexpected death or a death under unusual circumstances (gunshot, stab wound) occurs outside the hospital, it's considered a coroner's case. If the patient had a long medical history or had recently been seen by their doctor, chances are good that the coroner would release the body over the phone to the funeral home. In this case, the coroner did release the body over the phone and a funeral home (the wife's choice) came out to retrieve the body. Needless to say, this incident put a real damper on the wedding reception and people started filing out left and right. Soon it was only the sobbing family that was left. We had cleaned up our mess and had placed a sheet over the body. Ironically, the patient didn't "go to the hospital, over his dead body," just the funeral home.

The construction of the two new fire stations, approved by voters, was under way. The sites had been cleared and surveying stakes were in place. One morning, Gene Whiteside (a volunteer and owner of the local tow company and junk yard) stopped by the headquarters station with an Odyssey (a type of dune buggy) and asked us if we wanted to take it for a spin. The area directly behind the station (where the new station was being built) was all dirt, so we took our turns kicking up dirt and dust.

After we were done, we noticed that several of the surveying sticks had been knocked over or broken. We did our best to put them back where we thought they should go. To this day, if you drive onto the driveway of the station, you'll notice the station is cockeyed.

We received a call one Saturday morning for a child with scalding burns. We arrived to find a 4–5-year-old male screaming and crying from second degree burns (several were "weeping fluid"), from his navel and legs to his feet (including his genitals). The parents had been in bed sleeping and the child turned on the TV and was watching Bugs Bunny. Bugs Bunny was boiling carrots for breakfast so apparently the child thought he would do the same. The child filled a large pot of water, somehow got it on the stove, then turned on the burner (they were all on). He then went to the refrigerator and got several carrots and put them in the pot. After several minutes of boiling, he tried to pull the pot from the stovetop, and it overturned burning him with the boiling water. We put the child in burn sheets, and I started an IV with a butterfly catheter. "Is it going to hurt?" he asked. "Not as much as the boiling water," I told him. He didn't even flinch. We gave him morphine in small increments and took him to Harborview Trauma and Burn Center. He spent many weeks in the hospital, undergoing debridement and skin grafting. He made a full recovery. Remember parents, kids will say and do the darndest things.

We received a call to check on an elderly woman. The elderly woman had been talking to her daughter and began coughing uncontrollably, then the phone went dead. We arrived to find the elderly female on the floor surrounded by large clots of blood. We also noticed that she had large clots of blood coming from her mouth. As we were about to start CPR, the phone rang, and it was the patient's daughter. The daughter told me that the patient had terminal lung cancer and did not have long. The daughter also stated that the patient had DNR (Do Not Resuscitate) orders on the refrigerator. I told the crews not to start CPR. I called the E/R doctor and that was it. I walked out to the living room and one of the firefighters asked me, "What's on your cheek?" I walked into the bathroom and looked in the mirror to find I had a large blood clot sticking to my cheek. Lesson learned. Always check the mouthpiece of a patient's phone before using it.

We received a call on October 31, 1982 (Halloween), for a female with "chest pain." We arrived to find an older woman laying on her bed with a "little chest discomfort." The patient was just about to leave for the airport to visit family, when the onset occurred. The patient was cheerful and appeared to be in no distress. We had just put her on the EKG monitor, and as I was talking to her, I noticed her eyes roll back. I looked at the monitor and the patient had gone into ventricular fibrillation. I delivered one shock and she converted into a stable rhythm. "Oh, I must have dozed off," as she adjusted her wig. We transported her, and she was released about a week later. For several years thereafter, she would send us a huge Hickory Farm basket on Halloween.

We received a request for "mutual aid" from a neighboring department to our north (Dist. #4, Snohomish), for a smell of smoke in a large building (Dalgety Storage). When we arrived, we observed a long building (roughly one city block long), with nothing showing and a lot of fire rigs standing by. A walk-through was done, and the smell of smoke had dissipated. Still unsure, Fire Chief Bob Merritt ordered that an inspection hole be cut in the roof. Chief Merritt, Chief Eastman, a couple of Snohomish volunteers and I went onto the roof to cut the hole. The roof was a flat, hot tar roof and felt sturdy when we walked on it. The inspection hole was cut, and no smoke (or even the smell of smoke) was apparent. We shifted our attention to another part of the roof. I happened to turn around and noticed what looked like a blowtorch coming out of the inspection hole that had just been cut. "Look at that," I mentioned to the two chiefs. We all looked at each other and down the ladder we went. The cause of the fire was determined to be an electrical fire in the attic area of the building. Due to heavy insulation, the fire had been put in check. Once the hole was cut in the roof, the fire took off. Several interior attack lines were deployed, but due to the construction and maze-type layout of the building, extinguishment was difficult. At the time, the storage was full of recently harvested corn that also impeded advancement of hose lines. Bob Bigger and I advanced a 1½-inch line (a 2½-inch line would have been the hose of choice, but obstructions made it impossible to maneuver), and we were met with a wall of fire (by this time, the building was well involved). We attacked the fire until the alarm bells on our breathing apparatus began to ring. We stayed for another couple of minutes (we felt confident that we had enough time to get out by just following the hose), then attempted to exit the building.

At this stage of the fire, the ceiling was collapsing, and large amounts of insulation had fallen to the floor covering our hose line. We attempted to locate the hose but couldn't. We tried to back track the way we thought we had come in but took a wrong turn. By this time, our bottles were nearly out of air, and we didn't have a clue where we were (this incident was way before PASS (Personal Alarm Safety System) devices, IMS, (Incident Management System), "May Day," or emergency locator buttons on the radios). By this time, I had disconnected my low-pressure hose from the regulator and shoved it inside my coat, (there is a saying in the fire service, "Don't die in a fire with your mask off, die with it on"), and we were crawling aimlessly trying to get out. It was so hot, dark, and smokey, you couldn't see your hand in front of your face.

We came to a T in the wall and went right. We continued to crawl until we could hear some shouting. We crawled towards the shouting and soon we could see flashlights shining at us. As we crawled towards the light, we fell off a loading dock. Bob and I both landed on our backs, landing air bottle first. Let me tell you, there is no more eerier feeling than falling in the dark and not knowing when you're going to hit. This loading dock was only eight feet high, but it felt like an eternity to land. We were lucky, had we gone left at the T of the wall, we would have crawled right into the bowels of the fire. I had several close calls in fires, but this one was the worst. Bob and I escaped major injury (I still have a bad back from it). Saint Florian must have been watching out for us. By this time, the fire turned from offensive to defensive and all crews were ordered out from the building. We set up monitors and deck guns and did the familiar "surround and drown." Except for a small portion of one end, the building was destroyed. The building smoldered for several days. Today, an indoor soccer arena and restaurant/bar occupy the site.

A major portion of Fire Dist. #7 was considered rural. Many farms meant many barns. During my career, we had multiple barn fires. Late one night, we were dispatched to a barn fire approximately two miles from our headquarters. As we pulled out of the station, you could see a "large glow" in the area. When we arrived, we found a large barn fully involved. Sheep were running out of the fire engulfed in flames while others that had escaped were running back into the flames. As we were advancing hose lines, hysterical sheep kept running into us. Every so often, we would hear gunshots from the SCSO deputy (who had arrived before us), putting sheep out of their misery. By the time the sun was coming up, the fire had been extinguished (a total loss), and we surveyed the scene. In front of the barn lay several dead sheep (some killed from the fire, others euthanized), and so many dead sheep in a heaping pile under the rubble inside of the barn that you couldn't count. I am an avid animal lover, and this one hit hard. On a positive note, a dozen or so survived uninjured.

On another animal-related incident, we were dispatched to a small barn fire (I would describe it as a large, shed fire). When we arrived, the owner had most of the fire out. The weather had turned cold, and the owner had put a small electric heater in the shed to keep some chickens and a calf warm. Apparently, the calf had knocked the heater over and it landed in wet hay. The fire smoldered for a while and then ignited. All the chickens were accounted for, but the calf was dead. We pulled the calf out of the way and wet down the smoldering shed. I was walking past the calf, when I thought I saw it try to breathe. Thinking I was imagining it (and wishful thinking), I watched the calf and it tried to breathe again. Thinking *What the heck?* I grabbed the ventilation kit out of the medic unit. I grabbed the largest endotracheal tube out of the kit and attempted a "dactyl" (using my fingers) intubation. There are only two openings in the throat (trachea and esophagus), so I had a 50 percent chance of putting it in the right opening. Luckily, I put it through the trachea on the first attempt. I inflated the cuff, connected the BVM with oxygen, and started ventilating the calf. I had my partner take over ventilations as I examined the calf. Not expecting any results, we just watched the calf, hoping it would do something. Suddenly, we saw the calf try to breathe, then make more attempts to breathe. Finally, the calf was taking breaths in between our attempts to ventilate. Next thing we knew, the calf opened its eyes and attempted to get up. (We later learned that it was male from the owner. I should have checked.) Soon, the calf wanted up and was trying to pull away. I deflated the cuff and removed the endotracheal tube. The calf got up, and though a little wobbly, stood on his own. The owner came over, and seeing the calf standing, began to cry. (I even had a tear welling up.) She said, "This must be a sign. I'm never going to have him butchered." Lt. Andrews asked dispatch to contact an emergency vet clinic, explain the situation, and ask what the vet would recommend. Dispatch came back and said, "The vet recommends you give him 100 mg of Lasix." I drew up 100 mg of Lasix (a diuretic) and injected in his rump roast. The owner stated she would put some blankets in the house and the calf would sleep inside. I stopped by the next morning, on my way home from work. The calf was out frolicking in the backyard as if nothing had happened. Hopefully, she never turned him into hamburger.

M-71 was dispatched to a "sky diving accident" with Fire Dist. #4 down in the valley. Harvey Airport was located just south of the Snohomish River, East of Hwy 9. Harvey Field offered sky diving and lessons. When the weather is nice, on any given day or evening, you could watch sky divers jump out of perfectly good planes and return to earth onto the large grass area of Harvey Airport. This incident didn't end safely at Harvey Airport. It ended tragically in the large corn fields, west of Hwy. 9. The partner of the deceased sky diver described what happened. They had both exited the plane and were free falling. When it came to deploy their chutes, the victim's chute opened only partially. He tried to cut the chute away so he could deploy his reserve. Having no luck cutting away the chute, the partner yelled at him to deploy his reserve. The victims last words were, "I'm afraid it's going to wrap around my main chute." "Pull it!" the partner yelled, as he deployed his own chute. The victim deployed his reserve, and sure enough, it wrapped around the main chute. The victim hit the ground and was killed instantly. There was nothing to do, so we waited for the corner to arrive. The coroner arrived and began obtaining information. It was a gory scene, so a sheet had been placed over the victim. A deputy came walking up and made the comment to the coroner, "He must have hit pretty hard; there's blood way over there by your van." The coroner walked over to his van and noticed some blood next to his front tire, The coroner backed up his van and we were shocked to see a flattened heart. The impact of the fall was great enough to expel the patient's heart from his body. The coroner had run over it as he arrived. A small towel was placed over it while the coroner finished his business. Later the patient (and his heart) were taken away.

We were called to Fire Dist. #8 for a "heart problem." When we arrived, Dist. #8 personnel had already been on scene, taking vitals and giving oxygen therapy. The patient was a male in his mid-50s and had a history of hypertrophic cardiomyopathy (enlarged heart). The patient had been in and out of the hospital multiple times over the previous two years. The patient was severely short of breath, had a slow weak pulse, and low blood pressure. The patient also had pulmonary edema (fluid in the lungs). The patient was showing classic signs of heart failure. The patient quit talking to us and soon was unconscious. We placed him on the floor and CPR was initiated. I was just about to intubate, when the patient started moving around and trying to push our hands off his chest. He started talking about how he didn't want to die and how much he loved his family, then he stopped talking. CPR was reinitiated, and after about 20–30 seconds of chest compressions, he started talking again. "I need to say goodbye to my wife," he said, starting to cry. We asked where his wife was, and we were told she had run to the neighbor's house because she couldn't watch. A firefighter ran next door and got his wife. He had prepared her the best he could at what she was about to see. This scenario repeated itself several times, although it took longer CPR before he would respond again. His wife was near his side when he mouthed "I love you," and that was it. Intubation, IV, several rounds of cardiac medications with no response. Generally, if a patient is dead outside of the hospital from a medical cardiac arrest, we leave them for the coroner or the funeral home. In rare occasions, we will transport cardiac arrest patients to the hospital while life-saving measures are being done. This was one of those rare occasions. But as predicted, much wasn't done for him in the E/R, and he expired.

We responded to Mill Creek one afternoon for a "gunshot wound to a juvenile." Because of the location, there was some confusion on whose jurisdiction it was (Fire Dist. #11, Silver Lake, or Fire Dist. #7), so both departments were dispatched. The incident ended up being our jurisdiction, as a chain-linked fence separated us from Fire Dist. #11 (they could have jumped the fence if they wanted to). I waved to them as we went through the front door. The patient was located upstairs in a beautiful, luxurious home. The patient was laying on the floor in a puddle of blood. The patient and a friend (whose parents owned the house), had been playing with one of his parent's guns (a .357). The classic "I didn't think it was loaded" occurred. The friend pulled the trigger striking the patient (11–12-year-old male) in the right lower quadrant and exiting out of the side of the left upper quadrant (if you remember your anatomy class from high school, there were a lot of vital organs in the path of that bullet). I had my partner go down to the medic unit and hang two IVs of Ringer's lactate and I had another member run down and get the MAST pants and backboard. The patient was pale and diaphoretic, and I didn't think we would get him downstairs before he arrested. We placed the patient in the MAST pants, inflated the legs, then the abdominal section then maneuvered him down the winding staircase and into the rig. Total on-scene time was eight minutes.

In route to Stevens Hospital, we started the two IVs, drew blood for type and cross match, and "beat feet" for the hospital. Traffic was heavy and we made it to the hospital in 17 minutes. In the E/R, they hung blood and immediately took him to surgery. Even though the patient had extensive injuries, he survived and made a full recovery. Years later, I got cussed out by a Mill Creek police officer who had also been on the scene. Apparently, the kid grew up to be a prolific burglar and drug dealer.

We responded into King County with Bothell Fire Department early one morning for a male with "uncontrollable bleeding." The patient had just been released from the hospital for a heart valve replacement and was on blood thinners. The patient had gone to the toilet to move his bowels and started reading the paper. The patient said that he had an itch on his testicle, so he scratched it. While scratching, he felt a "little bump" and started picking at it. The patient said he was on the toilet for about 15 minutes and went to flush the toilet and saw blood all over the inside of the toilet. He looked down and noticed that there was blood "spurting" from his testicle. We got out some gauze and applied direct pressure to the injury, but it continued to bleed. Finally, I took a pair of hemostats (roach clip to you hippies), and with great care, I clipped the hemostats onto the "bleeder," (using as little scrotum skin as I could) and stopped the bleeding. As a precaution, we started an IV of Lactated Ringers and transported him to Evergreen Hospital. The E/R doctor decided the "bump" was a little wart that had grown atop a superficial artery and lacerated it by picking off the wart. The patient had the little bleeder cauterized and sent home.

One rainy, cold night, we were dispatched to a car/pedestrian accident in the parking lot of the Paradise Lake Church in Maltby. Eric and I responded in the medic unit, and volunteers from Sta. #4 responded in the engine. We weren't given much information about the call, and I mentioned to Eric, "car/pedestrian accident in a parking lot, can't be that serious." Wrong. When we arrived, we found people huddled around a 4–5-year-old boy. People were screaming and crying, yelling at us to "do something."

The victim and his mom had just left an event at the church and were heading to her car. Someone came out of the church and yelled to the mom, "You have a phone call". The mom told the child, "Stand right here and don't move. I'll be right back." While the mom was inside, someone got in an SUV and drove forward. Unfortunately, the child was standing right in front of it, and due to the high profile of the vehicle, wasn't seen by the driver. The driver stated she felt a bump as she pulled forward and immediately stopped. She got out and to her horror, saw two little legs sticking out from under the vehicle. The driver started screaming and several bystanders came running over. One bystander pulled the child out from under the vehicle, and not wanting to hurt the child any further, waited for us to arrive. I pulled out my penlight and shone it on the child and knew immediately that he was in cardiac arrest.

We slid a backboard on the child and immediately put him in the back of the medic unit. Eric and a volunteer were in the back setting up an IV as I intubated the child. Chief Eastman had arrived at the scene and offered to drive the medic unit to the hospital. As we were leaving the scene, I noticed the patient's mom in the front seat. Someone had helped her into the rig while we were working in the back (I would have never allowed it). Now the mom was screaming while watching and listening to everything that was said and done in the back. As were going to the hospital, we were being thrown around as the chief was trying to pass traffic at the same time as consoling the mom. When we arrived at Evergreen Hospital E/R, we wheeled the patient into the brightly lit room, and it was at that time I regretted transporting the patient. Brain matter along with blood was all over the backboard. If I would have seen the extent of his head injury, I would have never started treatment.

We responded to Mill Creek for an "intentional overdose in a young female." The patient was a 15-year-old female who had gotten into a "fight" with her boyfriend. Several hours earlier, she had ingested a "large amount" (possibly a whole bottle) of Tylenol. When her mom got home from work, the patient told her mom that she took the whole bottle "to show him." The patient was stable and talking coherently, so I called the E/R and asked if they wanted us to give ipecac, (to induce vomiting). The E/R doctor said to hold off, that if the patient had taken as many as she said and due to the time frame, ipecac would do no good. "Get her in here ASAP," the doctor said.

One thing about overdoses, you can never believe the patient. Some patients say they did when they didn't, and other patients will say they didn't, when they did. We always treated the patient as if they did. We transported her to the hospital without incident. In the E/R, the first thing they did was a gastric lavage (pump the stomach), which the patient fought, with a return of many, many pill fragments. Next came the activated charcoal (to absorb as much of the pills as possible). Unfortunately for this young girl, Tylenol poisoning is not a quick event. Tylenol poisoning attacks the liver causing liver failure. While I was writing my report, I heard the E/R doctor talking to the University of Washington Medical Center (U.W.) about putting the patient on an "emergency status" for a liver transplant. The U.W. said no. Since the patient had attempted to commit suicide (even though I'm sure she didn't mean to), she was automatically rejected. She died a week later.

Another little tidbit of advice I would like to give to EMTs, (as well as new paramedics), don't get "tunnel vision." Look at the whole picture. We responded to an "elderly male, weak and not feeling well." We arrived to find an older gentleman sitting in a lawn chair next to a large pile of split firewood. The patient said he had been splitting the wood for the past several hours and started feeling nauseated and like he was going to "pass out." It was warm and I asked the patient if he had been drinking any fluids. "No," he said. The first thing that came to mind was heat exhaustion, or dehydration. The patient was pale, diaphoretic, and cool to the touch. His blood pressure was 80 by palpation, but his heart rate was 50. I was thinking maybe he had a bradyarrhythmia that was causing the hypotension.

We put the patient on the cardiac monitor, and I was surprised to see him in a slow rhythm (sinus bradycardia) and not a heart block. The patient was so diaphoretic that we had to take off his shirt. I noticed some red "blotches" across his mid-section, but nothing obvious. We laid the patient down in the shade and put him on oxygen. I talked to the E/R and the doctor also suspected dehydration but was suspicious of the brady-cardia. He told me to give the patient a fluid challenge of normal saline, and if that didn't work, give him .5 mg of atropine. As I was reviewing the patient's medications, I noticed he was taking a beta blocker (Inderal), which could have accounted for his low heart rate. We gave the patient a fluid challenge of a liter of saline while en route to the hospital.

The patient felt "a little better," but not his normal self. I contacted the E/R doctor again and told him what had been done. The doctor told me to hold off on the atropine (a drug to speed up the heart), as he suspected the patient might be having an M.I. (myocardial infarction), and he didn't want to increase the heart damage by speeding it up. We got the patient to Evergreen E/R without incident. The E/R sent the blood we drew to the lab. While they waited for blood work, the doctor gave the patient another fluid challenge of 500 ml. No change. A 12-lead EKG revealed a sinus bradycar-dia without any ST changes. The lab results came back, and the hematocrit (red blood cells) was very low. The doctor thought with everything else going on, the patient could also be anemic. The doctor ordered that the patient be given a unit of blood. The patient received the unit and said he felt "better, but not great."

The doctor ordered an ultrasound of the patient's abdomen and found the problem. The patient had severely injured his spleen, causing internal bleeding. Every time the patient split a piece of wood; he was thrusting his left elbow into the area of his spleen. The patient was imme-diately taken to surgery and his spleen was removed. The surgeon said it was one of the worst injured spleens he'd seen that didn't result from a car or motorcycle accident. The patient made a full recovery. One day he came into thank us, but we weren't working. The crew on duty thanked him and told him they would pass it on to us.

We were dispatched to an "elderly female, unconscious," in Mill Creek. When we arrived, we found an elderly female in cardiac arrest in the kitchen. While CPR was initiated, I was asked by SNOPAC to pick up the phone. The patient had been talking to the 911 operator when she went unconscious, so the operator kept the line open. The dispatcher said she felt there was another patient in the house. The patient in cardiac arrest was "gasping for air" on the phone stating her sister wasn't breathing before the phone dropped. One of the crew members searched all the rooms, but no other patient was found. We worked the cardiac arrest for nearly a half hour to no avail.

The fire dispatcher called into the home and asked me if we could make one more sweep of the house, as she was sure there was another patient. The rooms were searched again, but again nothing was found. I found a narrow door that looked more like a closet door than an entry door. I opened it and found some stairs. I turned the light switch on and walked down the stairs. Sure enough, there was another patient. The patient downstairs was the twin sister of the patient upstairs. The first patient had gone down to check on her sister (who had complained of not feeling well the night before) and found her not breathing. The stress and exertion of running up the stairs possibly contributed to her cardiac arrest. The sister downstairs was cold to the touch, and nothing was done for her. Ironically, one of the sisters had made the news after performing CPR on the other sister years earlier.

One morning, we were performing a pump test at an industrial site. Before the owner could start leasing space in a newly constructed building, it had to be proven that there was enough gallons per minute (GPM) water flow as required by the National Fire Protection Association (NFPA) for occupancy. The site had a large retention pond with a small structure that housed the fire department hook-up to "draft" from the pond. The owner of the building had called earlier and stated that he had to fly out of town for an important meeting. He would have a representative on site. The plan was to hook hard suction to the fire department connection and draft water from the pond then spray the water back into the pond using the deck gun. The test required five minutes of uninterrupted flow and so many GPM. The pump was primed, and water started flowing. Things were going well for about the first three minutes, until the flow from the deck gun decreased. The test was halted, and we started looking for a cause of the decreased flow. Pump damage? We disconnected the hard suction from the engine and noticed a thick puree of blood, guts, tails, and gills. The owner had failed to mention that he had put thousands of dollars' worth of Koi in the pond. By drafting out of the water, all the Koi were sucked into the suction intake of the engine. The intake screen acted like a blender and killed all the fish (or a large portion). The intake screen became so infested with guts, that it restricted the flow of water. After an hour of cleaning, we conducted the test again. This time we went the whole five minutes. This time, the test passed. It was estimated that between $7,000–$10,000 worth of Koi were destroyed. Expensive miscommunication.

Once the new fire stations were built, Fire Dist. #7 implemented a "resident program." This program allowed people who were interested in becoming full-time firefighters experience and a place to live. Each resident had to attend recruit school, followed by more training, obtain their EMT certification, and finally be trained to be a paramedic assistant. In return, the resident was assigned to a shift and would be on duty every evening that the shift assigned was to work. Some of the first residents were Janet Jaeger (first female firefighter in Snohomish County to be hired, who retired at the rank of battalion chief), Roger Werst, Paul Guy, and Mark Toycen, to name of few. The reason I remember those names is because at one time they would be my Paramedic Assistant. At the time, the work schedule was a "modified Detroit." One on, one off, one on, one off, one on, four off. The resident program was very successful, and well over 150 residents went on to become full-time firefighters, either at Dist. #7, or around the whole State of Washington.

Today, Fire Dist. #22 (Getchell Fire Department under Chief Travis Hots) also has a highly successful resident program. We had quit using

Barker's Ambulance, when they started sending us $25 cancellation fees. A new ambulance company (Shannon Ambulance) started renting space in one of our old stations and we started using them exclusively for BLS transports. Shannon Ambulance only paid their employees for 12 hours of their 24-hour shifts. The company felt they shouldn't have to pay their employees "to sleep." If the ambulance crew went out once during the night, they would be compensated for a 24-hour shift. Since Shannon only responded upon our request, we would request them anytime we went out the door during the night. Even though we knew we would be transporting, we knew the crew would get paid for a whole shift.

One morning, we were dispatched to an "unknown medical problem," in a housing development known as "Mays Pond." SCSO was already on the scene as we arrived. We noticed a deputy sitting on the front porch, consoling a sobbing woman. As I approached the deputy, he told me the patient was in a backroom, dead. I walked into the bedroom and was amazed at what I saw. There was blood covering every wall as well as the bed and the carpet. There was a male victim sitting on the floor, propped up against the bed, pale and cold to the touch. There was no obvious trauma on the victim. I walked outside and talked with the female. She stated that she and the victim were going through a heated divorce, and the victim had dropped their kids off at her house the night before. She had been worrying about his mental health, as the acrimonious divorce proceedings had "changed him." One of the kids had left an item in his car so she drove over to pick it up. When she knocked on the door, she got no answer. She used her key to get in the house and found the victim.

Since the victim was a "big man," we figured the coroner would need some help removing the body. When the coroner arrived, he examined the body and could find no wounds. To get the body in the body bag, the coroner attempted to straighten the arms (they were drawn up towards the chest). The body was so stiff, the coroner had to resort to standing on one of his legs and with all his weight, pulled the arm down straight. One down, one to go. He did the same thing to the other arm. As he straightened the arm, he noticed something and said, "What the hell is that?" On the patient's arm was a small, deep laceration. The victim had cut down deep enough to sever an artery. The victim then walked around the bedroom "squirting blood" all over the walls, carpet, and bed. The victim then died of exsanguination.

The coroner mentioned that this was his second case of the day involving exsanguination. Just two hours prior, a psychiatrist had rented a motel room and had covered the floor and bed in plastic. He then placed a waste basket on the floor, next to the bed. Next, he laid on the bed with his head over the wastebasket. Using a Bic razor, he cut into his neck until he lacerated his jugular vein. He proceeded to bleed out into the wastebasket.

We assisted the coroner with removal of the body. As we were leaving the scene, I wondered if the female was crying for her soon-to-be ex-husband or, was she crying in relief that he hadn't taken the kids with him. In my career, I responded to dozens of suicides (hanging, intentional overdoses, gunshot wounds, carbon monoxide poisoning, car into brick wall, but the most bizarre is to come later). One thing all these suicides had in common: they left behind a grieving family.

There are times when a conscious patient must be intubated, referred to as an "elective intubation." This includes patients in severe respiratory distress such as fulminating pulmonary edema, stroke patients that cannot maintain their airway, and patients with facial and respiratory burns. We all know that if you stick your finger down your throat, you will gag. Do it long enough, and you'll vomit. Trying to stick a laryngeal scope into the throat will elicit the same response. To eliminate the "gag reflex," we would give a depolarizing neuromuscular blocker, (paralytic) a medication called Anectine (succinylcholine), to temporarily "paralyze" the patient. Other medications such as etomidate and norcuron are used in programs around the United States. When giving a paralytic agent to a conscious patient, it is imperative that you explain the procedure thoroughly. After the medication is given, the patient will be unable to move or breathe (the diaphragm will be paralyzed) but will be able to see and hear. Sometimes the patient will be premedicated with valium, versed, lidocaine, or magnesium to reduce the transient fasciculations (involuntary muscle contractions). Once the fasciculations have stopped, the intubation can be performed. After several minutes, the medication will wear off, and depending on level of consciousness, the patient may "buck the tube" (reject). A repeated dose of the medication or more sedative (Valium, Versed), may be given. Upon being extubated, patients may complain of body-wide aches and pains as the body has just gone through a workout that has affected every muscle.

In 1984, Valley General Hospital in Monroe had requested through the county to establish their own paramedic program (Medic 10). This would be a hospital-based system that the county eventually approved. Steve Dutton (my buddy from Longview), Craig Whitfield, and Bob Hutchison were the original paramedics hired. I also started working there on a per-diem (part-time) basis as a fill in. Vern Sevey, Glenn Phipps, and John Jacobson were ALS, (intubation and IV certified), and were partnered with the paramedics. One day, I was paired up with another per diem EMT, Randy Shelton (Randy was a lieutenant with Fire Dist. #4). We were dispatched to a "head on motorcycle/vehicle accident" on Old Monroe/Snohomish Highway. The WSP had been pursuing a male on a stolen motorcycle. Attempting to pass a car, the motorcyclist collided head on with an oncoming vehicle. The impact was so great, the motorcycle was embedded in the front of the car and the drive line had separated from the car as well and was laying on the ground. The patient was thrown over the vehicle and landed and rolled (the WSP trooper described it as an "Evel Knievel landing after a failed attempt"), roughly 200 feet.

When we arrived, we found the victim in a "heap." "He's dead," I told Randy as we got out of the rig. As I walked up to the patient, I noticed both femurs were obviously broken (from striking the handlebars while being ejected), along with lower leg fractures and bilateral arm fractures. I felt for a carotid pulse and amazingly, he had one. In the position found, his airway had been blocked off. A simple tilting of the head opened the airway, and the patient began to breathe, though labored. We placed the patient on a backboard and applied the MAST for all the leg fractures. We secured the arm fractures as best we could and loaded him up. Just as we were departing the scene, a bystander started beating on the backdoor of our vehicle. He handed me something that looked like a dandelion and said, "I think he'll need this." I thanked him and closed the door. "What is it?" a volunteer asked. "Just his thumb and a tendon," I told him. The detached thumb was the least of his problems, so I tossed it in a plastic bag and put it in an ice pack.

Because of the patient's severe facial trauma, I was unable to intubate. I pulled out a scalpel and performed a cricothyrotomy (an incision through the skin, puncture the cricothyroid membrane and insert a tube). Although dramatic looking (cutting a hole in someone's throat), they are very easy to do. I performed several over my career without any complications. A cricothyrotomy should not be confused with a tracheostomy. A tracheostomy takes longer and is more difficult to perform. Surgeons are the experts for doing a tracheostomy.

Unable to get a peripheral IV (due to all the trauma), I inserted a subclavian and external jugular IV. I always carried suture material in my pocket (from my days of suturing in the Air Force) and secured both the "cric tube" and subclavian in place. Simply taping in place provided a better chance of being "pulled out." Suturing, then taping, provide a lesser chance. This patient had "multisystem trauma." Any one injury could be fatal. We figured his abdominal and possible chest trauma would kill him before his head trauma. With his airway protected, we concentrated on fluid replacement. By the time we arrived at the hospital. We had infused 4 liters of Ringer's lactate.

We got the patient to the hospital alive (I didn't think we would), but unfortunately, he died two hours later on the operating table. I would like to add something here. In our demographic area, we were a long way from the hospitals. At times, we could be 45–60 minutes away from definitive care. I've given two doses of aminophylline, (a drug given to Chronic Obstructive Pulmonary Disease, or "COPD" to improve their breathing by relaxing the bronchioles in the lungs), to a patient while transporting, where urban departments don't even carry the drug because they are so close to a hospital. I've always been aggressive in my treatment. I live by the motto "Do no harm," but I would not stand back and watch someone die. If my patient was alive, I would do any and everything in my power to maintain this. If my patient was dead (but viable), I would "throw the kitchen sink" at them to bring them back (you can't be anymore dead). No, I do not have a "God syndrome." I was proficient and confident in my abilities and believed in what was best for my patient. I didn't do invasive procedures because I could or attempt to "look cool." I did them because, as a last resort, they had to be done. I have never claimed to be a doctor, but I had been trained in some things that a doctor may do. I did not diagnose what the problem was; I might have had an idea, but I treated what I saw. I had been accused of being a "renegade," but if I could keep my patient alive, I didn't give a shit. Some paramedics may never do a procedure like I've done in the field. Some have. It's just the way it is.

Later that night, Randy and I responded to a "vehicle into a tree." The police had been chasing a subject in a stolen truck. The police had lost track of him and discontinued the chase. Several minutes later, witnesses called 911 to report that a truck had run off the road and collided with a large tree. When we arrived, we found the truck, (with severe front-end damage), but no patient. There was blood noted on the floorboard, so we knew the patient was injured. Witnesses stated they saw a tall male with dark long hair exit the vehicle and run away. They also observed the patient to be limping. Police canvassed the area for 30 minutes or so, when a deputy located the patient in a ditch about a half mile from the scene. We arrived and found the victim chest deep in water and hypothermic. The patient tried to escape by swimming away. He made it to a shallow area and managed to make it to the road before he collapsed.

While shining a flashlight on the patient, we noticed that the patient had bilateral open ankle fractures with protruding bones. The bone ends were flat. The patient was high on PCP and had been running on the road abrading the bone ends as he ran. The patient was combative, and typical of PCP users, super strong. The patient's feet continued to "flop" all over as he struggled. I contacted the E/R doctor and explained what we had. Since we couldn't start an IV and give a sedative, the doctor ordered 5 mg Haldol be given IM, and if there were no results in 10 minutes, give another 5 mg.

By this time, the deputies were sitting on the patient as I gave him the 5 mg of Haldol. While attempting to put him on a backboard, he became combative again. Another 5 mg of Haldol was given. Finally, the patient began to calm down (but continued to have episodes of rage), and by the time we arrived at the E/R, he had "mellowed out" considerably. In the E/R, the full extent of his injuries could be observed. The patient had algae, dirt, and rocks embedded in his bones and his tibia and fib-ula were a few inches shorter than they should have been. The E/R doctor immediately said that he couldn't be treated there and that he would have to go to Everett General. While the doctor was talking to Everett General Hospital, an IV was started and irrigation of the bones and feet begun. We transported the patient to Everett General and an orthopedic surgeon met us at the door. The surgeon took one look at the injuries and said, "Those can't be saved; they're going to have to come off." The patient was taken to surgery, and both feet were amputated. I never found out what the patient's outcome was.

At the time, as far as I was told, E/R doctors did not have to be board-certified emergency room physicians. As long as you had "MD" after your name, you were eligible to work in the E/R. One day while work-ing a per diem shift at M-10, the E/R was busy, so we went over and gave them a hand. One of the nurses working that day was Jan Hartson. Jan was a great nurse and a lot of fun to be around. A patient had been brought in with chest pain and shortly thereafter, went into cardiac arrest. The doc-tor was summoned, and I was starting an IV as he walked into the room.

Without hesitation, he grabbed the paddles, charged the paddles to the highest setting, and delivered a shock. Normally, when defibrillation is needed, the person delivering the shock announces, "I'm going to shock, everyone stand clear." This command is followed by a 360-degree survey of the patient to make sure nobody is touching the patient. Not this time. As I was supporting the patient's arm, starting an IV, the shock was delivered. The only thing I remembered was seeing a "bright flash." Apparently, I fell backwards, striking the wall and sliding down to the floor. For several seconds, I didn't know where I was. My ears were ringing, and I had tingling in my hands and fingers. I looked up and saw Jan standing over me with a grin on her face saying, "Hey, are you okay?" By this time, the doctor looked like a chicken with his head cut off. He was so flustered that one of the nurses took him out of the room. He never worked in the emergency room again. The patient was resuscitated and transported to Everett General, where she made a full recovery. To this very day, every time I run into Jan, she calls me "Zap." Another great nurse who worked in the E/R was Genevieve Jelnik. She was a sweet woman whom we referred to as "Mom" because she always took care and stood up for us. She worked at Valley General for many years. Tragically, she was killed in a head-on accident on "death" Hwy. 2.

One day I was working at Dist. #7, and we invited Medic 10 to come to the station for dinner. Steve Dutton and Glenn Phipps were working that day. Eric and I along with a couple of residents were making dinner. While eating, I drank a glass of milk. Several minutes later, I had to go to the bathroom. I sat down and had to go again. Steve mentioned something about a "bladder the size of a gerbil." I came back, and again I had to go. By this time, Steve, Eric, and Glenn burst out laughing. "How does that milk taste?" Steve asked. By this time, it dawned on me what was going on. Steve had squirted 200 mg of Lasix in my milk. Apparently, he was getting me back for the prank I pulled on him in Longview as well as the curly hairs I had drawn on his "fake" leg. They were right when they gave furosemide its brand name, Lasix (LAsts SIX hours).

Steve would go onto prank me one more time. Before moving up from Longview, Steve married a fellow paramedic, Diane (who went by the nickname "Due"). Steve asked me if I would be his best man, so I drove down to Longview. A picture was taken of Steve and me standing at the altar. After the wedding I drove home. After moving up to Snohomish County, Steve took the picture of us standing at the altar and blacked himself out of the picture. He wrote on the picture: "Hi, my name is Brian and I have AIDS. At this time there is no cure for young men like me, so will you please donate the next time the AIDS Society comes knocking on your door?" (Rock Hudson had just died, and the new disease was all anyone could talk about.) Steve made several hundred copies of my "AIDS Poster" and hung them in every E/R, nurses lounge, and hospital entrance. He even started putting them in map books of every ambulance, aid car, and medic unit in Snohomish County. I would run into people I didn't even know, and they would say "Hey, aren't you the guy on the AIDS poster?" For several years, these posters kept popping up. Steve eventually gave up being a paramedic and went on to be an undercover narcotics agent. I haven't seen Steve in probably 30 years. Last time I saw Steve was on TV when he was protesting the killing of whales. I've had my revenge planned for 30 years. Just biding my time.

A new volunteer by the name of Dave Cato had just joined the department. Dave would come up to the station and hang out with us all day. One day, Chief Eastman jokingly mentioned to Dave, "Since you're here all day, you might as well buy yourself a uniform." Dave did. One day, Dave and I got into a long discussion, and I asked him if he wanted to make the fire service a career? "I'd love to, but I have a criminal record." A couple of years earlier, under the influence of alcohol, Dave robbed Sambo's restaurant (now Motel 6), on Evergreen Way in Everett. It wasn't armed robbery, so he was sentenced to 3–5 years in the Monroe penitentiary.

Dave said he remembered his first day walking down the aisle at the penitentiary and making eye contact with Charles Rodman Campbell (mentioned earlier). The first words out of Campbell's mouth were, "I'm going to make you my little bitch." First thing Dave did was to make a shank. Dave swore if Campbell ever got near him, he'd stick him. After two and a half years, Dave was released for good behavior. Dave was upfront with Chief Eastman about his criminal past. Chief Eastman believed in giving people a second chance, so Dave was allowed to be a volunteer.

One day, someone called in sick. The chief noticed Dave out washing the chief's car and asked him if he wanted to work the day shift. Without hesitation, Dave answered yes. This opened the door for Dave. Soon he was hired full time to work the day shift. Dave became my partner, and we became close friends. Dave was an excellent partner and always one step ahead of me. Coming back from a call one day, Dave asked me, "If you ever committed suicide, how would you do it?" Jokingly, I told Dave, "I would take all the morphine, Demerol, and Valium we carry, inject it into an IV bag, start an IV on myself, turn on some music, and open up the IV." No muss, no fuss. And with that, the conversation turned to something else.

One day, Dave came into the station and noticed that he had been taken off the medic unit and assigned to the engine. Dave mentioned to the lieutenant that he always worked the medic unit and didn't want to be on the engine. The lieutenant would not relent. Dave walked into the chief's office, threw his badge on his desk, and said, "I quit" and walked out. Needless to say, after all of us heard the news, we were shocked. I was especially bummed because Dave was such a good partner, a good friend, and a good person. We later learned that Dave had been having financial problems, along with other personal difficulties. Dave had changed and didn't come around the station anymore.

One morning I came into work and was told by the chief that I would be "Acting Lieutenant" for the shift. Things went smoothly. We responded to several calls and did some training and a lot of paperwork. Next thing I know, it's 1700 hrs. and the day workers had left. On his way out, the chief told me, "Don't burn the station down." Don Laird would be my partner for the night shift. It was a quiet night with no calls. The next morning, I was in the dispatch office and Don walked in and said "Hey, Pud," (Don always called me "Pud"; Zelmer Pud sounded like Elmer Fudd), good joke with the med kit." I asked him what he was talking about. "It's gone." I knew it could not have been left on the scene of a call, because we hadn't had any overnight. I went out to the medic unit, and sure enough, it was gone. I told Don to check the locked narcotics compartment. All our controlled substances (morphine, Demerol, Valium, and phenobarbital) were gone.

I walked into Chief Eastman's office and said "Chief, we have a big problem." The Chief looked at me and said, "we don't have problems, we have opportunities." I then told him "Well, we have a big opportunity." I explained the medical kit and all the controlled substances were missing. Chief Eastman turned white. "Nobody leaves the station," the chief said as he spun around in his chair to make a phone call. I went upstairs and told the outgoing crew not to leave and the oncoming crew not to touch any of the apparatus. I was scheduled to work a 24-hour shift at Medic 10 starting at 0900. I called the crew quarters and told them I would be late, without going into detail. One of the crew would hold over until I got there.

The SCSO arrived and took statements from everyone who had been in the station. I was asked if I had heard anything unusual, and I did recall hearing some running in the hallway in the middle of the night. (The station was a two-story building a with living area, kitchen, individual sleeping rooms, bathroom, and workout room. On the first floor was a reception desk, community meeting/training room, dispatch office, office space, and the apparatus bays.) I just figured it was someone in a hurry to get to the bathroom. After all the statements were given, people were allowed to leave the station. As I was walking out, I happened to hear the chief say to the deputy, "I think it was Dave Cato." I thought *Bullshit, I don't even think Dave lives around here anymore.*

I arrived at Medic 10 90 minutes late. Around 1700 hrs., one of the full-time paramedics (Cindy Coker) arrived and told me I could go home. Cindy lived in Marblemount (roughly 90 miles away), and it was snowing heavily at her home, and she didn't want to get "snowed in" as she had to work the next day. Cindy told me that she would work the rest of my shift and I would get paid for it. Just as I was walking out the door, they were dispatched to a medic call with Fire Dist. #4.

I had just got home, and the phone rang. It was Rick Rauma. He asked me if I had heard the call that Fire Dist. #4 and Medic 10 was on. I told him no. "It's Dave Cato, and he committed suicide." I was stunned, as I dropped into a chair. Rick said he had no information, except that Dave was dead. Rick gave me Dave's address, and I drove to his house. By the time I got there, the fire department and Medic 10 had cleared the scene. All that were left was SCSO, the coroner and Chief Eastman. As I walked up to the house, Chief Eastman stopped me and said, "You don't want to go in there. You don't want to see Dave in this condition." I told the Chief that I wanted to go in. When I walked in, I saw Dave lying on the couch, surrounded by the medical kit and all the empty syringes for the one once-full narcotics box. Dave had filled the bag with medication, started an IV on himself, and "let it go." In the background you could barely hear music from his stereo. Dave looked very peaceful. I walked out and went home.

The next day, I contacted Dave's mom and asked her if she would mind if I attended the funeral arrangements. She responded with "please do." I contacted Chief Eastman and told him I was meeting with the family, and he told me to pass on to Dave's mom that anything she needed, the department was there for her. Several family members, the funeral director, and I attended the meeting. I was surprised at how much input the family requested from me. As the funeral director was itemizing charges, he came to the use of the hearse. The cemetery where Dave was going to be buried was also where the funeral home was located. The director quoted a price of $1500. Dave's burial site was less than two blocks from the funeral home. I piped up and told the director, "No, we don't need a hearse. I'll take care of it."

The funeral was scheduled for three days later. I lived about a mile from the funeral home, so on the day of the funeral, Bob Bigger (who was also hit hard by Dave's death, as they were also very close friends), drove our original medic unit (now used as an aid car) over to my house and we removed the stretcher and center mount for the stretcher and put it in my garage. Next, we washed the rig until it shone: Bam! Instant hearse. It was a nice, well-attended funeral service. And as six of us carried Dave for the last time, it started to rain (I'm sure Dave was laughing his ass off). There was a short gravesite service, and that was it. Dave was officially gone. We all went back to my house and pounded down the alcohol pretty hard. It was a sendoff I'm sure Dave would have loved. To this day, I regret giving Dave advice about suicide.

We were dispatched to a motorcycle accident with fire on Hwy. 9, two miles north of headquarters. As we pulled out of the station, we could see black smoke. When we arrived, the motorcycle was fully involved. The motorcycle fire had ignited a brush fire, and because of the wind, it was traveling at a rapid pace. The engine crew concentrated on the fire as we looked for the patient. The motorcycle had gone off the road into a ditch, and the rider was thrown clear, into some tall, dry grass. Fortunately for the rider, the wind was blowing the fire away from him. The patient was your classic Harley rider: big, long beard and wearing leathers. The patient had sustained a compound (open) fracture to his tibia/fibula along with numerous lacerations. The patient said he had been riding behind a truck that was full of small potted fir trees. The load wasn't secured, and one fell out. The patient (traveling at 60 mph) swerved to avoid the tree. The patient lost control and went off the road. While other members splinted the fracture, I started an IV. The patient was in a lot of pain. The patient was hemodynamically stable, and responsive verbally and alert. The E/R doctor ordered up to 15 mg of morphine for pain. By the time we got him to the hospital, he was in some pain, but didn't care. The patient ended up losing his leg just below the knee. The patient did receive a large settlement from the company that was transporting the trees.

I was working a per diem shift at Medic 10. We had already responded to a head-on accident with critical injuries, and resuscitated a child found face down in a pool (unfortunately, the child died two days later). We were called to the Index Wall in the city of Index, for a climber who had fallen with serious injuries. The "Wall" was popular with climbing enthusiasts and always busy. Our patient had a malfunction with his anchoring system and fell approximately 30–40 feet, landing on a ledge. A fellow climber had rappelled down to the victim from the top of the wall and was relaying information down to us on the ground. The climber said, "I'm not a medical expert, but it looks like he broke both legs and complains that his back hurts."

The patient was probably 60–70 feet up the wall, and there was no way he could be lowered down until he was stabilized. Eric Andrews (Chief of Gold Bar Fire) was in charge and looked at me and said, "Are you ready to go up?" I told Eric, "If God wanted me up there, he would have made me a mountain goat." "Get him rigged up!" Eric shouted. The most rock climbing I had ever done in my life was in high school, carrying kegs of beer down to the beach. This was a flat mountain wall. While I was being put in the climbing gear, the climber on the ledge set up a hoisting system. I unbuttoned my uniform shirt and people started stuffing IV fluids, IV tubing, catheters, blood tubes, bandages, dressings, and anything else I would need. I was connected to the hoist system and all the rescuers started pulling on the rope. Every time the rescuers would stop pulling, I got slammed into the wall. Finally, after several minutes, I was with the patient. I looked down and everyone looked like ants. The patient had an obvious lower leg fracture and a closed femur fracture on the other leg. Thankfully, there was enough room on either side of the patient to work. I radioed down to Eric everything we would need: Stokes, Hare traction split, cardboard split, backboard, cervical collar, and straps. By this time, another climber with medical experience had rappelled down to assist. After about 30 minutes of work, we had the fractures splinted, IVs running, and the patient secured to a backboard in the Stokes and lowered down. Being lowered down was definitely faster (and less painful) than going up. From the time we arrived on scene to the time we got the patient to the hospital was just over two hours. Not in the "golden hour," but under the circumstances, a pretty good time. The patient went to surgery, had all fractures repaired, and after several months of physical therapy was back climbing rocks. That climber owes his life to everyone that was on the scene. This was truly a "team effort" that was performed to perfection (well, maybe except for the dumbass mountain goat who didn't know how to climb).

It was April 7, 1986 (I remember because it was my daughter Nichole's seventh birthday, thus her "Golden birthday"), and we were celebrating her birthday at the station. Fire Dist. #3, (Monroe) had been dispatched for a "serious broadside accident with entrapment." Medic 10 would normally have responded but they were on another call. M-71 was requested. The accident location was at the traffic light where Hwy. 522 intersected with Hwy. 2. Normally this would be a 12–15-minute response time for us, but it was rush hour traffic on two major thoroughfares. When we got to Hwy. 522, traffic was backed up for miles. Luckily for us, traffic had been stopped at the accident scene, so we were able to travel eastbound in the westbound lane all the way to the scene. Chief Pat Vollandt (Monroe fire chief) informed us that they had numerous patients with minor injuries, but had an unconscious young female trapped in the backseat. When we arrived, there was stopped traffic for miles in every direction. The car the patient was trapped in looked like an accordion. The mom of the patient was turning east on to Hwy 2, when a large truck, attempting to beat the light, slammed into them broadside.

Due to the patient's unconscious state, I knew it would be best if the patient went to Harborview. As Monroe firefighters dismantled the car, I walked over to Chief Vollandt. "Chief," I said, "with all this traffic, there's no way this girl is going to make it to the hospital." I told the chief about a helicopter transport program I had recently read about that responded out of Boeing Field in Seattle and flew patients exclusively to Harborview. I told the chief, "I think they're called Airflight Northwest" (turned out, the name was Airlift Northwest). Chief Vollandt requested SNOPAC to contact Airflight Northwest and see if they would respond. Naturally, several questions were asked by the fire dispatcher, as no one (to my knowledge) had used them.

Finally, the dispatcher came back and said "Airlift Northwest is en route, with an ETA (estimated time of arrival) of 12 minutes. Who is the ground contact?" "I will be," said Chief Vollandt. The Monroe firefighters did an excellent job of cutting the car apart and getting the girl out. While the firefighters were putting the patient into the MAST pants (we used them as air splints for the two lower leg fractures; it seemed I always got the extremity fractures), I started an IV and gave the patient 50 mg of Anectine (2 mg/kg) and intubated her. I had just finished starting a second IV when we heard kind of a "buzzing sound."

At first, we didn't know what direction it was coming from. Suddenly you could see a little black dot in the sky from the southeast. As the sound got louder, the dot got bigger. Next thing we know, here comes this sleek-looking blue and silver helicopter. It flew over us, then did a 360-degree hover, dropped its landing gear, and landed 200 feet from the scene. It was by far the most impressive thing I had ever seen. We had the patient all packaged up by the time the blades on the helicopter had stopped turning.

Out of the helicopter came a flight nurse (Rose Andrews) and Dr. Michael Copass. Dr Copass came over to me and shook my hand and said, "I'm Dr. Copass, what do you have?" (I was stunned.) "Well, sir," and I proceeded to explain the mechanism of the injury, all that was found on the patient, and everything we did for her. Dr. Copass shook my hand again and said, "Good work." The patient was loaded onto the helicopter, and as quick as it arrived, it was gone. The patient regained consciousness after surgery. The next day, I bought a big stuffed bear and a get-well card and visited her in the hospital. She made a full recovery. Rose (the flight nurse) was on duty and took me on a tour of the hospital, until she was called away for another flight. Since that day, Airlift Northwest has become a regular fixture in Snohomish County. The company has expanded and has locations all over the State of Washington. On a sad note, several years later, the helicopter that responded to this call crashed in Puget Sound, killing the pilot and two flight nurses.

I was in the dispatch office at Sta. 71 when a frantic voice came over the radio saying, "Bad accident in front of Sta. 72, send help!" SNOPAC came on and said, "Last unit, can you repeat?" The voice came on again and said, "I'm a new resident at Sta. 72 and we witnessed a bad accident in front of the station, send help." A family, unfamiliar with the area, ran a stop sign at the intersection of 180th and 35th Ave. SE (kitty corner from Station 72). In the car (a station wagon) were the dad and mom in the front seat, three children in the backseat, and a two-year-old in the way back. The station wagon was struck broadside just behind the driver's door with major intrusion. During impact, all the rear windows were shattered. The impact caused the station wagon to spin 180-degrees, strike the curb, then landed on a strip of grass. Witnesses thought they saw "luggage" fly out of the car. We were halfway to the scene by the time we were toned out.

On arrival, we saw multiple bystanders trying to lift the car. I went over and they were yelling, "There's a baby under the car!" The two-year-old in the way back was the "luggage" witnesses saw fly out. The two-year-old had been sitting in a booster seat that was attached to the floor with a bolt. After striking the curb, the child was ejected, and the car came to rest on the child. I looked under the car and saw the child with the differential sitting right on the child's face. With the help of a few more good Samaritans, I was able to crawl under the car and grab the child's legs and pull the patient out. When I pulled the child out, I couldn't recognize a face. The child's face had been severely burned and "flattened." All I could make out was the child's blonde hair. Obviously dead, I placed the child on the grass away from the car. I had a volunteer grab a sheet and place it over the body.

I turned my attention to the child (4-year-old male), who took the full impact. He was unconscious with labored breathing, pale and diaphoretic. Airlift Northwest was requested. Upon exam, the patient had a large contusion with swelling on his left upper quadrant (most likely from the left elbow striking the area). MAST Pants, two large bore IVs, trauma bloods drawn, and intubation done as Airlift touched down. Again Dr. Copass approached me. This time he extended his hand and said, "Hi Brian, what have you got?" I explained everything to him. He shook my hand and said, "You guys do good work." He was right, everyone in our department did good work. Airlift took off (still a stunning sight), and we turned our attention to the minor injuries that the family had sustained: some minor cuts and abrasions (none requiring transport).

The coroner was having a busy day and would be at least an hour before he could get to the scene. I talked with him over the phone, and he requested us to remove the body and he would pick it up as soon as he could. With permission of WSP, we wrapped the child in a sheet and wheeled him on the gurney over to the station. It was a very somber time. We all took turns staying with the child until the coroner arrived. The 4-year-old required the removal of his spleen. He had also suffered numerous rib fractures and a closed head injury. Unfortunately, he had no cerebral perfusion and was taken off life support two days later. The child's heart and lungs were used in a transplant.

As resident firefighters moved out, others would move in. One resident was Kevin Ryan. Kevin was just a happy-go-lucky guy who loved to play his guitar and ride his bike. Because of his bike riding, Kevin had legs the size of tree trunks. One thing Kevin had battled for years was weight control. Kevin was always on the latest diet fad. Lose some, gain a little more. While a resident firefighter, Kevin was putting himself through paramedic school at Central University in Ellensburg, Washington. Kevin had discovered the latest diet craze, "Nutrisystem's." Kevin religiously followed the plan and after eight months, had dropped nearly one hundred pounds.

One Easter Sunday morning, Kevin was getting off duty. Someone had brought in a five-pound chocolate bunny. As Kevin walked by the bunny, he happened to snap of a chunk of the bunny's ear ("What the heck, I've done so well on my diet, what's a little chunk of chocolate bunny ear going to do?"). Kevin skipped down the stairs while eating the ear. As he was nearing his car, he couldn't stop thinking about the bunny. He ran back upstairs and broke off the other ear and devoured it. This went on until Kevin realized he'd just eaten the whole bunny. On the way home, Kevin decided it would be a "cheat day," so he stopped at a grocery store and bought a dozen Dove Bars. Soon, Kevin was spiraling out of control.

One evening, one of our members was getting married, so we all attended. Upon arrival at the reception, Kevin was missing. "I saw him in a Burger King drive through," said one guest. "I saw him in a McDonald's drive through," said another. Kevin never made it to the reception. The next time I saw him, I asked him what had happened. "I ate too much," he said. "I ended up driving down to Lake Washington and laying on the beach so I could breathe."

Kevin finished paramedic school and got hired at Medic 10. After a couple years, Kevin was hired at Fire Dist. #7 as a firefighter/paramedic. Kevin retired from Fire Dist. #7 and put himself through pharmacy school. Kevin now works part time as a pharmacist. You will not meet a gentler, kinder, bigger hearted person than Kevin. He wouldn't say "shit" if his mouth was full of it. To show what kind of character Kevin has, he adopts old and terminally ill dogs and comforts them in their final days. You are a good man, Kevin Ryan.

Late one night, we were dispatched to a "male unconscious" in Mill Creek. Upon arrival, we found a 60ish-year-old male in bed having a generalized seizure. The patient had been in a lovemaking session when suddenly he let out a yell, arched his back, and became unconscious. We moved the patient to the floor and soon the seizure stopped. Every couple of minutes, the seizures would start, then stop. While starting an IV, my partner took the patient's blood pressure. "This can't be right, I get 280/160." "Take it on the other arm," I told him. "290/170," he said. Three other members took the blood pressure and got almost the same readings. Again, another seizure. Since I intended to intubate, I gave the patient a quick 10 mg of Valium for the seizure, then intubated. I talked with the E/R doctor, and he said, "We better do something before the top of his head blows off. Give him some hyperstat, rapid IV push, and if the blood pressure doesn't drop in five minutes, give him another bolus."

It was obvious that we were dealing with a "brain bleed" (cerebral hemorrhage), and the prognosis was poor. The patient's blood pressure dropped to 210/130, so the patient was given a second bolus for hyperstat. Soon, the patient's pressure dropped to 160/100 and the seizures stopped completely. The patient showed signs of movement on one side, but nothing on the other. We got the patient to the E/R without incident. The patient was hooked up to a ventilator and taken for a CT scan that showed a bleed. A neurosurgeon talked with the patient's wife and told her there were two options. One, do nothing and see what happens, but something as a simple sneeze could kill him, or two, insert a shunt into his brain. The neurosurgeon strongly recommended the second option. The shunt was inserted, and after several months of hospitalization and physical therapy, the patient was sent home. The patient had numerous neurological deficits and was confined to a wheelchair, but he was alive. Several months later, we responded to the same address for a "man unconscious." We found the patient dead in his wheelchair. The patient's wife stated he had been doing "so good." She said she had just gone grocery shopping and found him in this condition. She said he was in the bathroom shaving, and as she walked out the door, she heard him sneeze.

* * *

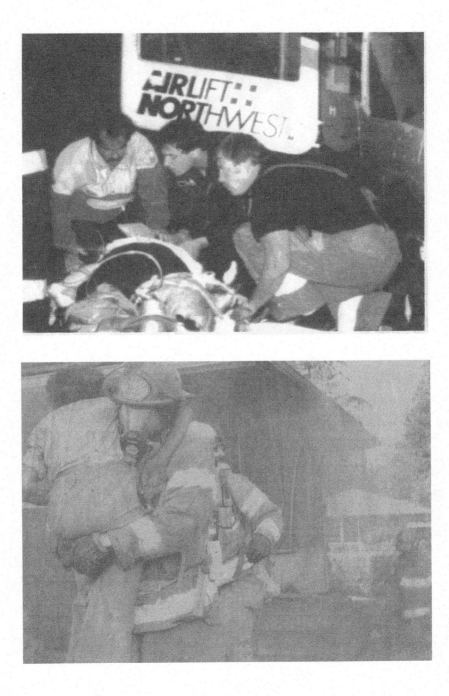

We were returning from the hospital on a beautiful Saturday afternoon. Mike Crockett was my partner, and a new resident, Mark Toycen, was riding as a "third man/observer." As we were driving east, I mentioned to the others, "I drive this route every time I go to work, and I've never seen anyone swim in that pool." (I was referring to an above-ground pool that was in full view from 180th St.) We had been in quarters 30 minutes when, God as my witness, we were dispatched to a possible drowning at that pool. As we pulled into the driveway, we saw two little bodies on the driveway next to the pool. As it turned out, the two little girls (ages three and five) had been visiting their grandparents. Everyone had just finished lunch on the deck on the opposite side of the house from the pool. The girls had been "hounding" the parents to let them go swim. The mom finally relented and told the girls, "You can go swim in 10 minutes." The girls started jumping up and down.

After several minutes, the mom noticed the girls weren't around. "Oh my god," she said, as they all started looking through the house. The grandfather ran out to the pool but did hear or see any splashing. He was just about to go back in the house when a "sick feeling came over him." He ran to the pool and climbed the ladder. There he found both girls face down in the water. He yelled for family members as he pulled the girls out. Neither one was breathing. I distinctly remember walking towards the patients and noticing how quiet it was. You could have heard a pin drop. Suddenly, the mother started screaming, "Oh my god, please save my babies, please, please, please!"

It was just my partner and me and a brand new, inexperienced resident looking down at two children in cardiac arrest. I immediately called for a second medic unit and more manpower. We moved the girls next to each other, and as I bagged both patients, Mike and Mark did chest compressions. Within five minutes, we went from three rescuers on scene to close to 30. We had SCSO officers coming from all directions, volunteers, and off-duty firefighters arriving in their personal vehicles and three engines arrived. Soon, there were too many people on the scene. I was able to get both girls intubated and an IV started on the five-year-old. Paramedic Glenn Phipps arrived with his partner on Medic 10, and I told Glenn to take the three-year-old. Both Glenn and I had to intubate the girls a couple of times as the tubes were getting pulled out. After several minutes of CPR and medications, both girls regained a pulse. Unfortunately, both had fixed and dilated pupils. Because we didn't want to overwhelm one emergency room with two critical children, Medic 10 took their patient to Evergreen Hospital, and we took our patient to Everett General. Glenn's patient passed away several hours later. Our patient was eventually transferred to Seattle Children's Hospital and survived through the night. Unfortunately, she passed away the next day. You ask any rescuer, doctor, or nurse, kids are by far the most heartbreaking patients to treat. Chances are the health professional have kids of their own. I had way too many heartbreaking incidents involving kids. A week later after the double-drowning incident, I drove past the house with the pool. The pool was gone.

Fire Dist. #7 is located in the "convergence zone" of Snohomish County. Winds coming off the Pacific Ocean split when they hit the Olympic mountains. The winds travel around the mountains and converge (or meet) just north of the King/Snohomish County line, and this affects weather patterns roughly 30 miles to the north and 60 miles to the east. Rain and snow tend to be heavier in this swath of land. This became apparent a week before Thanksgiving in 1985. A major snowstorm had passed through the convergence zone. It was unusual for the time of year, the amount and how long the snow was on the ground. Some areas received 18+ inches of snow. If you traveled 20 miles north or 20 miles south, there was no snow.

Early evening on the day before Thanksgiving, Fire Dist. #4 was dispatched to a "male unconscious" on the most southern end of their fire district (and roughly two blocks out of our district). Because of the heavy snow and ice conditions, Dist. #4 estimated it would take 20–25 minutes to arrive. Normally it would take us three minutes to get to the scene, but because of the conditions, it took us 10. Marge Gogal was my partner and we slipped and slided all the way to the scene. As we pulled up to the scene you couldn't make out where the driveway was. Just like school buses, our medic unit was equipped with "automatic chains." We estimated where the driveway was and made it as far as we could, then stopped.

I got out and was met by the patient's wife who pointed in the direction of a small barn (after shining a flashlight in that direction, I approximated it at 80 yards away from the medic unit). The wife told me that her husband had gone to split some firewood and had been out for at least 20 minutes. I asked Fire Dist. #4 their ETA. "Fifteen minutes," they answered. I requested manpower from Dist. #7 (the engine arrived just as Fire Dist. #4 did). I told Marge that I was going to try to get the patient to the medic unit and for her to set up an IV and get the intubation equipment ready.

After walking, stumbling, and falling in snow up to my knees, I reached the patient. He was face down in the snow. I rolled him over and wiped away all the snow he had in his nose and mouth. This guy must have been a peanut lover because he had a paste of it coming out of his nose and mouth. The patient wasn't breathing. The patient was dressed as if for the Arctic, as he had on several layers of clothes, gloves, and a thick, fur-lined coat. A smarter person would have just said, "He's dead," and left the body there for the coroner. I've never claimed to be the sharpest tool in the box, so I grabbed the patient by his hood and started dragging him. Dragging the body was difficult but made more difficult by all the snow that was piling up around him. His body was like a snowplow, so every 10 yards or so, I had to stop and remove the snow piling up around him. Finally, I heard sirens getting closer. Everyone showed up after the work was done.

The arriving crews put the patient on a backboard and put him on the gurney (by this time, I thought I was going to die). Members tried to ventilate the patient, but because of all the peanut paste, they couldn't. I tried intubating, but I too couldn't see through all the gunk. Suctioning didn't do anything. I performed a "Cric," but even after inserting the tube, we couldn't ventilate him. After cutting through layers of clothing, Marge was able to apply the EKG leads: Asystole (flatline); pupils fixed and dilated. "That's it, were done," I said. I called the E/R doctor, got the approval, and it was over.

I walked up to the house to talk to the wife. By this time family members had arrived. "He's gone," I told her. She started crying and said, "I figured he was." Since the patient had no pertinent medical history, this was going to be a coroner's case. I requested the coroner through SNOPAC. Normally, SCSO would arrive on the scene and standby until the coroner arrived. SNOPAC advised there were no SCSO units available, and the coroner would be calling into the residence. The phone rang and it was handed over to me. "Hi, this is (so and so) from the coroner's office. I have an unusual request; my travel time is going to be over two hours. Could you take the body to the station, and I'll pick it up there?" I told him okay, so we took the body back to the station.

We placed the body on a table we had set up in the bay (still on a backboard and covered with a sheet). As we were cleaning the medic unit, a new resident came into the station and saw the sheet. "What's that?" he asked. I explained that it was a cardiac arrest that was unsuccessful. "I've never seen a dead body, can I look?" I told him, "Sure, he's not going to bite you." The new resident was nearing the table (again, as God is my witness), and the patient's arm dropped from the table. I swear the kid jumped 10 feet into the air. "Go ahead, take a look," I said. "Nnnnnnnnnnnnnnn, no, no," he stuttered as he hightailed it out of the bay. Poor kid had his chance.

It was just before Christmas, and we received a call for "intentional overdose," in Mill Creek. The patient was despondent male who had taken an unknown amount of Imipramine (tricyclic medication, used for depression). The patient said, "I want to die, I have no one in my life." The patient was going through a heated divorce and his soon-to-be ex-wife would not let him see his children. The patient said he "swallowed a whole bottle of the medication." If the patient had, in fact, taken the amount he said he did, he was in big trouble. The patient was becoming drowsy, and I noticed his EKG rhythm had become irregular and wide.

Naturally, the patient lived on the top floor of an apartment with steep stairs. I told everyone in a low voice, "We need to get him downstairs, now, before he arrests." We decided holding off on treatment until we got him downstairs and in the back of the rig. Just as we were about to go downstairs, the phone rang, and you could hear a child's voice. "I love you, Daddy. I love you, Daddy." I told the patient that we had to go right now and that he could talk to his children at the hospital. By this time, the patient was crying, saying, "I love you, I love you," as I took the phone away from him. He looked me right in the eye and said, "I don't want to die."

I was talking with the patient's estranged wife as the rest of the crew started manhandling him down the stairs. All of a sudden, one of the firefighters yelled, "He's seizing." I told the wife I had to go. "What's going on?" I heard the wife say as I hung up the phone. I made it outside to witness the patient projectile vomit. We still had three more flight of stairs to go. I grabbed his head and tried to turn it to the side, just as another stream of vomit splashed on the ground. By the time we got him to the asphalt, he was in cardiac arrest. In between the episodes of vomiting, I was able to intubate him. By now, the patient was in a wide idioventricular rhythm without a pulse. We gave him two boluses of sodium bicarbonate (because of the tricyclic), epinephrine, atropine, and even started an Isuprel drip. ("heart not doing well? Give Isuprel.") We continued CPR and drug therapy for nearly 30 minutes as the QRS complexes, (the electrical impulses seen on an EKG monitor), got wider, until he was in asystole. This was a classic tricyclic overdose. The patient goes along, goes along, then boom, over the cliff and that's it.

Two shifts in a row, we were called to serious auto accidents with Fire Dist. #4 on Hwy. 2. The first was early in the morning for a car that had gone head on with a semi. We were advised that they had one dead and one critical, unconscious female with entrapment. Fire Dist. #4 had already requested Airlift Northwest. As we were approaching the scene, I told my partner, "Look out," as we almost ran over the deceased driver. The vehicle he had been driving was a Firebird with a T-Top; it had drifted over the centerline and struck a semi nearly head on. The unrestrained driver was ejected through the open T-Top and landed several yards away from the vehicle near the fog line. The impact was so great that the driver's shoes were still on the accelerator and brake pedals.

District #4 firefighters were using the "Jaws of Life" to cut the car away from the female victim. The vehicle's firewall was compressing the patient's legs against the seat and preventing extrication. The firefighters couldn't estimate how long it would take for extrication. This was probably one of the worst head-on accidents I had seen, where the front occupant was still alive. There was so much intrusion that we couldn't visualize anything from her chest down. A Dist. #4 EMT was assisting ventilations with a bag mask. There was no way I was going to be able to intubate the patient orally because of the position of her head against the seat, so I lubed up an endotracheal tube and nasally intubated her. Unable to start an IV in her arm, I started one in her external jugular. Airlift had landed on the highway (no Dr. Copass) and awaited extrication. After 25 minutes of hard work, Dist. #4 Firefighters finally had the patient out (kudos to you all), and on a backboard. As expected, the patient had multiple leg fractures as well as a possible pelvis fracture. With a close head injury, some of us suspected she wouldn't make it to Harborview. MAST pants were applied for the lower leg fractures, and the patient was flown to Harborview. Although the patient lost one leg, she eventually recovered and was released from the hospital.

The second incident involved a Cadillac that broadsides a small car. When we arrived, Dist. #4 had just extricated a 14-year-old unconscious female. The patient was in respiratory arrest and personnel were having difficulty ventilating with a BVM. Attending to the patient was Dr. Simon Whitney (Fire Dist. #4 medical director). "I'm quite sure she has a C-spine injury, and we dare not move her head," he said. I inserted a laryngeal scope blade in the patient's mouth but could barely fit it in. The patient had a small mouth and braces. "Won't work," I told Dr. Whitney, "I think we need to 'cric' her." "That sounds appropriate," Dr. Whitney said. I made a cut, punctured the cricoid membrane, and the tube was in. I had just sutured the tube in place, when the patient began to vomit. We transported the patient to Everett General Hospital, where she died of a herniated brainstem.

A new fire commissioner was elected to the board. His first act was to discontinue our medic unit responding to Fire Dist. #8 (Lake Stevens). My last response for that district was for an "unconscious female," just as the sun was starting to come up. Eric and I had been up all night on calls, so we were both pretty tired. At the time, the initial standard protocol was to administer 0.4 mg of Narcan (narcotic reversal drug), and if they didn't respond, narcotic overdose was ruled out. Next, one bolus (50 ml), D50W was administered. If the patient didn't wake up, insulin shock and hypoglycemia could also be ruled out. Because of the immediate response these two drugs had, intubation was not done until after the drugs were administered. I had just given the Narcan and there was no response. Eric handed me the amp, (a large glass syringe) of D50W and that also produced no response. We'd eliminated two possibilities, now it could a million other reasons. I was turning towards the med kit, when I noticed a gold-colored box on the floor. D50W comes in a blue-colored box. I had just given the patient 50 ml of sodium bicarbonate. It was completely my fault. I should have verified the drug I was giving. Complacency and fatigue had gotten the better of me. As luck (or divine intervention) would have it, the patient was unconscious from a tricyclic overdose, and sodium bicarbonate was what she needed. Per doctor's orders, the patient was given a second bolus of sodium bicarb, intubated and transported. The patient eventually recovered.

I came into work one morning and noticed five times the usual number of vehicles in the parking lot. A young girl had gone missing the evening before, so our training/community room became the operations center to find her. The report was a young girl was last seen getting off the school bus and walking up the driveway to her house. When her mom came home, there was evidence of a break-in. Snohomish County Search and Rescue was called in and coordinated the search. A tip line was set up and the calls started coming in: "I saw her walking in Seattle," "I saw a group of kids in Everett, and one of the girls looked like the picture I saw on TV," were some of the hundreds of tips that were received. And of course, the "You'll never find her, she's dead," and "abducted by aliens" tips had to be filtered out. Our job was to respond to calls, but also assist with the search. All other scheduled training, inspections, or station maintenance were put on hold.

A psychic had arrived and "felt her presence by a lake, near her home." A small lake was searched and dragged. Nothing found. My partner and I had been searching in a wooded area several hundred yards from the missing girl's home. A bloodhound had gotten a "hit" in an area where it looked like the dirt had been disturbed. My partner and I were given shovels and we carefully started digging. After a few minutes, a news crew had shown up and started filming us dig. While digging, the reporter started asking idiotic questions like "Do you think she's buried right here?" and "What are your feeling right now?" I looked at the reporter and her cameraman and simply asked her, "If this poor girl is buried here, do you really want us digging her up on the evening news?" "Our viewers have a right to see breaking news," she said. I shook my head and went back to digging. Fortunately for us (and unfortunately for the "viewers"), nothing was found. For the next three days, the fire station was a beehive of activity. Every legitimate tip was investigated. By day four, hope was dwindling and by day seven, the search was called off. The case was still considered "active," but until new, convincing evidence was presented, the case became "cold." The girl's remains were found nearly a decade later, 20 miles north of her home on the Tulalip Indian Reservation. A person of interest was finally captured, convicted, and sentenced to life in prison.

Every doctor, nurse, firefighter, paramedic, EMT, police officer, and dispatcher has a handful of calls that they just can't forget. The following is one of mine. It was early morning, and we were returning to quarters after transporting a patient. As we were pulling into the station, we heard a neighboring department get dispatched to a patient with "abdominal pain." Approximately 20 minutes later, we were dispatched to the same call. I was a little surprised that we were called that late into the call. Normally, we would be requested immediately. We arrived to find a 35-year-old black male (I only mention skin color because it is difficult to observe perfusion and or paleness or perfusion in people of color), sitting on the couch, doubled up in pain. The patient had just gotten home from a "night on the town," that included dinner, drinking, and dancing. The patient stated the pain started shortly after he got home and described the pain as "tearing and traveling to his back." He rated the pain as a "10 out of 10." The patient's only medical history was hypertension (which he was taking medication for), and a gunshot wound to the abdomen 20 years prior (the bullet had been left in, due to its proximity to the spine).

The patient was diaphoretic, had poor capillary refill on his finger-nail beds, and was short of breath. Other signs included supraventricular tachycardia (SVT), with a rate of 160 and a blood pressure of 80/40. "Triple A," (abdominal aortic aneurysm), was my first thought, but the patient was only 35. Too young, I thought, but he did have history of hypertension, and his description of the pain and location were classic signs and symptoms of an aneurysm. Myocardial infarction? The patient did not complain of chest pain, and again, he was only 35. Could the bullet have dislodged and lacerated a vital organ?

We laid the patient supine on the floor and placed him in the MAST pants and inflated the legs. Two large-bore IVs of Ringer's lactate were started and rapidly infused. Blood pressure was up to 110/palpation, heart rate down to 120. The abdominal pain had somewhat subsided, so we prepared for transport. I noticed that the patient had quieted down considerably. Vital signs were pulse 100 and blood pressure was down to 90/palpation. Suddenly, I saw pink froth coming out of the patient's mouth and filling the non-rebreather mask we had put on him. *Shit*, I thought, *did we fluid overload him, and now he's in heart failure?* "Start suctioning and check for a pulse," I told my partner. "I can't feel a pulse." CPR was started. The patient was intubated but fulminating pulmonary edema kept filling the tube. By this time, the patient was in an idioventricular rhythm that deteriorated into asystole. I had been in constant contact with the E/R doctor and after 45 minutes of efforts, he instructed us to stop. We had emptied the medical kit, (and then some), into this patient without any results and it hit me hard. The autopsy report came back saying the patient suffered a severe diaphragmatic myocardial infarction (DMI), with resultant cardiogenic shock. Although nothing was mentioned about the treatment he received, I'm sure I pushed him over the edge.

In January 1987, I was sent to the Washington State Fire Academy as a fire instructor for Class 87-1. The academy is located off I-90 outside of North Bend. It's situated a couple of miles off the interstate up in the foothills. Our medical director (Dr. John Orozco) felt I needed some time off the medic unit due to a rash of incidents, requiring invasive procedures (including central IV lines). The academy was an intensive 10-week training course that departments would send new hires to. Recruits were taught every aspect of firefighting, including hazardous material, live fire, etc. The academy had props that with a turn of a valve, could ignite a vehicle, a large tank, and even the fuselage of an airliner jet into an inferno. It was a very impressive and realistic setting for the fire personnel that attended.

For me, the academy was actually 12 weeks. Instructors had to report two weeks earlier than recruits to prepare lesson plans and do hands-on training of the subjects that the instructor was assigned to teach. When I reached "the gate," (the main entry, approximately two miles from the academy), there was a foot of fresh snow on the road leading up. The road had not been plowed yet (the academy had their own dump truck with a plow), so I inched my way up the road. I passed several elk and deer as I drove, and I managed to make it up to the facility without driving over the many embankments that you encountered on the narrow road.

I went into the main office and was greeted by an older gentleman who looked like Popeye. He was wearing a stocking cap and an old navy colored coat, and he had a beard. "Hello, I'm Gene Eggebraaten, and I'm the academy drill master." I shook his hand and introduced myself. Gene Eggebraaten had retired from the Seattle Fire Department as a chief officer. Chief Eggebraaten had been the academy drill master since it opened in 1984. The chief stayed in a camper down by the "flam pad tower" (flammable liquids props control tower), during the entire academy. The chief directed me to a classroom where I had a set of green overalls that had two fancy red patches on the arms and a green baseball cap that had the same patch.

One by one, instructors walked in: John Fanning and Dave Reilly from Federal Way Fire; Dan Bausch from Auburn Fire; Roy LaQuette and Mike Collins from King County Fire Dist. #11 (Rat City). Mike was the instructor coordinator (a liaison between the recruits, instructors, and the administration of the academy). We went to work on our assignments that took up much of the first day. Most of the instructors had brought up campers to stay in during the academy. Training days ran from 0800--1700 with an hour lunch break. Recruits were assigned four to a pod, and instructors (who didn't bring campers) shared a furnished trailer.

I was assigned ladders and search and rescue. For the next 10 weeks, it was my responsibility to teach recruits, ladder nomenclature; one-, two-, and three – man carries (flat, beam); ladder raises; attic ladders; 10-foot, 12-foot, and 14-foot straight and roof ladders; 24-foot, 35-foot, and 55-foot extension ladders; locking in while working off ladders; auditorium raises using 55-foot Bangor ladder with tormentor poles, up and over on Bangor ladders; carrying charged and uncharged 1½-inch and 2½-inch hose lines; carrying equipment up and down ladders; tying off ladders, rescue of conscious and unconscious victims down ladders; rescues using the Stokes basket; and bridging, to name a few.

By the time I left the academy, I knew how many rivets were in each ladder. The drill tower was five stories high and included small and large rooms for fire attack, standpipe system, sprinkler system, and a floor with separate rooms that simulated a hotel. Search and rescue entailed one-, two-, and three-man searches, right wall searches, searches using tools, marking of doors after a search, rescue of conscious and unconscious victims and various rescue techniques involving conscious and uncon-scious firefighters.

On day 2 of instructor orientation, it was sunny, but only 10 degrees. All the apparatuses were covered in snow and the hoses were frozen stiff. It was so slippery, every couple of steps and you were on your keister. It was decided to move into the warm classroom and "chalk talk" the evolu-tions. The two-week orientation went by quickly. I had just gotten home on the Friday before recruit school (which started the following Monday) and called headquarters to see how many recruits our department was send-ing up. While I was on the phone, I heard in the background a call for an "unconscious female" at the Albertson's store. The store was only three miles from my house, so I thought I would go down and lend a hand.

When I arrived, I was directed down one of the aisles where I found the crew doing CPR on a rather large female. Kevin Ryan was the para-medic in charge. Kevin was having difficulty establishing an IV and asked if I would put in a central line. "I can't," I told Kevin. "Remember, I was sent to the Fire Academy as an instructor to give me some time away from paramedic procedures." Kevin explained that he tried several "sticks" but couldn't get a line. "I'll tell you what," I said to Kevin, "I'll put in a central line, if you take credit for it." "That sounds good to me," Kevin said. I put in a subclavian and Kevin went to work. After working on the patient for almost 30 minutes, Kevin called the doctor and was advised to stop. Since this patient was going to be a coroner's case, any IV, endotracheal tube, or flutter valve would have to be left in place. Any unsuccessful IV marks had to be circled.

As I was about to leave, Kevin came up to me and said, "Hey, Pud," (yes, he called me that, too) "I just don't feel right putting myself down for the IV, when I didn't do it." "They'll hang me, Kevin," I told him. "I'll document why it was needed; I think you'll be okay," said Kevin. I took heat for it, but nothing ever came of it.

On day 1 of recruit school, it was sunny and warmer than usual. Most of the snow had melted. Most if not all of the recruits had arrived the day before. Because of the size of the recruit class, several had to bring their own campers to sleep in. All the instructors met with Chief Eggebraaten before he went in to talk with the recruits, Chief Eggebraaten looked sharp. He had shaved his beard and had a short haircut. The chief was also decked out in his "Class A" uniform that he wore while with Seattle: black pants and shoes so well shined that you could see your reflection; his black coat, one sleeve covered with so many gold Maltese crosses and the other sleeve covered in gold stripes; and on his head a perfectly white cap with a black visor and a gold badge. I was sure he would make a great first impression.

The chief was scheduled to speak for an hour, covering rules and regulations, formation line up, raising and lowering of the flag, military bearing, and what to expect for the next 10 weeks. All instructors while lecturing in the classroom were required to wear their respective department uniforms, with tie and shined shoes. On the drill field, we wore the green overalls and baseball hat. When involved with live fire, search and rescue, and ventilation, we were required to wear bunker gear. I was first up to lecture at 0900 hrs. While the Chief was giving his presentation, I got dressed. In the instructors' quarters, we had a full-length mirror and a lint remover. We were expected to "lead by example." I looked in the mirror and started from my shoes up to my head: shoes shined, black socks (you never wore white socks with your uniform), dark navy pants, black belt with Maltese Cross, dark navy tie with silver and red tie clasp, silver Lieutenant bars on the collars, badge, and hair recently cut and combed. I walked like Frankenstein back to the instructor's room so my uniform wouldn't get wrinkled.

A couple of minutes before I was scheduled to speak, Chief Eggebraaten came in and told me not to enter the classroom until exactly 0900 hrs. Instructors would always enter the front of the classroom from a side door. I'll admit, I was a bit nervous. I had instructed several EMT classes and several fire training classes in the past, but this was different. Inside the classroom were 36 recruits. Some had experience; some had none. A few recruits had even paid their own tuition and rented bunker gear from the academy to attend. The bottom line was passing the academy was a condition of employment. Fail the academy and you're out of a job.

I walked through the classroom door at exactly 0900 hrs. Once the door opened, someone yelled, "Instructor entering the classroom," as they all rose and stood at attention. It blew me away. As I walked to the podium, I wasn't sure what to say, so I just said, "Sit." I introduced myself and explained a little bit about my background. The first thing I asked was, "Who here seated has never carried or worked from a ladder before?" A few hands went into the air. I know what a drag it is being lectured on something you already know about. In this room were recruits with not one iota of ladder work. I knew just how basic I had to get. I looked at the recruits that raised their hand and told them, "I was once like you."

As I was looking around the room, memorizing faces to their name placards on their desks, I noticed that none of the recruits wore a badge. Badges would be presented to the recruits at their graduation, and traditionally "pinned" by a spouse, family member, or friend. My lecture lasted three hours (with a couple of 10-minute breaks thrown in). The recruits were excused for lunch, and I changed back into my "Jolly Green Giant" outfit. I was done lecturing for the day. For the rest of the day, I was down at the drill tower, getting everything ready for the next day's hands-on training. The afternoon classroom lectures would include safety and hand tools followed by introduction to fire hose.

I can't recall Lt. Collins ever lecturing. His job was mostly administrative along with drill ground supervision and overall operation of the recruit class. Lt. Collins answered to Chief Eggebraaten, and we (the instructors) answered to Lt. Collins. One of Lt. Collins's responsibilities was to make out the weekly roster. Every week he had to select a new group leader, who oversaw all the recruits, led calisthenics, and was responsible for formation discipline and marching. Every week, Lt. Collins had to select squad leaders, responsible for all recruits in his squad. Each squad had seven recruits. The squad leader reported to the group leader, who reported to the instructor, who reported to Lt. Collins, who reported to Chief Eggebraaten.

As you can see, there was a chain of command from the top to the bottom, and a chain of command from the bottom to the top. In the fire service, the chain of command is strictly enforced. It's highly inadvisable for a firefighter to circumvent the chain by going straight to the chief. At the academy, each squad was responsible for raising the flag in the morning and lowering it in the evening. Each squad leader (and recruits in his squad) were required to know all the steps and commands, along with folding the flag. Any mistakes and the whole squad received a demerit. After a set number of demerits, the recruit was expelled from the academy.

Every morning, the recruits would fall out at exactly 0800 hrs. for physical training (PT). The group leader had his watch synchronized with Lt. Collins's watch. Recruits better not be 10 seconds early, and definitely not be one second late: 0800 meant 0800. Physical training consisted of stretching, pushups, sit-ups, whatever Lt. Collins felt like, and finally a "brisk" mile run around the drill field. After PT, the recruits had to shower, get in their uniforms, then eat breakfast. The faster the recruits finished their morning run, the more time they had for breakfast. If there was a lecture, all recruits had better be in the classroom sitting at attention at 0900. If it was hands-on training down at the drill field, all recruits were required to be in full bunker gear, at attention in formation by 0900. If you were ill, you'd better be on your deathbed. If you were injured, you'd better be on your deathbed. After three absences, you were expelled.

Every morning, the recruits took a written test of the topic they learned the day before. Passing score was 70 percent. If the recruit failed three exams, they were expelled. Every Wednesday afternoon, representatives from the recruit's department (usually training officers), would meet with their recruit and go over what they learned and if there were any problems. Any problems got the instructor of that squad involved. Fortunately, we didn't have any problems. At 1600 hrs., training would stop, and the recruits cleaned and maintained the equipment and performed maintenance around the grounds.

During this hour period, each recruit would meet with the instructor responsible for their squad. Any problems, illnesses, or injuries would be reported then. Chief Eggebraaten had eyes in the back of his head. One day, he was talking with a technician who was working on the water reclamation pump, over a football field away from the training tower. As the recruits were performing rescues off the ladder, we all heard a booming sound, so loud that it was probably heard at the ski resort on Snoqualmie pass. "What in the helllllllllllllll are you doing?" Because of the echo, you didn't know what direction the yell was coming from. I told all the recruits to stop what they were doing as I canvassed the area, looking for the source. Finally, I noticed a subject coming towards us. It was Chief Eggebraaten. One of the recruits had taken off his helmet (which I had not noticed, but the chief had). Chief Eggebraaten proceeded to verbally tear the recruit apart, up one side, and down the other. After his rant, the chief was beet red. While walking past me, the chief gave me a big wink. I knew deep down inside; he was a softy.

As I mentioned earlier, the academy had a water reclamation pump system. All water sprayed made its way into drains that led back to the pond. A pump system would distribute water back to the hydrants situated all over the drill field. The recruits were advised to never drink the water out of the hoses. The water was contaminated with diesel, jet fuel, and God knows what other contaminants. Recruits were given bottled water. By week 6, lectures were over, and the recruits were spending the whole day down at the drill tower doing hands-on training. Each squad would spend 90 minutes at a station (ladders, ventilation, live fire, salvage and overhaul, search and rescue). Every morning, the recruits were told which rooms to stock for the day. The academy utilized pallets for fire load. Companies would truck unwanted or broken pallets up to the academy and they were stacked six feet high for several hundred feet, usually four deep. Ground level fires were simple to do. The "high rise fires" were a bitch, not only extinguishing, but stocking.

The recruits were doing quite well, but there seemed to be something missing. On the Monday morning of week 7, Chief Eggebraaten had a meeting with the instructors. The chief felt the recruits were becoming too complacent and "chummy" with the instructors. The chief demanded more discipline. He had noticed that not one "dying cockroach," sit-ups, pushups, or running had been ordered to a recruit who had "screwed up." A "dying cockroach" was a form of humiliation. If a recruit made a mistake, that person was required to find a puddle of water, lie on his/her back, and with legs and arms in the air, squirm around and yell, "I'm a dying cockroach, I'm a dying cockroach for—" (whatever they had done wrong). "Dying cockroaches" had been a staple in past academy classes, but we were under the impression that we were there to teach, not treat recruits like children. I asked the Chief if maybe "it was too late in the program to tear someone down, then build them back up?" "You should have started earlier," was his reply.

For the next four weeks, the recruits did their fair share. Week 8 was dedicated to flammable liquid fires. Week 9 was "Night Ops" fires. The recruits had the day off and the from 1900 to 0700 recruits did "multi-company drills," utilizing every aspect of training they had learned. Live fire with search and rescue, coordinated ventilation with entry, rescues from floors using ropes and ladders, forcible entry, down firefighters in unknown locations, aerial operations, salvage and overhaul: Every night presented a new scenario. It was very impressive. If you didn't know better, you could actually mistake the drill for a real three alarm fire.

Week 10 was dedicated to preparing the recruits for the state final written and practical exam that would be held on Thursday. Thursday morning, the recruits took their final written exam (they were allowed 90 minutes) and spent the rest of the day being evaluated on different tasks. By the end of the day, all 35 recruits (one had been expelled weeks earlier for chronic disciplinary problems) had passed both the written and practical. Per tradition, after test day, all the recruits, instructors, and the chief went out for pizza and beer. During dinner, several of the recruits had too many "libations" and were becoming boisterous. As the chief was leaving, he warned the recruits that they "had one more day, so be responsible and be in bed at a reasonable time." Some of the recruits did not heed the chief's advice. They arrived back at the academy "whooping and hollering" at all hours of the night (now early morning).

Normally, on the last day of class, the recruits would clean out their pods, clean out the drill tower, and be gone from the academy by 1100 hrs. Graduation would then be that evening. Due to a scheduling conflict, the graduation was re-scheduled for the following night (Saturday). Chief Eggebraaten was so pissed with the behavior of a few, and since technically, there was still one day left of the academy, he decided to take advantage of it. The chief ordered all recruits to fall out for PT. After a longer than normal "brisk run," the recruits were ordered to report to the flammable liquids "props," (burning cars, tankers and railroad cars) in full bunker gear, including breathing apparatus. The instructors were not immune. Apparently, the chief felt the instructors had not done enough to "curtail" the rambunctious behavior, so we got to partake. Fortunately for me, I was assigned to the flammable liquids tower. The tower sat about 25 feet in the air, had a roof, and a lookout of 270 degrees (the back of the tower was treed).

Inside the tower, sat a control panel with switches and lights that controlled every flammable prop on site. Each prop was individually controlled, or if you wanted to shut down the whole system, you just pushed a large red button. My job was to babysit the large red button. I had several beers the night before (as most of the instructors did) and had a splitting headache. I put on a pair of sunglasses and tried to stay awake. From my vantage point, I could see every recruit. Every now and then, I would see a recruit bend over and heave his guts out. After about three hours, the chief remarked, "I think you get my point." And with that, the academy was over. The recruits fulfilled their responsibilities, and instead of heading for the gate at 1100 hrs., they were out by 1500 hrs.

The next night was graduation—a lot of happy, relieved new fire-fighters. Chief Eggebraaten was the host speaker and looking dapper. All the instructors stood up on stage in our "Class A" uniforms, congratulating each graduate as they walked off stage. A lot of family members meant a lot of pictures. The instructors were even invited to be included. I truly enjoyed my time at the academy. I learned a lot, especially about leader-ship. The experience gave me a different, but better perspective of the fire service. But I was tired of the commute, being away from the family for extended periods of time, and I was ready to get back to work. I didn't have to wait long; I was scheduled to be back on shift the next day.

As I walked into the station that Sunday morning, I had hoped to "ease back in" to station life. I noticed several breathing apparatuses on the work bench that needed repair. As a certified technician, it was my job to repair the departments air packs. I would like to clear up a misnomer. The air tanks that we carry on our backs are not oxygen tanks. They are full of air. Air we breathe contains 21% oxygen, 78% nitrogen, and 1% other gas-ses. When we inhale, the body absorbs 16% of that oxygen and exhales car-bon dioxide. Oxygen itself is not flammable; as an oxidizing gas, it makes other things flammable.

The crew was cooking a "welcome back breakfast," and like typical firemen, we scarfed it all down (requiring a loosening of the belt). We had just finished, when we got toned out for a "house fire with subject trapped." The fire was approximately two miles from the station. Hearing the call, Chief Eastman responded from home and upon arrival at the scene, reported an 1800 square foot, single-family, one-story residence 75 percent involved. The chief then came back on the air and stated, "Bystanders report one occupant trapped inside." The fire was located just before the infamous "Charles Campbell murder house," well over 1400 feet down an old, narrow, overgrown gravel road.

Knowing that we would be blocked in for several hours at the fire scene, I had my partner pull over on the main road and park. My partner said he would bring down the med kit as I donned my breathing apparatus. I started jogging towards the scene and at the halfway point, I heard the engine slowly coming down the road. I had reached a fenced pasture and had two options: either continue running down the gravel road for another 800 feet and follow it up and around the pasture or cut through the pasture and run less than 300 feet. Going by the old adage the quickest way to two points, is a straight line, I chose to cross the pasture. I climbed the fence and was a quarter of the way, when I heard a noise. I looked to my side to see a bull charging at me. The bull was a long way off but had the angle of pursuit to make it interesting. I ran as fast as I could, but the breathing apparatus slowed me down. It must have looked hilarious watching someone run for their life being chased by 800 pounds of snot and fur. As his horns got closer, I ran faster. I was able to make it to the top rail of the fence, as the bull slammed into it. The force threw me over the fence, landing me on my back and the air tank. The impact knocked the wind out of me and brought back memories of falling off the loading dock.

After a few seconds, I was able to get up and limp over to the chief. "There's no way he's alive if he's in the back of the house," the chief said. "Search the kitchen and go back as far as you can." By this time, the engine had arrived, and one of the firefighters stretched a pre-connected hose line from the engine. I put on my mask, turned on the air, and heard the familiar "ding, ding," as the bottle fully opened. Smoke was down to the floor, and it was hot. "Nobody can survive this," I thought as I started my search.

I was doing a right wall search when I entered a room, hotter than the kitchen. As I continued, I felt something as I was sweeping my legs. I crawled over and felt a face, then two arms. I grabbed the victim by his collar, but it ripped off in my hand. I pulled out my hose strap and secured it under his arm pits. I crawled back to the wall I had just come from and followed it out the same way I came in. A couple of times along the way, I had to stop and move obstructions the victim was getting hung up on. Rescuing a victim from a fire is not delicate. More times than not, the victim is going to suffer lacerations from broken glass, contusions from hitting obstructions and abrasions from "rug burns." As I was coming out, the hose line was coming in.

I pulled the victim from the house, onto the grass. As soon as I took my mask off, I could tell the patient was dead. The "death stare" and the severe facial and respiratory burns was the first clue. I immediately loosened my breathing apparatus and plopped on the ground. Not only was I trying to catch my breath, but I was also trying to keep the large breakfast down. The fire was eventually extinguished, and because of the head start it had, the fire was considered a total loss. The cause was determined to be a chimney fire that had extended to the attic. The victim's cause of death was attributed to the fire.

Early evening, April 24, 1987 (I remember the date because it was the night before my son, Kyle, was born), we responded to a T-bone accident at Hwy. 522 and Fales Road. This intersection was notorious for high-speed "grinding accidents." While en route, we were advised that WSP was on the scene, reporting several minor injuries, and one unconscious driver with entrapment. Airlift Northwest was requested. When we arrived, we went to work extricating the driver using the jaws of life. We covered the driver with a blanket to protect him from all the flying glass. The patient was extricated and intubated, and IVs were started. Airlift arrived and landed several hundred feet south of the accident scene (again, a very impressive sight). Two flight nurses got out that I did not recognize. I came to find out that this was their first day on the helicopter.

The patient was loaded up on the helicopter and it slowly lifted off. Instead of turning around and taking off the way he came in (there was no wind), the pilot slowly hovered north. Suddenly, we heard an immediate increase in power and the helicopter immediately climbed vertically. The helicopter then went out of sight, and eventually reappeared and headed south. Eric and I looked at each other with bewildered faces. The pilot then came on the air after getting the shit out of his mouth and stated, "I'd really appreciate it if next time you can tell me about the wires we almost hit." We knew the wires were there, as the pilot should have. The wires were perfectly visible when the helicopter landed. The light had faded as the sun was going down and it was "assumed" that the pilot was going to rotate and go out the direction he came in. For some unknown reason the pilot chose to fly out in the direction of the wires. It could have been a disaster. Not only would the flight crew and the patient have perished, but also several bystanders who had stopped at the accident scene would have been were in the direct line of fire had the helicopter crashed.

Later that same night, we responded to a "motorcycle accident with impalement" on the Hwy. 522 off-ramp to Hwy. 9. Washington State Patrol was pursuing a rider on a reported stolen motorcycle. Instead of continuing east on Hwy. 522, the rider decided to exit the off-ramp. The motorcyclist miscalculated, and instead of staying on the asphalt, he hit the curb and was ejected. The motorcyclist hit an alder tree and was impaled with a branch in his left upper quadrant. The patient was unconscious. Airlift again was requested. This time the landing zone and surrounding area was so lit up, the Space Shuttle could have seen it from space. The impaled limb was cut and stabilized, patient was intubated, and two IVs were started. The patient was airlifted to Harborview where he died in surgery. Tragically, there was a miscommunication. The rider had not stolen the motorcycle but was given permission to ride it. A roommate had noticed the motorcycle missing, so he reported it stolen. The rider did have a warrant out for his arrest, so that is probably why he fled.

It was a beautiful Thursday night in August 1990. It was Volunteer Drill Night, and I was assigned to teach a rescue drill off the roof of the station utilizing ropes, Stokes basket, and our aerial ladder. Volunteers from neighboring departments were also in attendance, so it was a large group. I climbed onto the bed of the ladder and made my way to the tip. The plan was to raise the ladder, then extend the fly section so it extended just over the parapet. The ladder was raised, and just as it was being extended, I repositioned my feet. As I adjusted, both feet slipped off the rung and I immediately felt pain. I raised my hand and yelled "stop."

Thankfully for me, Rob Fisher (the turntable operator) sensed something was wrong and stopped the extension. I looked down and could see that both of my feet were pinned between the fly section and the next section of rungs. I also noticed a little puddle of blood pooling on the asphalt below. The force of the hydraulic system had no problem ripping open my rubber, steel-toed bunker boots and tearing open my feet about three inches from my toes. I noticed blood "spurting" out of my left foot. The pain felt like someone had just smashed my feet with a sledgehammer. Nauseated and sweaty, I tried to support myself on the rails of the ladder. "Slowly retract the ladder!" I yelled down to Rob. I could hear the increase in the motor's RPMs as the fly section slowly retracted. Soon I was able to free my feet. I was hesitant to look, but curiosity got the better of me. The left boot (which bore the worst damage) was shredded, with blood escaping at a pretty good pace. The right boot was torn open, and I could see two toes angulated. Next thing I know, I'm being assisted down the ladder with the help of Rich Shrauner and Phil Smithson. I was placed on a gurney, and my partner, (Jeff Chittenden) started an IV. My boots were taken off, wounds and fractures treated, and off to the hospital we went. I don't know if I pissed Jeff off in another lifetime, as he only gave me a total of 5 mg of morphine.

We arrived at Stevens hospital and were met by our medical director, Dr. John Orozco. I was immediately given a "buttload" of morphine. My two right toes had been dislocated, so they were put back in place by an orthopedic surgeon. My left foot, on the other hand, was a topic of discussion. I had sustained a five-inch-long, two-inch-wide ripped wound. Muscle and tendons were visible and there was concern that there might be some nerve and tendon damage. After a lengthy debate, it was agreed upon to simply suture the wound closed. After thorough irrigation, the wound was closed. I was given pain medication, told to have the wound checked in the morning and sent home. The next day, I had the wound checked and was then sent to headquarters to fill out paperwork. I was told that I would be off work for at least three weeks.

The next day (Saturday), my left foot was throbbing, and I was in a lot of pain, so I ate pain pills and kept my foot elevated. My wife had to work that evening, so she took the kids and me over to her mom and dad's house to babysit us. By this time, I was not feeling well at all. I was freezing, nauseated, and had a temperature of 104 degrees. My foot had swollen up to the size of a small watermelon. I knew there was something wrong when I couldn't eat the Peanut Buster Parfait my wife had brought home. "We need to go to the emergency room right now," my wife said. Reluctantly, I agreed.

I was wheeled into a treatment room, when a smiling Dr. Orozco came in. When Dr. Orozco saw me, the smile went away, and he turned white. "Shit, I knew it," were his first words. An IV was started, and I was immediately given Dilaudid, and I went cross-eyed. I was in pain but didn't care. I was sent to X-ray and then wheeled back to my room. Dr. Orozco came in and drew two lines on my foot and ankle with a marking pen. "You have gangrene gas in your foot," he said. "This line here"—pointing to the middle part of my foot—"is where the gas is now. If it gets to this line (ankle), we're sending you to the hyperbaric chamber at Virginia Mason in Seattle." I asked him, "What if it goes past the line on the ankle?" Dr. Orozco drew a third line. "If it gets to the third line, you may lose your foot." Kind of a sobering thought. But I didn't care, I was high on Dilaudid.

A nurse walked in and hung a piggyback IV of a potent antibiotic. The medication burned so bad that I could feel it march up my arm with every drip. I ended up rubbing all the hair off my arm as I subconsciously tried to ease the burning sensation. Dr. Orozco mentioned that he saw a foreign object in the X-ray of my foot. "We're going to open up your foot, remove the object, irrigate, then put a drain in your foot," said Dr. Orozco. You could barely see the sutures; the foot was so swollen. Dr. Orozco took a scalpel and cut the middle suture. My foot popped open like a popping fresh dough canister. Dark, greenish red fluid started pouring out. Even though the visual effect was disgusting, I had immediate pain relief.

For the next 20 minutes, my foot was irrigated. Dr. Orozco, using a magnifying glass, started probing around in the wound. "Hand me some tweezers," Dr. Orozco said to a nurse. He dug deep into the wound and pulled out a small black chunk of rubber with fabric attached. "There's the culprit," he said while showing it to me. It was small piece of my bunker boot. I was sent back down to X-ray; the gas had traveled to between the first two lines. A drain was placed in my foot and the wound left open. Another IV of antibiotics was infused and I sat in the E/R for two hours. After a third X-ray was done, the gas had traveled no further.

Thinking the worst was over, I thought I would be sent home. "Oh no," Dr. Orozco said. "You have a major infection, and you'll be admitted for at least three days." Wrong. It turned out to be seven days. It's true what they say, "Want to sleep? Don't go to a hospital." I had nurses and fungus doctors coming into my room every 15 minutes. The infection I had in my foot was the same type of strep that killed Muppet creator Jim Henson. I became very popular with the infectious disease doctors. I was sent to surgery to have dead tissue debrided from inside of my foot. After seven days, I pleaded and begged to be sent home. The doctors relented, on the condition that I keep the wound clean and dry. I was good for a week. A week later, Harold Smith and I went to an EMS Conference in Yakima. Went golfing, drank beer, and got my foot wet and muddy. Thankfully, nothing happened. Ironically, the week before my incident, an Everett firefighter

(Don Schwab) had experienced the exact same incident. Due to my accident, our department disallowed the practice of being on the ladder when it was raised and extended. The only permanent effects I have from my foot injuries are two ugly scars and the ability to know when the weather's going to change.

In February 1991, I had a major decision to make. The Everett Fire Department had announced that they were hiring four lateral firefighter/paramedics. I was a lieutenant paramedic in a great fire department with high seniority and the good possibility of being promoted to battalion chief. On the other hand, if I wanted this new position, I would be joining a department at the lowest seniority level, having to go back to the State Fire Academy as a recruit and be on probation for one year. But I would be making a dream come true, to become an Everett firefighter/paramedic. I knew it would be a difficult first couple of years but decided to give it a try.

The hiring process was going to be another "wham bam, thank you ma'am" event. The department had four openings (two firefighter /paramedics and two entry-level firefighters), for the upcoming fire academy, scheduled to start in late April 1991. Since the Everett Fire Department was a municipality, it had to abide by civil service requirements. There would be a four-step process: written exam, physical agility test, an oral board, and finally a chief's interview.

Before I go any further, I would like to give some advice to people who are thinking of getting into our profession. I have been through many testing and promotional opportunities, as well as being on several oral boards myself, and this is what I found successful for me. Granted, everyone has their own opinions and experiences going through the processes, but these worked for me. First (depending on the department, they may do little things to trip you up), read the employment application thoroughly before you fill it out. Probably the most important are the instructions. Read how they want you to fill it out. If the applications say, "Fill out in black ink," **use black ink.** This is purposely done to see if you can follow a simple direction. If you use blue, red, green, or even pencil, I guarantee that your application will be tossed in the trash.

Second, be truthful. You'll be amazed at how many applicants will falsify or omit information requested. You will be found out. Departments go to great lengths on background checks and 99 percent of the time, they'll catch you in a lie. I've heard of recruits that have finished the fire academy only to be terminated because of discrepancies on the application that don't match the background check.

Third, don't wait until the last minute to turn in the application. Applications are normally time stamped. Even though it's not a disqualification to get your application in at the last minute, it may make an impression. Is the applicant eager for the job, because he got it in early? Or does the applicant really care by just meeting the deadline? Another important reason for getting the application in early is mistakes. Say you forgot to sign the application. Maybe the city will notify you and let you sign it, or let you fill out a new application. Once the filing is closed, you're out of luck.

Oral boards can be tricky. Sometimes they're straightforward, other times not. I had two incidents that reflected "trickiness," both involved the use of the chair for the "interviewee." The first involved being seated. Normally when you walk into the room, the head of the oral board will say, "Please be seated." Other times, nothing will be said. If you're told to be seated, sit. If not, stand next to the chair and wait to be asked, or ask "May I be seated?" This, along with the next one I'm about to mention, are double-edged swords. The oral board committee is looking to see if you are taking the initiative to sit (which could be construed as arrogance) or is the applicant polite and waits to be asked. I personally have waited or asked to sit. The second scenario involved the chair being placed several feet from the table. Do you take the initiative and move the chair closer to the table, or do you sit where the chair is located? My personal advice would be to move the chair closer to the table (but not right to the table) and ask (or be told to sit). My advice for dress apparel is neutral color suits. It does not have to be a $2000 Armani, just a simple matching suit. No flashy colors, and definitely no bling. Be confident, not arrogant.

If you're going to bring in a resume, bring one for everyone. Just a couple of sheets for easy reading, not a novel. When seated, keep your legs uncrossed and sit upright in the chair. If the chair has handles, rest your arms palms down on the handles. If no handles, fold your hands in your lap (this prevents "talking with your hands"). When asked a question, if you didn't hear it properly or are confused, just say, "Sir, could you please repeat the question?" Never answer a question you're not sure you heard right. If you understand the question, take a few seconds to absorb it (don't blurt out an answer before the questioner is done), then look that person in the eye as you are answering. Make sure to make eye contact with all the other members while answering. Speaking of answering questions, answer the question to the best of your ability, then stop. Never expound on your answer, unless asked. To do so only opens you up to the possibility of going off track and becoming a "babbling buffoon." When you are told to leave, if possible, go up to each member of the committee, look them straight in the eye and while shaking their hand, tell them, "Thank you for your time." Do not look away until they've acknowledged you. If they attempt to stand while shaking your hand, encourage them to remain seated. Handshakes should be firm. Don't try to squeeze milk out of their hands, and definitely don't offer a "dead fish" handshake.

On the day of the testing (physical agility in the morning, written in the afternoon), the process had to be changed. There was frost with ice in places on the drill field asphalt, so the written was held first, and the agility test was held in the afternoon. There were 25 applicants that showed up to take the test. The written was a general knowledge civil service test that would be 25 percent of the overall score. I felt good walking out of the test. We met at the drill field at 1300 hrs. for the agility test. The ground was wet from crews drilling there earlier. The Everett Fire Department agility test was one of, if not the most, strenuous tests in the state. Applicants had only a 30 percent chance of passing. If you passed the test, you've accomplished something.

There were several off-duty firefighters running the test. The first event was shoulder loading a 2½-inch bundle of hose with a rope attached to a tire with concrete that was weighted at 100 pounds The objective was to pull the hose and tire 60 feet, cross a line, and pull it back 60 feet to the starting line. Time allowed: 45 seconds. I was first in line. Time started when you crossed the starting line. I was all ready to go, took my first step, and fell on my face. The asphalt was slippery, and I could not gain any traction. I stood up and tried again: down on my face again. I got back up and started taking short, choppy steps until I got going. After crossing the halfway point and heading back, you were met by a force that nearly threw you on your back: The dead weight of the tire stopped you from advancing until you could get it moving again. I crossed the finish line in 35 seconds. We lost four applicants at that station.

Next was the overhead lifting of two pieces of equipment. There was an eight-foot ladder that was made to simulate the weight of a 24-foot ladder. The other piece of equipment was two cement blocks with hooks to simulate the weight of a smoke ejector. The objective was to lift the ladder, place it overhead onto brackets on the wall, then move to the other side of the room and do the same with the blocks of concrete. Next, you moved back to the ladder and placed it on the floor, and then back and lowered the concrete to the floor. This was to be done four times. Passing score: 30 seconds. Everyone passed that station.

Next it was the 2½-inch hose carry up five flights of stairs then down. The hose was weighted to 150 pounds and if anytime you held on or touched the hand rail, it was a five-second penalty. Passing score: one minute. By the time I came down, it felt like my legs were on fire. We lost five applicants at this station. The final station was the "fatigue o' meter." This prop was a continuous rope that was inserted in a series of pullies. The rope was tensioned to a weight of 45 pounds of resistance. Passing score:

240 feet in one minute. Both feet had to be on the ground and at least one hand on the rope at all times. This was by far the most difficult station; you were still trying to catch your breath and still had the burning sensation in your legs from the stair climb.

As I stepped up, I met my future best friend, Scott Dunn. Scott's first words were, "You look like a softball player. Do you play softball?" "Yes sir, I do," I answered as I walked up to the rope. Scott quickly went over the rules and told me the clock would start as soon as I touched the rope. I started pulling as hard and as fast as I could. The whole time, Scott's talking about softball. At the halfway point, Scott yelled "30 seconds." I looked at the meter and noticed I was approaching 200 feet. I thought to myself, *30 seconds left; I'm giving it all I've got.* Scott finally said "Stop." I was surprised to see that I had pulled 308 feet. I passed. We lost another four applicants.

I was so tired and sore that I went and sat down. Human Resources member Nick Alvanos thanked us for participating and that we would hear within the next week how we did and what would come next. True to his word, I received a call from Nick stating I was scheduled for my oral board in two days, and would I be able to make it. "Yes, sir," I told him. Two days later, I was walking through the door that would either make or break me. When I walked in, I noticed a long table with three individuals on either side, and two on the far end. The oral board was made up of union representatives from the Everett Fire Department, HR personnel, a city councilman, a doctor, and a retired businessman. The oral board went well, and I finished high enough to qualify for the chief's interview.

A week later, I got a call for the chief's interview. I met with Fire Chief Terry Ollis and Assistant Chief Howard Huglen. They asked me a variety of questions and finally Chief Huglen said, "I see you've been an instructor at the state fire academy. This job requires successful completion of the academy. Are you willing to go?" "Yes, sir," I told them. I shook their hand and out the door I went. It was out of my hands now. I received a call a week later from Murray Gordon, the Deputy Chief of Emergency

Medical Services. He congratulated me and told me that barring any medical issues, I was hired. I didn't tell anyone until I passed my physical. I was then fitted for new uniforms and was told my first day with Everett would be April 22, 1991. I gave Chief Eastman my two weeks' notice and told him my last shift would be April 19.

As excited as I was to be going to Everett, I still had some reservations. I was leaving a great department that I truly loved. I had so many great times, great calls, and fond memories. I was leaving great people: Chief Eastman, Chief Jim Evans, Battalion Chief Eric Andrews, Battalion Chief Gary Meek, Rick Rauma, Bruce Young, Kelly Downes, Jeff Chittenden, Janet Jaeger, Carol Wisman, Mark Toycen, Mike Crockett, Kevin Werst, Roger Werst, Randy Weiss, Bob Bigger, Kevin Ryan, Rob Fisher, Scott Dorsey, and Ralph Provenzano. For those of you I have missed, thank you from the bottom of my heart.

THE EVERETT
FIRE DEPARTMENT

The first week on the job was mostly orientation, donning breathing apparatus and preparing for the state fire academy that was scheduled to start the next week. Out of the five of us (Dick Roundtree, Bill Stopoulous, Dave Wilson, Sam Herrin, and myself), I was the only one with academy experience. The academy had changed since I had attended as an instructor. Chief Eggebraaten had retired, and the schedule was now four 10-hour days, Monday through Thursday, 0700–1700. We had a large class (45), which required more instructors.

From day 1, the academy was a disaster. Disorganization, miscommunication, poor morale, an instructor coordinator on an ego trip, and a record-setting number of injuries. To be honest, to this day, I cannot remember any of the instructors that taught us except for one, Lt. Tom Marino from the Auburn Fire Department. That man epitomized the Fire Service. Lieutenant Marino was an ex-Marine, in great shape, with a plethora of knowledge. I credit Lt. Marino as the "glue" that kept the academy together.

The main reason for the disorganization was the training was done in reverse. The drill tower was going through a major repair because of severe spalling of the concrete due to so many hot fires in the burn rooms. Instead of learning all the basics first (hose handling, fire behavior, etc.), we started with the more advanced and dangerous flammable liquids training. On multiple occasions, we would be scheduled for a classroom lecture only to be told at the last minute that a "window of opportunity" had opened to use the drill tower. We definitely learned to "overcome and conquer." Another obstacle was competing with other organizations for use of the drill tower and flammable liquid props.

During the second week, we were attacking a liquid petroleum gas railcar fire. It was raining with high gusty winds. One of the members received second degree burns on his neck, chest, and abdomen from steam burns. Due to the severity of the burns, he had to drop out of the class (he did return in a future class and completed the academy). One morning we had access to the drill tower. We were divided into groups and lined up. We were told to hold onto the person in front of us and not to let go. It was the responsibility of the person in front of you to make sure that you were always there. As you entered the drill tower, you were required to slap the door and say "Recruit (your number and last name), entering the building." When you exited, you did the same thing. I was last in line when we entered the building, and after slapping the door and making my announcement, an instructor told me to let go of the recruit in front of me. I was led out a separate door and told to lay under a large red tarp that had been placed on the asphalt. After several minutes I was joined by several other recruits. Soon, all you could hear was yelling and screaming from the instructors. "Look at that tarp, under it lies members that *you killed!*" Every group had not insured that the last person was accounted for. One by one, each recruit had to lift the tarp and verbalize, "I'm sorry that I killed you." Next, they had to go over to an instructor sitting in a chair wearing a gray wig, a shawl and holding an American flag and verbalize "I'm sorry, Mrs. Jones, I killed your son." It was a very sobering lesson.

Late one evening, the instructor coordinator decided it would be fun to have all of the recruits fall out in formation and stand in the pouring rain for 30 minutes. I don't think much was learned. But the incident that brought to light all the BS that was going on happened one morning during week 5. All the recruits had fallen in for inspection after breakfast. The instructor coordinator was pouting about something, so he ordered us all to "fall out" and get our breathing apparatus masks and helmets and be back in formation in five minutes. During the academy, each recruit usually has three or four uniforms that are used for day-to-day activities. One uniform, however, is considered the "holy grail." This uniform is used only for inspection. This uniform, along with the boots, are meticulously cared for. Worn for 10 minutes, then back in the plastic it goes. We were all wearing our holy grail uniforms when we were ordered to perform sit-ups on the wet asphalt until told to stop. Next, we were told to run in place. Several minutes later, we were ordered to put on our helmets and breathing apparatus masks and "briskly" run down to the drill tower while in formation. Once down at the drill tower, we were again ordered to perform sit-ups in the soot-filled puddles of water. Next, we were told to go to the third floor and perform a "right wall" search of the entire floor while "mooing like cows." After we were done, everyone had abrasions to their knees along with some lacerations to the hands (we weren't wearing gloves). Needless to say, everyone's uniforms were trashed. Union officials from several departments got involved and threatened legal action if this type of "harassment" wasn't stopped. From that point on, things changed. I was told (by a reliable source) that until the "change," the instructors would watch the first 30 minutes of "Full Metal Jacket" to get "pumped up." The disorganization continued until finally, graduation day came, and we were done. Thank you, Lt. Tom Marino.

After graduation, we all spent a week at our own drill field performing evolutions and learning the "Everett Fire Department Way." The academy taught you the basics, but all departments do things "just a bit different." My first assignment as a "probie" was on Ladder 5, (L-5). L-5 was a "quint," (five functions), meaning it carried hose, had a pump, carried ground ladders, had an aerial, and had an adjustable nozzle on the tip of the ladder. My officer was Capt. John Burgy and my driver was Mike Cyrus. I would be assigned to a ladder and various engines throughout the city for the next four months as I got my "probie book" finished. Since I was hired as a firefighter/paramedic, I had a reduced time, (six months), to get my training done because I was to be assigned to the medic unit soon. Entry-level firefighters had nine months to finish theirs. The "probie book" was a "thick as a brick" binder that had every conceivable topic of the fire service. To pass probation, you had to keep your nose clean and have every topic of the probie book signed off by your officer.

During Probation, you are expected to keep the station clean, answer the phone, and greet anyone who walks into the station. Most importantly, you are expected to have coffee ready by the daily "station tone test" at 0700. Also, during probation, you are not allowed to watch TV or eat at the "round table" (where all the regular firefighters eat). If you're not doing your station chores, you are expected to be in the training room working on your probie book. Captain Burgy was a good officer and a great cook. He could make a gourmet meal with three dollars. When on shift, the first thing he would do in the morning would be to find the shopping section of the paper and plan the evening dinner.

Captain Burgy was very frugal. If three stores had Roma tomatoes on sale, he would go to the farthest one, just to save two cents. Being out in the public with L-5 could be embarrassing. At a stoplight, while in the jump seat, I would motion or mouth "Close your window" to the passenger or driver of the vehicle next to us. During initial acceleration, a large plume of black smoke would make its way into their car. Sometimes I was successful, a lot of times, not.

My next assignment after L-5 was Engine 4 (E-4). E-4 was located in a small building across from Forest Park. Station 4 was a quiet station that was surrounded by trees and flowers. You could eat lunch in the back and feed the birds and squirrels. Shortly after I did my time at Sta. 4, it was shut down and relocated to a larger two-story station, built three miles away. Because of its size, it had a lower-than-normal bay door. Only one engine ('68 Mack) could fit in the station. The water tank on the engine had to be full. If the tank was less than full, the beacon ray on top of the engine would be torn off as it left the station.

In November 1991, I was assigned to Medic 5 (M-5). At the time, there were only two medic units, M-1 and M-5. The city was split in half, with M-1 covering the central to north portion of the city while M-5 covered south. M-5 was busier than M-1, due to the fact that they provided mutual aid coverage to Fire Dist. #11 (Silver Lake), and the city of Mukilteo. Several years later, a third medic unit, M-6, was added. My first shift was busy. We ran 23 calls in a 24-hour period. I was partnered with firefighter/paramedic Mike Lambert. Mike was a knowledgeable and well-respected instructor around the county in both EMS and fire-related training. Mike was also known to go "strictly by the book."

Who did what on the medic unit was left up to the medics. Some crews preferred to alternate calls with one being the driver and on the next call, the driver would be patient man. Other crews preferred to rotate positions after each shift. The patient man was considered the "officer." He was responsible for making decisions about patient care, talking on the radio, tending to the patient in the back of the rig while transporting, filling out all the paperwork, and making entries into the daily log. The driver was responsible for performing the daily rig check, any basic maintenance on the vehicle (replacing burnt out lights), patient skills (IVs, intubation, medication administration), restocking supplies, clean-up, and washing the rig the next morning.

On our first shift, Mike chose to be the driver the whole shift. Mike performed a lot of skills; I performed a lot of paperwork. I only worked with Mike for two shifts. He was promoted to captain shortly thereafter. My new partner and I were working on Thanksgiving and just as everyone was about to sit down for dinner (I ate in the training room), we received a call for a male with "chest pain." We had to leave all that delicious look-ing food. The patient looked to be in considerable pain, diaphoretic, and pale. Vitals were normal, but his presentation screamed "M.I." The patient had been seen for the exact same thing the day before in the E/R. and sent home. "Cap," my partner said to the officer on the engine, "he can go AMB" (ambulance). I'm thinking, *No, no, we need to treat him and transport.* I knew for a fact that all my partner was thinking about was the tasty meal we left behind. I turned to my partner and mouthed "Are you sure?" He nodded yes.

I was advised when I first started, while on probation, you are to be seen, not heard. Half of me wanted to say something; the other half wanted me to shut up. I remained silent. The patient was transported by private ambulance. Five minutes after returning to quarters, the "third rail" (non-business line) rang and I answered it. "Hi, This is C.J. in the E/R. I just wanted to let you know that patient you just sent in by ambulance is hav-ing a 'big time' M.I. They're sending him to the cath lab now." I shook my head and all I could say was, "I knew it." C.J. went on to say that she "didn't think anything would come of it since the doctor who treated and sent the patient home yesterday was the same doctor treating him now." The patient survived and we dodged a huge bullet.

Because of civil service rules, each rank was a classified position. Once a member reached a certain "time in grade," they were eligible to take a promotional exam. To become a paramedic or an engineer you were required to have three years on the job. To become a captain or a fire inspector, you needed five years on the job. All promotions required a writ-ten test, a practical exam, and an oral board. At the time, chief officers were appointed and classified as "E Employees" (exempt), meaning they were contractual employees and not covered by the International Association of Firefighters (IAFF). The chief officers came under the heading of PERS (Public Employees Retirement System) and did not have the job security that IAFF employees had. Chief officers' positions are at the whim of the mayor and can be terminated at any time.

One shift, I came into work and was partnered with a firefighter EMT/ALS (Advanced Life Support). EMT/ALS receive additional medical training that includes starting IVs, endotracheal intubation, and the MAST pants. EMT/ALS personnel cannot give medications. My partner had called in sick and no other firefighter/paramedic was available to work. Currently, there were several Everett firefighters attending paramedic training at Harborview in Seattle, but they weren't scheduled to graduate for another nine months. The battalion chief (Tom Haugstad) had to deal with a first. There had never been an EMT/ALS paired up with a paramedic on probation. My partner for the shift was John Tanaka. John is an incredibly knowledgeable and hardworking individual (you'll hear more about John later). We had responded to several run-of-the-mill chest pain and breathing difficulty calls previously, treating and transporting without incident. We were so busy; we hadn't been back to the station all day. We stopped at a fast-food place on the way back to the station. Just as we ordered our meal, we were dispatched with E-6 to the very far end of the city for a "woman in labor." I asked John if he had ever delivered a baby. "Not yet," he said.

When we arrived, E-6 had the patient on oxygen and getting a set of vitals. The patient was in a considerable amount of pain. I asked the patient the typical questions concerning her pregnancy. She told me that she was diagnosed with placenta previa and that she was scheduled for a Cesarean section the next day at Stevens Hospital in Edmonds. As I was talking with her, I had John start two large-bore IVs of Ringer's lactate. The patient was adamant, pleading and crying that she needed to go to Stevens Hospital. "My doctors are waiting for me right now," she sobbed. I looked at the captain (Gene Kent) and asked him to call an ALS ambulance with a nurse. Several minutes later we were told that Shannon ALS Nurse Ambulance was unavailable, and AMR, (American Medical Response), had an ETA of 90 minutes from Tacoma. I told the patient that we would transport her to Everett General. Simultaneously, every family member spoke up: "she has to go to Stevens." Transporting a patient out of Everett in an Everett Medic Unit was taboo. It had never been done. The patient was becoming more hysterical as her vitals were deteriorating. Again, I looked at Capt. Kent and asked if we could take her to Stevens Hospital. In all reality, the location of the patient's house, distant wise was the same if we transported her to Stevens or to Everett General. "I'll contact the battalion chief," Capt. Kent said. After a couple of minutes, Capt. Kent whispered to me, "These are that B/C's exact words, 'Get your ass down there, drop her off, and get your ass back here.'" Thankfully we transported her to Stevens. After dropping her off, she was taken to surgery for a C-section. The patient went into disseminating intravascular coagulation (DIC), requiring 50 units of blood. After a couple of days on the critical list, both mom and baby survived. Yes, we got our "asses back" in a hurry.

One February morning, Tim Ross and I were on M-5 when we responded with mutual aid with Fire Dist. #11 for a "burn patient" at the AM/PM mini-mart on 128th St. SW. We were advised to meet them at their station near Mariner High School. We pulled into the parking lot just as the aid car was arriving. One of their firefighters opened the backdoor to their aid car and smoke started rolling out. It looked like a scene out of Cheech and Chong's "Up in Smoke." On the stretcher was a 400-pound male burned from head to toe. Reportedly, the patient had walked into the AM/PM, purchased a pack of cigarettes, a lighter, and five dollars of gas. A witness stated that he was putting gas in his vehicle when he smelled smoke and noticed flames "rolling" under the overhang roof. He stopped pumping gas and looked over to see a subject walking away from a van, fully engulfed in flames. Several bystanders saw the individual on fire and wrestled him to the ground and tried to smother the flames with blankets. The cashier in the store noticed what was going on and shut off the emergency pump switch and grabbed an extinguisher. After the flames were nearly extinguished, the patient stood up and started to walk away. He reignited. He was again wrestled to the ground and finally extinguished. He kept repeating the same line, "I was pumping gas when it overflowed and was ignited by a lit cigarette on the ground."

Upon observation, the patient had third-degree burns to 99 percent of his body. His arms had even begun contractures, (stiffening of the arms). Airlift was requested. There was no place to start an IV. The patient was charred. I told Tim that I was going to put in a central line. "Go ahead, he said, "I hear you're famous for them." To find the landmarks, I had to scrape off charred skin. I was then able to get the central line in. Tim said, "He needs to be intubated." But since the patient was still conscious, we had to "knock him down" with two vials of Anectine. As I inserted the blade, I could smell the pungent odor of burned flesh. Amazingly, the intubation was easy. As we dumped the fluids into the patient, he started to come around. Tim gave him 20 mg of morphine. Airlift landed and was amazed at the size of the patient. "We'll have to leave some equipment here to lighten the load," said the pilot. The patient had received nearly five liters of fluid by the time he left. As the helicopter was straining to lift off, Tim asked me, "How long do you give him?" "Two hours," I said. Two hours and ten minutes later, he was dead. Upon investigation, it was found that the patient had severe financial difficulties. The incident suggested that the victim's wife would sue the owners of AM/PM. It was determined the patient died of self-immolation. The wife denied ever being involved. When we got back to the station, everyone complained how much we stunk. Tim and I ended up putting our uniforms in trash bags and throwing them away.

Probation came and went. I was allowed to eat at the "big boy table" and watch TV. Soon, new "probies" were hired, and they got to experience the joys of probation. Some of my best times were spent at our "old headquarters," located at 28th and Oakes Ave. The station was several decades old and housed a lot of memories and traditions. One of the traditions was a brass pole that ran from the second floor to the apparatus bay. It didn't get used much. If you used it, you polished it. The headquarter station housed

E-2, Aid (A-2), and M-1. Brian Campbell and Kyle Griffiths were assigned to A-2 and Scott Dunn (ALS) and I were assigned to M-1. I seemed to get more than my fair share of "kinky calls."

One morning, just before getting off shift, A-2 and M-1 were dispatched to a man unconscious. When we arrived, we found a male, sitting in a chair dead, with a pair of women's panties on his face and a can of brake fluid in his hand. Good old "huffing," (inhaling fumes from and aerosol can to achieve a "high)." There was nothing to be done so I called for the Everett Police department (EPD), to respond. They got to babysit the "sniffer" until the coroner showed up. I responded another time to an old beat-up house in the north end. The call came in as a "possible hanging." When we arrived, we found a "very prominent" individual hanging from the neck, dressed in drag, with a cucumber up his rectum. Apparently, his erotic asphyxia idea wasn't so smart.

Early one morning, we received a report of "a house fire across the street, people trapped." Generally, when you receive a report of fire "next door to" or "across the street from," it's a legitimate fire. The fire has been seen by someone. Tim and I were on M-5, and since we were the first medical unit on the scene, we were tasked with search and rescue. The house was a split level with heavy fire in the far end of the house. There was a report of a young girl, her grandfather, and a dog in the house. As we went through the front door, the smoke was down to the floor and hot. Tim "thought he heard a noise in the basement," so he went down stairs, and I went up. While doing a left wall search, I kicked something that felt pliable. I crawled over to the area, and I felt what seemed like a body. After groping around, I felt a face. I pulled out my hose strap and secured it around the victim. Before leaving, I reached out and swept as far as I could with my leg (rule of thumb: if you find one victim, there's a good possibility of another).

Unable to locate anyone else, I found my way back to the stairs. As I dragged the victim down the stairs to the front door, I ran into Tim. "Look what I found," Tim said, holding on to a dog. "Look what I found," I told

Tim, as I dragged the victim out. My victim was the grandfather, who was in respiratory arrest. As we were placing the victim on the gurney, I told the captain of Engine 4, (E-4) that the girl had to be upstairs. Another search and rescue team was sent in. Just as we were loading our patient up, I heard over the radio, "We have another victim." It was the 12-year-old granddaughter, who was found less than 10 feet from where I found the grandfather. Even though it only took three minutes to locate her, that was three minutes too long for her to be exposed to that hot, smoky environment. We transported our patient to Providence Hospital, where he died several hours later. The granddaughter (who sustained facial and respiratory burns) was airlifted to Harborview and released several weeks later. The dog that Tim rescued was seen running around the yard playing with a toy an hour after the fire.

A week later, while working on M-1, Scott and I responded with Engine 2, Engine 1, Engine 3, and Ladder 1 to a well-involved house fire. It was raining and the wind was blowing so hard, the house next door ignited. The crew of E-2 located a victim, and Brian Campbell dragged him to the front door. All firefighters remember their first "grab," and this was Brian's first. Scott and I carried the victim out the front door and onto the gurney. As soon as we got the victim in the back of the lit medic unit, I could see that nothing could be done for him, but we tried anyway. After 20 minutes of resuscitative measures, the patient was declared dead. In the paper the next day, it was mentioned that "paramedics failed to revive the victim." To this very day, Campbell still flips me shit that I failed to revive his "grab."

On a rainy evening, one fourth of July (there's a saying in Washington that summer starts on the fifth of July), Scott and I were headed to Memorial Stadium to watch the annual fireworks show. Just as we pulled in, we were dispatched as mutual aid to Fire Dist. #11 for a "T-bone" accident. A liquor control board agent had been following a vehicle that he suspected was being driven by an impaired driver. The agent had been following for a couple of miles and called 911 to report the driver. The longer the agent followed the car, the more the car "weaved" into oncoming traffic, nearly causing several accidents. As the agent was approaching a major intersection, he watched the vehicle run a stoplight, and at high speed, broadside a truck. The truck then veered into a light standard.

Naturally, the intoxicated driver was not injured but the occupant of the other vehicle was unconscious. Fire Dist. #11 did a fantastic job of extricating the patient and had him "packaged up" when we arrived. From the time we arrived until the time we started transport was three minutes. I notified the "local hospital" that we were transporting a "trauma alert" and gave a quick assessment of what we had. The patient was intubated, and two large-bore IVs had been started. The patient was becoming difficult to ventilate and had a noticeable tracheal shift to the right. A flutter valve was inserted into his left chest with an immediate release of air and blood. From time of call to transport to the hospital was 22 minutes (well under the Penner half hour).

When we arrived at the E/R, we went into the trauma room and there was no one there. I tracked down a nurse and her first words were "We weren't expecting you." Apparently, it was shift change and there had been a "miscommunication." Strike one. A "trauma alert" was announced, and everyone came running. The E/R doctor asked about the flutter valve that was still in the patient's chest. I explained the tracheal shift and the difficulty ventilating. "Chest tube," the doctor said to a nurse. The doctor made an incision and as soon as he penetrated the intercostal space, a "river" of blood came pouring out. The doctor immediately stuck his finger in the hole to stop the escape of blood. Scott came in the room and told me we had another call. We responded, but got cancelled so we returned to the E/R.

I walked into the room and the doctor still had his finger in the chest. By this time, the doctor was visibly irritated. "Where is that blood I ordered and where is the damn surgery team?" Several nurses looked at one another. "I didn't page them, I thought you did," one nurse said to another. "I didn't call for them, I thought you did," said another nurse. Another miscommunication. Strike two. The patient died in the E/R from a lacerated lung. To make matters worse, Scott got chastised by one of the nurses for "traumatizing" the patient's family. Apparently as they were walking through the E/R entrance, they noticed the patient's clothing hanging out of a trash can outside of the E/R. I guess that was more horrifying than the fiasco witnessed in the E/R. Strike three.

There was an individual who lived in Everett (unknown where) who had a real disdain for the fire department. Every time an engine or medic unit drove by him, he would give "both barrels" of the middle finger. He would yell, curse, and sometimes walk out onto the street to get his message across. Once he jumped out in front of the medic unit I was driving code to the hospital. I had to slam on the brakes just to avoid him. We were in a training class at Sta. #1 one afternoon, when we got toned out for a fully involved house fire on the north end, just down the street from Everett General Hospital. E-2 arrived and while attacking the fire, Rich "Opie" Shrauner and Bruce "Crankshaft" Henshaw pulled out a naked male. The male was unconscious with extensive burns. Brian Murril and I arrived on M-1 and started treating the patient. By this time, the patient was in cardiac arrest. After several minutes, we were able to resuscitate the patient and transported him up the street to the hospital. The patient was transferred to Harborview, where he died several hours later. During overhaul of the burnt-out shell of a house, several boxes of child pornography were found. The clincher? The victim was our "bird flipper." Karma sure can be cruel.

We were working a cardiac arrest, possibly from a heroin overdose, upstairs at the Hodges Building (a less than desirable apartment), on Hewitt Avenue. I had started an IV and stuck the needle into the carpet as I always did. I made a habit of sticking the "sharps" in soft objects so I could inventory what drugs I had administered, and more importantly, to prevent people from getting "stuck" by exposed needles. As I was reaching for something on the carpet, I felt a sharp pain on my fingertip. I noticed blood on the fingertip and looked down to find the IV needle sticking out of the carpet. Under the carpet was concrete. The needle bent up as I stuck it in the carpet. We had given the patient enough Narcan and cardiac medications to sink a ship without success, so we stopped.

My next concern was irrigating my finger. I had been wearing gloves, but that didn't stop a needle. I went through the patient's wallet to get an identification and found an "AIDS Outreach" card. I contacted the E/R doctor for advice. I spoke with Dr. Cindy Marcus, who was a lawyer as well as a doctor. "Draw a red top blood tube and get to the E/R," she told me. For the next two hours, M-1 was out of service while I had bloodwork done and AIDS awareness counseling. I was prescribed AZT and sent back to work. I was starting my four days off, and by day 2, the AZT was making me sick. I became so nauseated and weak that if I walked to the mailbox to get the paper, I had to stop twice to rest. After five days, against the advice of the doctor, I quit taking the AZT. I was told that I had a 1 in 250 chance (.004%) of contracting HIV, so I was willing to take my chances. I was told to have bloodwork done every six months for three years. I never tested positive.

In the early 90s, a prolific arsonist was on the loose. He was suspected of starting 107 fires in Snohomish County as well as King County causing $30 million in property damage over a six-month period. He was also suspected of starting a fatal fire that killed 3 residence in a nursing home in Seattle. An FBI profiler described the arsonist as being male, white, between the ages of 25–40, well dressed, with neat hair. The profiler went on to say the suspect would not strike in wet weather (mess up his hair) and would only light the fires between 1900–2230 hrs., (so he could get home in time to see the late news). The arsonist was an opportunist (used available combustibles, like paper and cardboard, lighter), and started diversionary fires (start a small one, then travel somewhere else and start a larger fire). Most likely, the arsonist would park in the avenue of travel to watch the fire department go by.

For weeks, Everett firefighters were paired with Everett police officers and conducted "arson patrol" between the hours of 1800 and midnight. A major clue was uncovered after a fire in an abandoned warehouse. It had recently snowed, and a footprint was discovered. A person of interest was identified and arrested. Paul Keller was tried, convicted, and sentenced to 107 years in prison For many years, Paul Keller was suspected of starting the Everett Community College fire in 1987. That fire resulted in the death of 18-year veteran Gary Parks and $8 million in damage. Paul Keller adamantly denied he had any involvement. In March 2021, Elmer Nash Jr. admitted to starting the college fire to cover up a burglary. Nash (12 years old at the time of the fire) was sentenced to 10 years in prison.

During my career, I was often asked if I had ever treated or responded to calls that involved schoolmates. Yes, I have seen several who have been killed in car accidents, suicides, and drug overdoses. Several classmates who had been popular, athletic, and intelligent, with great potential in life who took a "left turn" at the intersection of life instead of a "right turn." One day while in the locker room, as a senior in high school, I was lacing up my football cleats and heading out for a Monday practice. Our team had just beaten a very good Cascade High School football team the previous Friday night. I had scored two touchdowns and if I wasn't so clumsy (I tripped at the 10-yard line), I would have scored a third time.

As I was closing my locker door, I noticed one of our underclassman football players looking at me. The player's name was Charles "Chuck" Kent. Chuck was short, overweight, and an introvert. You could tell he wasn't comfortable around people and would stare at the ground while he talked. "Hey, Chuck," I said as I closed the locker door. Chuck immediately turned red, and while fidgeting with his helmet said, "I just wanted to come over and tell you what a great game you had Friday night." I was completely blown away. I felt 10 feet tall. I was so flattered that I didn't know what to say. "Well, thank you, Chuck," I said as I tapped him on his shoulder pad. I went on to tell him how the line did a great job of blocking, and I just carried the ball. Chuck looked up and had a great big smile on his face. For the rest of my senior year, I made it a point to seek out Chuck and say hello. He always responded with a big smile.

Brian Murril and I were on M-5 when we got a report of a possible male unconscious. We arrived about the same time as EPD. I was standing behind the officer at the front door of the apartment while he tried to make entry. The door seemed to be blocked so I helped the officer push the door until it opened enough for me to fit in the opening. I noticed a body sprawled out on the floor pressed up against the door. I pulled on the patient's legs to move the body and the door finally opened fully. I noticed a large pool of blood under the victim's head and when I felt for a pulse, the patient was cold to the touch. Nothing for us to do. Upon further examination, the patient had been shot in the face and head at least five times. The patient looked familiar. EPD went through the patient's wallet and found a driver's license. Charles Kent was the patient. It had been 20 years since I had last seen Chuck. He had lost weight, but still had that friendly smile on his license. I was stunned. How could anyone do something so barbaric to such a nice "kid" (as I fondly remembered him). This killing was up close and personal. I never found out all the particulars of what happened, but EPD learned that Chuck was divorced and that his ex-wife's current boyfriend was under suspicion of molesting one of Chuck's kids and that Chuck was scheduled to testify in court. Again, I never heard an outcome. RIP Chuck.

One night, my partner (who shall remain nameless in this case) and I responded to a "male weak with shortness of breath." On arrival, we found an elderly male, sweaty, pale, and moderately short of breath. The patient also complained of chest pain. The engine crew had arrived first and had started oxygen therapy. One of the firefighters said that he couldn't get a blood pressure or a pulse. We put him on the EKG monitor, and it showed ventricular tachycardia. My partner, (who was the patient man, and who thought giving an aspirin was aggressive treatment), frantically said "I have to go call the doctor for an order of lidocaine." I mentioned giving the patient some Valium and cardioverting (shocking) him. "No, I don't feel comfortable with that. I'm going to go talk with the doctor." As he left the room, I started an IV.

"Is he in the kitchen baking a cake?" the engine captain remarked after my partner had been gone for several minutes. "Screw it," I said as I gave the patient some Valium. I took the paddles, turned the "synch" button on, and delivered a shock. Cardioverting a patient is not the same as defibrillating someone. With defibrillation, the provider charges the paddles, applies the paddles (or patches) to the chest, and pushes the buttons. The provider is in control of the shock. In Synchronized Cardioversion, the machine is in control of the shock. With the synch button on, the machine is looking for a prominent electrical beat to "synchronize" with to deliver a shock. The provider is just as surprised when the machine delivers a shock as the conscious patient is. If the patient converts to ventricular fibrillation, you just turn off the "synch" button and defibrillate. After delivering the shock, our patient went into a sinus rhythm and his vitals immediately improved.

I was just giving the patient a bolus of lidocaine when my partner came back in the room. "The doctor wants the patient to have Valium then cardiovert," my partner said. "Done," I told him as I was setting up a lidocaine drip. By the time we got the patient to the hospital, he was in stable condition. I apologized to the patient for the pain we caused. "What pain?" the patient said. Good old Valium. It's like drinking a case of beer and waking up not remembering what you did the night before. Needless to say, my partner was pissed at me. "How dare you, embarrassing me like that in front of everyone?" he said. "Lead, follow or get out of the way," I told him. Thankfully, this paramedic left the department soon after. Last I heard, he was a sales representative for some company.

Brian Murril and I were working early one morning on M-5 when we were dispatched to a breathing difficulty in E-6's area. It was an address where we had "frequent flyers," (people who call 911 several times per month for minor ailments). While riding the elevator up, we heard E-2 and M-1 get dispatched to a shooting with multiple victims. The captain on E-6 told us to respond with M-1 and he'd call for an ambulance. It only took us five minutes to get to the scene because we used I-5. The shooting started with a party where a male had been hitting on a girl. The girl spurned his advances, so the male slapped the girl. Several male attendees picked the male up and threw him out the front door. The male threatened to go home, get a gun, and "waste all of them." Several people laughed at him and told him to get the hell out of there. Several minutes later, the male called into the house and told them "that he was on his way with a gun." Again, attendees scoffed at him. The male did come back with a shotgun. The shooter came in through an unlocked basement door and confronted the girl who had been sitting on a couch with a male friend of the shooter. The shooter aimed the shotgun at the girl's face and said, "You got a problem with me, bitch?' "No, I don't have a problem with you," she said. The shooter stepped back and proceeded to shoot the male on the couch in the arm, blowing off his elbow. The shooter then walked up the stairs just as a male was opening the door. The male took a point-blank shot to the abdomen. The gunman then proceeded through the house taking random shots at people as they fled out the door and windows. The gunman then fled out the back door.

"Scene is secure, scene is secure," EPD called over the radio. "Send aid in immediately," another officer announced. (As it turned out, the scene was not secured. The shooter was later found hiding in some bushes outside the house with a loaded shotgun.) M-1 took the patient who had a severely bleeding arm wound. We took the gunshot to the abdomen. Several other patients were being treated for minor pellet and glass wounds. When we walked in the kitchen, the smell of gunpowder, Doritos, and beer was in the air. A light haze of smoke was also still lingering. Our patient was laying on his side in a fetal position. As we rolled him onto his back, I found the source of the Dorito and beer smell; it was oozing out of his gunshot wound. Our patient had sustained about a baseball size shotgun blast just below his diaphragm in his right upper quadrant. We were only six blocks from Everett General Hospital, so we put the patient on a backboard, "scooped and ran." We were able to announce a trauma alert before we transported to get the ball rolling. The E/R was not used to us coming in with a trauma that did not have IV access or intubated. The doctor immediately grabbed a laryngeal scope and attempted to intubate him while he was conscious. As the patient gagged, internal organs started bulging out of his gunshot wound. Even as an IV had been established, the doctor tried to intubate the patient without a paralytic. "How about some Anectine," (paralytic), a nurse suggested. "Fine," he said. Even after the patient was paralyzed, the doctor couldn't get him intubated; an anesthesiologist had to do it. Our patient went to surgery and survived. Over the years, that same patient had several setbacks and doctors predicted he would not live a long life. The patient with the arm injury suffered a permanent, disabling injury As for the shooter, he claimed "steroid induced rage." He was found guilty and sentenced to 30-plus years in prison.

Brian and I were on M-1 and just before shift change, we were called for an "imminent birth" in an alley behind the Monte Cristo Hotel. We searched the area for 15 minutes without finding a patient. The dispatcher advised us that it could be a hoax, as the reporting party sounded like "a child." As we were returning to quarters, I happened to catch a glimpse of something behind a bush. "Turn around," I told Brian. We went around the block and sure enough, there was a small figure moving around. I went up to the patient and thought, *This is a 12-year-old girl, not someone in labor.* "It took you long enough," she said. "I called 20 minutes ago." This "child" was actually 24 years old and weighed "70 pounds soaking wet." The patient said her "water" had broken an hour earlier and that she was in severe pain. "I need to go to the hospital right now," she said. We placed her in the back of the medic unit when she started screaming, "It's coming, it's coming." I told her I would have to check for crowning. I couldn't believe how small her "baby bump" was. "Have you been under the care of a doctor" I asked her as I placed a sheet over her. "No," she said. "How many times have you been pregnant?" "This is four," she said. "How many live births?" "None," she said. When she spread her legs, I don't know what was worse, the sight or the smell. This woman had so many vaginal warts, she looked like a sea urchin. She also had many festering sores. I got on the phone to the doctor to describe what we were bringing in. "Do not let her deliver vaginally," the doctor said. "Go directly to labor and delivery." We went straight upstairs and transferred her to a hospital bed. The nurses all reacted the same way I did. The patient had a Cesarean section, and the baby was stillborn. Gravida 4, (number of pregnancies), Para 0, (number of live births).

Joey "Cocoa Puff" Means, and I were working one night on M-1 when we received a call for a "car/pedestrian accident" at the Howard Johnson. When we arrived, E-2 and A-2 were already on the scene. As we pulled up, I noticed a male leaning against a short cement "knee wall," wearing white paints, covered with blood. As I walked up to the patient, I noticed his femur sticking out of his pant leg. "I'm okay, go take care of her," he said. I looked over and could see a young female laying on her back with multiple extremity fractures. I called one of the A-2 EMTs over and told him to dress the man's wound, tie his legs together and take him to Providence. I knew our patient, (female), had multi-systems trauma and would need to go to Everett General. Apparently, the couple had met on a plane the night before. She was a flight attendant, and he was a business-man. They hit it off, so he asked her out on a date. They had spent the evening drinking and dancing and decided to go out on the lawn and stargaze. As they were looking at the moon, someone ran over them, backed up, ran over them again, backed up, and took off. Witnesses described the vehicle as a "white Bronco." This was just after the O. J. Simpson "white Bronco incident." Investigators were trying to determine if this was a premeditated incident, or some drunk had gotten into his vehicle and inadvertently ran over them. It was never determined. We treated and transported this poor girl to the hospital where she spent the next eight months rehabbing and learning to walk again. No one was ever charged with a crime.

Early in my career with Everett Fire, I became a member of the Fire Department Honor Guard. Scott "Tay" Dunn, Scott Ames, Klaus Janssen, and I were the original members. No one was really in charge, so I stepped forward to be the organizer. Soon, Joe Paterniti, Curt Low, Jack Murrin, Naaman Midyette, Paul Gagnon, Jason Gianella, Rob Robertson, Mike Morton, Rich Mansfield, Sean Dickinson, Tim Hogan, Mike Lingrey, Dan Galovic, and Rich Couden joined. We represented the department in flag ceremonies, funerals, retirement dinners, 9/11 remembrances, and parades. Anytime an honor guard was requested, we were there. Any time of the day or night, I would receive a call. The hardest events to organize were funerals. It was always short notice (sometimes as short as eight hours). It was always difficult in the summertime. Members were either on vacation or had other plans. I kept "shaking the tree" until someone fell out. We had three levels of funerals. Level I was "line of duty death." This included pallbearers, bunting on the engine, casket draped with an American flag set on the hose bed of the engine, two ladders extended with a large American flag suspended, and a parade of fire apparatus from all over the state. Level II was "death of an active-duty member (not in the line of duty)." Depending on the circumstances, all of the above might apply. Level III was "death of a retired member." This included pallbearers, and a folded flag presentation.

Before every funeral, we would meet two hours before to practice marching, carrying the casket, and folding the flag (no matter what they say, no two flags are the same). We would then get dressed in our "Class A" uniforms. For gravesite burials, I would go out to the cemetery and survey the layout of the gravesite to see if there were any obstructions, how the casket would need to be rotated, and the placement of the casket mount. I was also in constant contact with the funeral director as well as a representative for the family. While I was at Everett, we had one Level I, one Level II, and twenty Level IIIs. It was a great honor to have served with this group of guys.

I was working out in the basement of Station 5 when we were dispatched to a "house fire with possible subject trapped." I was working with Steve Marth on M-5. When we arrived, the house was fully charged with smoke. Mark Anthony Hopkins (a photographer for the Everett *Herald*) was on the scene taking pictures when he told me that he thought an elderly female was trapped in the house. There was a hose line extended to the front of the house, so while Steve manned the nozzle, I entered through the kitchen, and I came upon the unconscious patient. We dragged the patient out to the front door, then carried her to the lawn. Battalion Chief Jim Schwartz was the incident commander and requested Airlift Northwest. Since the area was congested with trees and powerlines, a landing zone was established at a local elementary school approximately a mile away. The unconscious patient was 80 years old, and we knew her chances of survival were poor. She had sustained some minor burns to her face and hands, but she had soot noted in her nostrils down to the epiglottis. Steve intubated the patient and started two large-bore IVs. We transported her to the LZ, (Landing Zone), where she was flown to Harborview. Unfortunately, she passed away two weeks later.

One night, Brian Murril and I were working on M-1. It had rained so hard during the week that there was severe flooding in several parts of the city. In the northeast section of town was a large railyard where loading and offloading of boxcars was being done. Due to the flooding, a temporary onload/offload area was set up. A-2 and M-1 were dispatched to an "unknown medical problem" near the temporary site. There was a longer than normal response time due to miscommunication of the actual location. A-2 eventually arrived and immediately informed us of a "Code 4" (CPR in progress). As I got in the back of A-2, I noticed a 24-year-old male who was big enough to be a lineman for the Seattle Seahawks. This guy had muscles on top of his muscles. I also noticed that half of his head was missing. Blood and brain matter were all over the backboard and gurney. The patient's pupils were fixed and dilated, and the EKG monitor showed a wide idioventricular rhythm. "Stop compressions," I told the aid crew. This patient was obviously deceased.

The patient had been part of a crew that was offloading a boxcar when a strap broke, and a large turnbuckle struck the patient directly on the side of his head. I went out and looked where the injury occurred. The patient's helmet was broken in several pieces, and fragments of skull and brain matter littered the ground in almost a perfect line. You're probably asking yourself, "Why didn't you try to save him for organ donation?" The area hospital just didn't do them. It's one thing to have a patient on a ventilator in the hospital and a "harvest team" standing by to retrieve organs. It is a different story to bring in a brain-dead patient from the field.

While returning from a call, we were dispatched to an "unknown medical problem" near North Middle School. There we were met by EPD and several civilians. A young teenage male had gotten in a fight with his parents, and while running out the door, yelled, "I'm going to kill myself." When the male did not return, the parents became concerned and made phone calls to all his friends and neighbors to find out if they had seen him. They had searched the neighborhood without locating the teen. The fire department had been requested for manpower to help with the search. We had been searching for nearly an hour when my partner and I rounded a corner of the school and found the teen hanging from a rope tied to a basketball hoop. It was determined that the teen stood on a garbage can, tied the rope around his neck and kicked the garbage can away. The coroner estimated that he had been dead for a couple of hours.

It was the first week of September and you could feel the changing of the season. One morning around 0530, Phil Smithson and Bill Stopoulous were working on Aid 1 (A-1), while Brian Murril and I were on M-1. We were dispatched to a "woman in labor" in her front yard. The woman had been experiencing contractions "every couple of minutes" and felt her husband could get her to the hospital across town in time. The patient made it as far as her front yard when she "felt the head coming out." She dropped to her knees, and we found her in the head down, butt up position with the baby's head presenting. Two things jumped out at me as I approached the patient: first, the steam that was coming off the baby's head and second; the baby's head was "stuck" between the mom's buttocks. The baby's nose and mouth were impacted with the mom's fecal matter causing an airway obstruction. While Brian delivered the baby, Phil and I worked on getting the fecal matter out of the baby's nose and mouth. Finally, the baby started crying. What a wonderful sound. We turned the heat up to maximum and wrapped the baby in a silver swaddler and put a little cap on his head. Although the newborn was a little hypothermic, upon arrival at the hospital, both mother and baby were fine.

Early one morning, M-1 was dispatched to a female "vomiting blood." A-2 arrived and requested we "expedite." When we walked into the living room, there was a female in her 50s sitting bolt upright on the couch talking while blood "gushed" from her mouth. There was blood all over the couch, the patient, and on the floor. The female had a history of chronic alcoholism and the first thing I thought of was esophageal varices. There was nothing we could do for the patient except rapid transport. Two IVs were started en route to the hospital. After a five-minute transport to the hospital, she was dead. It was that quick. This was the same way my dad died.

Early one miserably rainy morning, A-1 was dispatched to a "man down." Lonnie Davis and his partner arrived on A-1 and immediately called for M-1 and announced, "Code 4." When my partner and I arrived on M-1, we found a Black male in his 40s laying in some shrubs with obvious severe traumatic injuries. Lonnie was looking over the patient when he said, "Holy shit, someone impaled him with rebar." I took a closer look and noticed a symmetrical shaped white "cap" near the victim's genitals. "Usually rebar caps are orange," I told Lonnie. Upon a closer glimpse, it was determined to be the head of the victim's femur. We determined the patient to be DOA and requested EPD. While waiting, we all gave our two cents' worth of what might have happened. The patient was located near a three-story building so my theory was he jumped or was pushed off the building. Lonnie stared at the victim's face and said, "I know where I've seen him before, we had a call on him about 12 hours ago after being assaulted." It was determined that the patient, after being assaulted, either sought revenge or the assaulter returned. The victim had been thrown out of a fast-moving vehicle, then run over. The crime had occurred somewhere else, then the victim was dumped where he was found.

Every person in our profession has that one call that puts them over the edge. I went on a call that nearly pushed me, but definitely pushed my partner that day, Chuck King. Chuck was one of the nicest, most compassionate people I've met. Chuck was one of the original Harborview-trained paramedics and had been for several years. At the time, Chuck had been with the department for over 30 years. Chuck was also an avid scratch golfer. For the shift, we had Bill Stopoulous riding as "third man," doing his paramedic internship. We were in a training class at Sta. 1 when we got toned out for a "gunshot wound." In route, we were advised that it was a "pellet gun" wound. Additional, updated information was relayed. This was in fact a large caliber weapon incident with "multiple patients."

When we arrived, there were multiple EPD officers, guns drawn, canvasing the area around the Pine Apartments. Scott Dunn and his crew on E-2 arrived just as we did. It was cold and raining hard. An EPD officer ran up to me and told me there were "multiple victims" that they were looking for. The shooter had not been located. The scene was in a large courtyard and as I ran up a small set of stairs, I found an adult male (in his 30s) lying on the sidewalk with brains and blood running down the cement. Half his head was gone. Code Black, (dead on arrival, coroner's case) I continued up the sidewalk and came upon a young boy (probably 10), shirtless, with a gunshot wound in the center of his chest. A bystander told me, "I just saw him take his last breath." I yelled for Chuck and Bill to put the boy on a backboard and get him in the medic unit. I heard an officer yell, "I've got one over here." I ran over and found a female in her 30s with gunshot wounds to each one of her extremities, one to the genitals, one to her chest, and multiple gunshots to the head. The *coup de grâce* was a gunshot to the mouth that took off the back of her head. But the worst was the five-year-old girl sitting next to the older female. She was wearing "Care Bear" pajamas and had gunshot wounds to the two bears heads on her chest. At that same time, I had a five-year-old daughter at home. Two more Code Blacks.

As there was nothing to be done for the three other victims, I returned to the medic unit where Chuck and Bill were working on the 10-year-old male. We were less than a mile from the hospital, so we just "scooped and ran." As we moved the young male over to the treatment table, we noticed a large exit wound to the patient's back, in line with the spine. The hospital did one round of resuscitative efforts, then stopped. One more Code Black. Before the shift was over, we found out what had happened.

The 30-year-old male I first encountered was the husband of the female with the multiple gunshots. The two children belonged to the deceased adult male and female. The husband had recently been displaying erratic behavior with delusional thoughts. The husband had accused the wife on multiple occasions of having an affair with a maintenance man. The husband had called home and didn't get an answer. He came home to confront his wife (whom he was sure was with the maintenance man). When he got home, the wife and her sister, along with the kids, had just got home from shopping. The husband threatened to shoot them all. He went into the bedroom and located his handgun and chased the family through the courtyard. 911 calls started pouring in of a "crazy man" yelling and shooting at people.

Investigators determined that the young male was shot first. One person who called 911 stated there was a woman on her front porch huddled in a corner with a small girl. She said she heard the male talking to the female, then made the comment, "Watch this slut." Next she heard the little girl say, "No daddy, no daddy, I love you." The reporting party then said she heard two gunshots. The reporting party could hear the mother screaming hysterically. "No, no, please don't," the wife pleaded. Multiple shots were then heard. The husband walked away, and a final gunshot was heard. To this day, I don't know what was worse, the description of events, or seeing the aftermath of three executions. When the coroner removed the father's body, they found the gun used in the murders. Several days later, a post-traumatic stress debriefing was held. Scott and I held our own. We went golfing and got drunk. Shortly after this incident, Chuck King gave up being a paramedic and was promoted to captain.

I was working M-5, and early one morning, we were requested to transport a patient that E-6 had evaluated. The patient was a 40-year-old female who had passed out from too much alcohol in a bathroom at a local Fred Meyers. As we arrived, E-5 and M-1 were dispatched to a head-on accident at the intersection in front of Sta. 5. Bill Searcy (Capt. of E-5), immediately called for a second medic unit as they had two (actually three) critical patients. One was the driver, an unconscious male, and the second was the pregnant wife of the driver, who was also unconscious. The driver of the other vehicle was a drunk, uninjured male. I met with the captain of E-6 and advised him of what was going on with E-5. He acknowledged what was going on but felt their intoxicated female should be transported by medic unit. I checked the patient's gag reflex (present), and I commented to the captain that she could be transported by ambulance. "I didn't call you for evaluation, I called you to transport," replied the captain. "I'll transport if you order me to," I said to the captain. "I'm ordering you," he said. As we were transporting, the E-5 captain came on the air again requesting our status. "We're transporting a BLS patient," I answered. Due to accessibility, the male driver was easily extricated, treated, and transported by M-1 in critical condition. The female, however, required extensive extrication and was transported by a private ambulance. Mother and baby died. We transported a patient a couple hours later, and found the drunk female, still laying on a gurney, snoring in the hallway. A few days later, I was called into the battalion chief's office and "orally admonished," for not using better judgment. I should have "broken away" from the minor call that I was on to the more severe call. I said nothing and took the admonishment. Nothing happened to the captain on E-6.

In 1999, I was promoted to captain. I was no longer assigned to the medic unit. My office became an engine or ladder truck. I preferred engine work over ladder work. I wanted to be in, close to the fire. Not over it. Even though I was no longer a "paramedic" in the city's eyes, I maintained my certification for another seven years, performing skills. I was working a "flip-flop" shift (I worked for someone, then they worked the next day for me), for Matt Hausmann on E-4. It was a Saturday morning (Saturdays were dedicated to station and vehicle maintenance) when we were toned out for a "commercial structure fire" at Food Services of America, located approximately one mile from our station. Jim "Vu" Venturo was my driver and Mike Masterson was my "pipe man." Mike had recently been hired and was our "probie."

As we were driving towards the scene, a massive plume of black smoke was visible hundreds of feet in the air. Battalion Chief Dave Neyens (responding from Sta. 1), saw the smoke from six miles away and immediately called for a second alarm. The 60,000-square foot, four-story building was under construction and two thirds completed. As we arrived, I observed one quarter of the west side fully involved from the ground level to the fourth floor. There were no organized roadways around the complex, just muddy, potholed construction access. There were several hydrants in the vicinity of the building, but it was unknown if they were in working order (as luck would have it, they were put in service the day before). Not knowing the hydrants worked, we laid a thousand feet of five-foot supply line, requesting the next in engine to "reverse out" to a known working hydrant on the main street.

Upon further investigation, the material on fire was 12-inch-thick Styrofoam attached to the exterior of the building. Welders had inadvertently ignited the material while working inside. The heat of the flames ignited several forklifts on the first floor. Because of the expansive area inside the building, every time a tire on the forklifts blew up, it sounded like a bomb going off. Mike and I "hand jacked" 400 hundred feet of 2½-inch line into the building and attacked the fire. Arriving crews attacked from the exterior. For more maneuverability, we attached a 1¾-inch "apartment pack" to the 2½-inch and extinguished the forklift fires.

It took nearly 30 minutes to extinguish all the fires and several hours of overhaul. Due to the heat, several large beams were damaged from annealing and had to be replaced. The total cost of damage was three million dollars plus an extra six months' delay of completion. When we returned to quarters, we spent the next several hours cleaning equipment and replacing hose. There was so much mud on the engine that we had to pressure wash the undercarriage and every "nook and cranny" before we could hand wash it.

Early the next morning, we were dispatched to a "possible house fire" in our station area. When we arrived, we found a large "mansion" at the top of a steep driveway with nothing showing. Mike and I entered the house and were met by the homeowner. He had just gotten home and was using the bathroom when he thought he heard "crackling" overhead. I directed a thermal imaging camera (TIC), at the ceiling and the screen turned "white" (indication of severe heat). I had Mike bring in a 1¾-inch pre-con-nect, and we opened up the ceiling. There was fire overhead. I reported to the battalion chief that we had a well involved attic fire, and we would need ventilation. L-1 was able to maneuver into place to reach the roof from the street. After a ventilation hole was cut, flames and smoke "boiled" out of the hole. It took us about 20 minutes to extinguish the fire. The fire caused several hundreds of thousands of dollars in damage, but a far cry from the three million dollars it would have caused had the house burned to the ground. Another several hours of salvage and overhaul. Another couple of hours of cleaning and reloading hose. It was Easter morning and as I left, I told Matt the Easter bunny had left him a basket in the hose tower. I failed to mention that it was several thousand feet of dirty hose.

I was working on E-5 one evening when M-5 and E-4 were dispatched to an "unconscious male." When E-4 arrived, Capt. Dan Taylor advised M-5 that they had a "Code 4." Several minutes later, E-5 was requested to the scene for "manpower." When E-5 arrived, we observed both crews working a cardiac arrest on a very large male. This patient weighed well over 500 pounds. Firefighter/Paramedic Dave Demarco (now the chief of the Everett Fire Department) was in charge of the patient. Dave had the patient intubated, but neither he nor his partner could establish an IV. The patient's girth and adipose tissue made it impossible to start a peripheral IV. The patient's neck had so many folds that an external jugular vein was not accessible. Dave asked me if I could start a central line. I was able to get a three-inch, 12-gauge catheter in his subclavian vein. Dave was able to give several cardiac medications and eventually, the patient regained a pulse and blood pressure.

The next challenge was getting the patient out of the house. While on a backboard, the patient's body overhung a good 18 inches on both sides. E-5's crew was tasked with making an opening wide enough to get the patient out. We were able to dismantle the glass slider, which gave us just enough width to remove the patient. As we lifted the backboard, it started to crack. We placed a second backboard for reinforcement. It took 10 of us (eight firefighters and two EPD officers) to manhandle the patient out to the gurney and down the driveway to the medic unit without dropping or tipping the patient over. We called for E-2 to meet us at the E/R to help offload the patient. We eventually got the patient into the cardiac room at Everett General. The doctor came walking in with the patient's records and announced, "This patient is a DNR." Apparently, the patient's orders had been on the refrigerator upstairs. The patient died several hours later. It was a noble try, but for nothing. We did return to the house and repair the slider.

Early one morning, E-5 was dispatched to a "2-11" at Kimberly Clark (formally Scotts Paper Company) down on the Everett waterfront. A "1-11" is a first-alarm response that includes three engines, a ladder truck, an aid car, medic unit, and the battalion chief. A 2-11 response (second alarm) includes all the rest of the city's fire apparatus (three more engines, a ladder truck, and a medic unit). Off-duty personnel report to Sta. 1 with bunker gear and man reserve apparatus. Surrounding departments "move up" to empty stations and respond to other calls in the city. A "3-11" (third alarm) sends all "move up" apparatus to the fire scene.

Kimberly Clark manufactured toilet paper, tissue, and paper towels. There were five large "paper machines" that ran 24 hours a day. When a paper machine was "down," it cost the company $10,000 per hour in lost revenue. Because of the dust and paper fibers constantly collecting on the machines, small fires were typical on a day-to-day basis. The plant had their own "fire brigade" that would extinguish these small fires. If we were dispatched to a fire at Kimberly Clark, we knew it must be something significant because the "fire brigade" couldn't control it. Paper machine #5 was always a problem. In my career, I had been on multiple fires at Kimberly Clark, and all, except one, were on paper machine #5.

When E-5 arrived, we were directed to take a 2½-inch line into the building, connect to a manifold, and attack the fire. My crew consisted of Driver Tom Morse, Pipe man Matt Sorenson, and myself. We had advanced deep into the building and could see a large orange glow through all the smoke. We knocked down the fire and because of the expansive room, all we felt was "cold smoke." Smoke was down to the floor and visibility was zero. We advanced further into the building and were met by more flames, but they were easy to extinguish. As we paused, two sounds were prevalent. The sound of running water, and the "booming" of five-ton rolls of paper falling from a 50-foot-high stack placed up against a wall. The sound of water was a broken sprinkler pipe that had been destroyed when several of the rolls of paper had collided with it. The broken sprinkler pipe was saturating all the rolls of paper, causing them to collapse, then roll. Several waterlogged rolls even crashed through the metal siding, causing considerable damage. It was eerie sitting in a confined area with no visibility, surrounded by rolls of paper flying right past you.

I radioed to the command officer that the fire was out and that the sprinkler system needed to be shut down. The water damage was perhaps 20 times greater than the fire itself. After several minutes, the sprinkler system was shut down. Ventilation was ongoing, and slowly the smoke dissipated. Surprisingly, damage was listed at only a hundred thousand dollars. The main damage was limited to the wall the rolls of paper took out, and the broken sprinkler system. Roughly 50 rolls that were waterlogged were recycled and made into new products.

On another occasion, we were called out to Kimberly Clark for a fire in the "flaw lot." This was an area where large rolls of paper that had "flaws" were stacked. Because of the friction generated by manufacturing, occasionally a spark or small burning ember would be captured in the large rolls. It could take days to weeks for these embers to slowly ignite from the inside out. On this occasion, a roll on the bottom stack eventually ignited and then ignited the rolls stacked around it. We could have dumped a million gallons of water on it, and it still would not go out. Finally, a front loader was brought in, and the pile was broken up. The fire was then easily extinguished.

I was working on E-6. M-6 and E-7 were dispatched to a "possible drowning" at Silver Lake. E-7 requested E-6 for manpower. It was a warm day just before the Memorial Day weekend and a large group of people had gathered for a day of fun at the main beach. There were "No Lifeguard on Duty" signs posted. A 20–30-year-old male was unaccounted for and there was suspicion that he might be in the lake. I have been on several of these calls where it turns out the subject had left, went to the bathroom, or was gone for other reasons.

When we arrived, everyone was out of the lake by the order of EPD. There was an EPD officer certified in scuba diving, in route to the scene. Because of the prolonged ETA (20-plus minutes), I recommended that we form a "human chain" and slowly walk out to our chest. There were more than enough people to accomplish this. I was told by the EPD Officer that "no one is to go in that water. You will only stir up mud making it impossible to see." By the time the diver arrived, the subject had been missing for over 30 minutes. After another 10 minutes of donning his gear, the diver entered the water. Not 10 seconds later, this purple, lifeless body emerged to the surface. The swimmer had been only 15 feet from shore in about four feet of water. The "human chain" would have been 25 minutes quicker. The patient was pulled from the water and resuscitated in the back of M-6. They were able to save his heart, but not his brain. He died two weeks later without ever regaining consciousness.

In February 2003, I went back to the state fire academy as an instructor/coordinator. The state had come to their senses and eliminated the January start time. Even though there were some days with snow, it was not the brutal cold that prevented anything from getting done (my true respect to Boston, New York, Chicago, and East Coast brothers and sisters). The state academy had changed in several other positive ways. First, the academy was taken over by the Washington State Patrol. Second, the state had hired full-time instructors from all over the state, specializing in certain aspects of the fire service. Third, there were upgrades and additions to the facilities, and finally (and in my opinion the best change), the program was labeled an "adult learning environment." No more humiliation, no more "dying cockroaches," and no more disciplinary calisthenics. You fuck up and you're done. Simple as that.

The drill master was Chief Frank Garza from the Tacoma Fire Department. Two great instructors, Capt. John Tanaka (Everett Fire Department) and Lt. Todd Plum (Port of Seattle Fire Department), were the two main instructors. I had 36 recruits I was responsible for. For the next eight weeks, I would be their mother, father, wife, priest, social worker, psychologist, and confidante. It was an absolutely fantastic time and experience. I learned some "new tricks" (yes, an old dog can), and even taught some "old tricks." For the most part, I was on the drill field all day, participating in live fires, multi-company drills, and even being the "dummy" for search and rescue operations.

As with previous classes, I had to select a group leader. I selected Brian Lamoreaux from the King County Fire Dist. #2, (Burien Fire Department). Brian was an ex-Marine and had the "it" factor. Brian was a true leader from the minute he was selected. Brian did such a great job, I kept him as permanent leader. Mr. Lamoureux (as I always called him) would often remind me that the "chair force," (Air Force), was not considered a part of the military. I would have to correct him and remind him that the Air Force was the "backbone" of the military. I'd also ask him if he preferred mustard or ketchup with his crayons. I did get my "tit in a ringer" once while at the academy. Lieutenant Jon Cahill from the Auburn Fire Department and I were instructing recruits in the heat and smoke trailer. Lieutenant Cahill was a very well-respected and knowledgeable instructor. I learned a lot from him. In past academies, if an instructor sustained damage to their helmet in a hot fire, it was considered a "badge of honor." Not anymore. Today, melting of helmets is taboo. Even though they are a valuable part of the protective equipment we wear, I've never been a fan of Nomex hoods. I'm from the old school; my ears tell me when it's too hot and time to get out. On this day in the trailer, I had my Nomex hood on and by the time I felt the heat on my ears, I knew it was time to get out. Once I got out, I noticed my face shield was completely melted and the helmet looked like a dragon's tail with all the blistering. The cold air immediately hardened the blisters, making them permanent. I had to fill out a three-page incident report stating how it happened and how I would prevent it from happening again. Other than that, time flew by and soon it was graduation time. All the recruits passed with flying colors, and most importantly, no one was injured.

On my first shift back from the academy, I was assigned to E-6. We had just sat down to eat dinner, and the evening news was on. The leading story was about a climber who had been killed while climbing Mt. Rainier. The dead climber was Jon Cahill from the Auburn Fire Department. I had just talked with him the week before. I was completely shocked and saddened. While I was in my office, trying to absorb Jon's death, E-6 was dispatched to a "patient assist," a stone's throw away from the station.

When we arrived, I was met by an older female (the mother of the patient), who was hesitant to give any information. As we walked through the basement, something caught my eye in a small room. From a distance, I thought it was the largest beehive I had ever seen. As I got closer, I could see this "beehive" was purple with weeping sores and had a little foot with a dripping sock attached to it. The mother took me upstairs to a small bathroom, where I found a mentally challenged female who weighed in excess of 600 pounds. The patient had attempted to sit on the toilet, when the floor gave way. The patient was pinned between the floor joists, and the distal circulation to her very obese leg was compromised. I was amazed that the patient was able to get through the small bathroom door because of her girth.

The only way we were going to be able to get her out would be to cut a large opening on the side of the house, shore up the supports for the floor, and cut the floor away. I called for A-6, L-5, and our Urban Rescue Unit from Sta. 4. I was trying to be discreet when requesting additional units as I did not want to get the battalion chief involved. Chiefs tend to "muck up" things, and I knew exactly what I wanted, and what needed to be done. The amazing thing through the whole extrication process, the patient did not complain or cry. All she was worried about was "having dinner" at the hospital. While L-5's crew was upstairs cutting the opening in the wall, my crew was in the basement shoring up the floor joists. We had run out of wood for the shoring, so I had Jamie Wall and his partner go to the Home Depot a couple miles down the street and get more posts and lumber in A-6. I told Jamie to find a manager, explain the situation, and get the wood. I told Jamie to tell the manager that the city would be in touch with them in the morning and pay for the materials. Because of the complexity and time frame of the extrication, I called M-6 for patient care. Because of all the rigs we had on the scene, it was time the battalion chief was notified. Soon, the wall opening, and all shoring had been completed.

The plan was to place the patient in a large cargo net, cut away the floor, and take her out the opening. I had one of the crew members upstairs "sound the floor" so I knew where to cut without cutting the patient. Using a Sawzall, I started cutting the floor away. I noticed blood running down the blade, so I immediately stopped. I had cut into one of her folds of adipose tissue and she didn't even feel it. The rescue crew had set up a hoisting and pulley system, and thankfully they did. After the final cut, weight and gravity dictated which way she was going: down. We were able to gently lower her down to the basement floor. It took 10 of us to get her out to the medic unit. Because of her size, we weren't able to put her on the gurney, so we took out the center mount and laid the patient directly on the floor. The cargo net was secured with hose straps. After a nearly three-hour extrication, the patient arrived at the hospital. Unfortunately, the patient had an adverse reaction to medication given by the hospital. Her skin began to sluff, and she was transferred to Harborview. She passed away several weeks later due to sepsis.

I was working on E-5 when I was assigned a new "probie," Chad Gallatin. "Chadly," as we called him, was one of the best firefighters I worked with in my career. Chadly was smart, respectful, hardworking, quick witted, and just a pleasure to be around. Chadly could do the best Barney Fife imitation. I loved working with Chadly. On our first shift together, we were dispatched to a house fire with flames visible. As we approached the scene, we were directed to go down a driveway that wasn't visible from the road due to trees. I yelled to Chadly, "Blind alley," and he got out of his jump seat and removed the first flake of the five-inch supply line. I had not noticed that Chad had gotten back on the engine. As I had mentioned earlier in this book, during a blind alley, the hose must be "heeled" in case the hose gets hung up in the hose bed. Chadly had not "heeled" the line, and sure enough, it got hung up in the bed.

When we got to the house, flames were rolling out of both gable ends of a rambler style house. When I got out of the engine, I noticed Chadly shoulder loading a preconnected hose line. I happened to look back at the driveway and noticed a five-inch coupling shining in the sunlight. I asked Chad, "Shouldn't that coupling be a couple hundred feet back at the road?" Without a word, Chad ran back and extended the supply line to the road. After the fire was extinguished, Chad couldn't apologize enough. All I could do was laugh. To this day, if I say the word "blind alley," Chadly turns red.

While a captain, my favorite crew and station was Sta. 2 on the north end of the city. My crew consisted of Driver Phil Smithson, Pipe man Chad Gallatin, with Mike Lande and Mike Calvert on A-2. Mike Lande went on to become a battalion chief and Mike Calvert went on to be assistant chief. Early one morning E-2 was dispatched to an "unknown medical problem" at a local nightclub. We arrived to find a 40–50-year-old female, visibly upset in a manager's office. I asked her, "How can we help you?" She replied, "I'm bleeding from my vagina." "Okay," I said." Is there a possibility of pregnancy?" I asked. "No," she flatly said. "Could you be starting your menstrual cycle?" I asked. Again, a flat no. After answering no to several questions, I asked her, "Why do you think you're bleeding?" She stated that she had anxiety and that her roommate was always "stealing my medication." The patient went on to say that she now carried her medication in a little plastic bag that she hid in her vagina. She was losing at blackjack and was becoming very anxious. She went to the bathroom to retrieve her medication and inadvertently lacerated "something up there" with her long fingernail. She did not want to go to the hospital but wanted us to put a Band-aid on her "cut." I told her that a Band-aid wouldn't work and recommended a tampon. A worker went to get one as we left. You can't make this stuff up.

I was working on E-1 with Mike Masterson as my pipe man. We were dispatched to an unknown medical problem in the parking lot of a local restaurant/hotel. When we arrived, we found a young Vietnamese male lying on his back with his intestines spilling out onto the parking lot. He had been attending a wedding reception when he got into an argument with another attendee. They took their argument outside and according to one witness, a knife was drawn. According to a second witness, a broken bottle was used. Either way, the patient was eviscerated. It was a pretty severe wound, the kind you might see in a Hollywood war movie. The patient kept trying to "scoop up" his intestines and put them back where they should have been. A lot of hysterical people were running around and because of a language gap, a lot of confusion. Through a translator, we were able to calm the patient down and treat his wound. After irrigating his intestines with saline, we covered the wound with saran wrap and applied a bulky dressing. He was taken to surgery and made a complete recovery. Due to uncooperative witnesses, no one was ever charged.

On our way back to the station, we were dispatched to the Greyhound bus station for an unconscious male who would soon be arriving by bus. We found a 20-year-old male in the back of the bus, not breathing. We got the patient off the bus and began respirations with a BVM. M-1 had just arrived, and as they were setting up an IV, I drew up some Narcan and injected it under his tongue. (I have a buddy, Dan Galovic, who would inject Narcan right under the chin into the sublingual space.) I told Mike (who was ventilating the patient) to be ready to turn the patient on his side in case he vomited. Being very familiar with Narcan, I knew what to expect. Mike was new, and he didn't. Approximately 30 seconds after giving the Narcan injection, I heard some rumbling from the patient's stomach. "Roll him now," I told Mike. We were quick enough to get him on his side, but Mike wasn't able to get his arm out of the way and the patient spewed vomit all over Mike. I don't know what surprised Mike more, the fast-acting Narcan or getting puked on.

In January 2007, I was promoted to Division Chief of EMS (Emergency Medical Services). It was a substantial increase in pay and instead of two silver stripes on my Class A uniform, signifying captain, I now had three gold stripes, which made me look like a tugboat captain. My work schedule was four, 10-hour days with Mondays off. The main reason I took the job was my right hip was shot. Even though I was in my 40s, I had the hip of an 80-year-old. Bone on bone. I got to the point that

I had to gingerly exit the cab of the engine. Now with an office job, I could get my hip replaced and not miss much work. My job as EMS administrator was to oversee the paramedics and EMTs of the department. We had a great bunch of employees so that made my job easy. I was the liaison between the department and the hospitals, as well as chairman of the Planning Committee for the Snohomish County EMS Council. I was also the chief infectious control officer of the department. I handled concerns and complaints from citizens and assisted my right-hand man, Fred Jaross, medical services officer, with training and planning. I was responsible for a multi-million-dollar budget, and had to keep the chief of the department, Murray Gordon, apprised on the latest trends and impacts involving EMS. In February 2008, I had successful right hip replacement (thank you Dr. Phillip Downer) and I was missing the fun of being out in the field. Being an "office shirt" just wasn't my cup of tea. I had to wait for a captain vacancy to come out of the office. In April 2008, I went back to being a captain. One month to the day of my hip replacement, I was back in the office, and two months to the day of surgery, I was putting out an apartment fire.

Phil, Chadly, and I were working on E-6 and had just sat down for dinner. We were dispatched to a "service call, assist EPD." As we were responding, SNOPAC advised us that EPD was on the scene at a local apartment complex and had requested our assistance but gave no information why. When we arrived, we observed no less than six EPD vehicles and several officers talking. I went up to a sergeant and asked him what we could do for them. He told me to talk to the officers down a corridor that turned to the right, then to the left. Phil stayed with the rig as Chadly, and I proceeded to another group of officers. At their feet was a male in his 30s, with the top of his head missing. Apparently, the subject had threatened someone in one of the units and come with a gun. The occupant had a larger gun and turned the victim's head "into a canoe." There was an impressive amount of brains, blood and skull "peppered" on the walls and a large pool of blood where the victim lay. "Can't get more dead than that," I told the officer. "That's one reason you're here," the officer said. (Police weren't allowed to pronounce death, even in the most obvious situations.) "The other reason is for you to clean up the mess." However, because of infectious diseases concerning "gored up" scenes, a policy had just come out stating the fire department was no longer permitted to "hose down" large amounts of blood and guts. There was a company in Tacoma that had a contract to deal with the cleanup. I wanted to oblige the police, but this was a new policy that was to be strictly enforced. We returned to quarters.

About an hour later, we got a call to go back to the scene and assist EPD. When I talked with the sergeant, he told me they had been in contact with the cleanup company, and they gave an ETA of six hours with a minimum charge of four thousand dollars. The sergeant told me he was getting heat from his commander about getting the scene cleared and could I do him a favor by spraying the brains away Because I could see that the sergeant was in a predicament, I told him we would do it. Chadly advanced the booster line and started spraying. We weren't aware that the crew the day before had put a protein-based foam in the tank for a large gas spill. The foam mixed with the blood and turned everything pink. Chad was able to wash all the remnants of death out into a yard. A couple hours later, we responded to a call past the apartment complex, and I noticed several cats feasting on the foam.

THE BEGINNING
OF THE END

Throughout my 35-plus years as a first responder, I have accumulated so many news clippings of calls that I have been on that they fill a large scrapbook. I have also accumulated so many graphic pictures of those calls that they fill a large photo album. I have used those photos in the many EMT classes that I instructed. I showed these pictures on the first night of class to let the new students know what they were getting into. Yes, I did lose a few students, but it was better to expose them early to what they could expect versus seeing the gruesome sights for the first time on a call. I also incorporated accident scene photos into presentations that I gave at local high schools (just in time for graduation). I'm sure several students thought twice about drinking and driving. My presentation became so popular, that I was invited back year after year.

On June 1, 2009, I was working an overtime day shift on E-1A with Driver Tom Morse and Pipe man Eric Watson. All the on-duty crews were tied up with mandatory training, so E-1A responded on all calls. We had just cleared a call, when we were dispatched to a "man down" on the Hewitt trestle. In my career, I had responded to hundreds of "man downs" and 99 percent were usually someone sleeping, or an intoxicated individual "sleeping it off." In our profession, the greatest invention ever made was the cellphone. In our profession, the worst invention ever made was the cellphone. Before cellphones, the reporting party would have to stop and use a phone, thus making it a hassle. "Man down" was rarely reported. With the advent of the cellphone, it is so convenient to dial 911 that the occurrence of "man down" has increased 300 percent. As we were responding, we were advised to contact the reporting party at the Home Acres Exit off Hwy. 2. We stopped at the exit, and I noticed a dump truck hauling gravel stopped several hundred feet down the exit. I walked down and met the driver. The driver was visibly shaken. The driver told me that as he was driving east on Hwy. 2, he thought that he had seen a body in a concrete triangulated barrier just off the exit. The driver was so sure that it was a body, that he proceeded east and turned around and went back into Everett and got back on the trestle. He got off at the exit and confirmed it was a body. The driver was so upset that he couldn't go back up the on-ramp. I told the driver that he didn't have to. I took his information to give to the Washington State Patrol as the reporting party. The driver went on his way, and I walked back up the off-ramp. When I got back to the engine, I looked in the triangulated area, and sure enough, there was a dead body. The height of the triangulated area was just high enough that a domestic vehicle driver could not see in but a high-profile vehicle driver could. I had Tom and Eric place traffic cones to shut down the exit and then had Tom block the right lane with the engine. Upon observation, we noticed jewelry, pieces of clothing, blood, skin, and hair along the side of the barrier. Inside the barrier was a young female who was obviously dead. She had been struck by a vehicle on the shoulder and the force catapulted her headfirst into a cement bulkhead approximately 30 feet away. Because of the location of the incident, I was unsure which law enforcement agency had jurisdiction. I advised SNOPAC of the exact location and the next thing I knew, I had Everett Police, Lake

Stevens Police, Washington State Patrol, and Snohomish County Sheriff's Office on scene. Prior to arrival of the first police agency, I asked Tom to take some pictures with his cellphone as I did not have mine. Tom took several pictures, and I asked him to send them to my computer. I passed along all the information I had to WSP, and we cleared the scene. Upon investigation, the victim was a 14-year-old female who had been missing for two days. She had been walking on the shoulder with a young male early Saturday morning when she was struck. I don't know if the young male has ever come forward. To this day, no one has ever been charged for the hit and run.

I was working another overtime shift on L-1 when we were dispatched to a "possible seizure" at the Everett train station. We were given the location as the south end of the station. E-3 was in the area, so they also responded. When we arrived, no patient could be located. As we waited for an update on the patient location, I noticed several people waving and yelling near the north end of the station. I walked down to the other end and was met by a chorus of "Where the fuck have you been?" and "What took you so fucking long?" I noticed probably 30 "freakish" looking people standing around a young female, kicking and taunting her. Apparently, one of the "freaks" was cussing and carrying on when the female asked him to "watch his mouth." The tough guy punched the female in the face, and she fell to the ground. In my opinion, the female then faked a seizure. As I talked to the female, I noticed she had "fluttering eye syndrome" and during the arm drop test, (when you lift a person's arm above their head, if unconscious, the arm will strike them in the face. If faking, the arm miraculously falls to their side). Her arm fell to the side and not on her face.

By this time, the rest of the crew arrived and began evaluating the patient. There were no medic units available (and in my opinion, she didn't need one). I called for a private ambulance to transport the patient. Upon arrival of the ambulance, I gave my short report to the ambulance crew and told them she was ready for transport. "I want to get a set of vitals before I get the gurney," said one of the ambulance crew. By this time, more people had arrived and the tension in the air was increasing. I told the attendant, "We have just examined her, and vitals are stable. Let's just get her out of here right now." "No, I want to get my own set of vitals," the attendant said. I then told the attendant that for the safety of the patient, "Get your gurney, now." "No," he flatly replied. I took him aside and looked him right in the eye and told him, "Get your fucking gurney, now." The attendant just stood there smirking at me. Out of nowhere, the other attendant walked up as we were "discussing" getting the gurney. I noticed the one attendant smirk and then nod to his partner. The one I had been talking to walked away from me. He walked towards the ambulance, with me following. I told the attendant, "I am not going to tell you again, get your fucking gurney." The attendant then said, as he was removing the gurney, "Yes, Captain, I'm getting my gurney, we'll transport right now." The patient was transported, and except for a split lip, she was fine and soon released from the hospital.

As L-1 was leaving, an EPD officer pulled up to my side and told me, "I want to let you know that those two ambulance attendants intend to file verbal threat and abuse charges against you, and they have it on tape." Apparently, a dash-mounted camera had just been installed on the ambulance and even though there was no video, the audio had been recorded. The only thing heard on the tape was me "yelling" at the attendant, and the attendant complying with my demands. I had been set up. "Good for them," I told the officer.

As soon as we returned to quarters, I went in and told the battalion chief the entire incident. When I was the division chief of EMS, I received multiple complaints about the ambulance company. On numerous occasions, the ambulance crew would walk into the scene, hands in pockets, without their gurney. It was their job, if called to transport the patient. Nothing more, nothing less. I had worked part time for ambulance companies in the past, and I knew why I was there: to transport. While a Division Chief, I had an incident one night where a homeless man wanted to go to the hospital. It was policy that a fire department unit must evaluate a patient before an ambulance could transport. A ladder truck was dispatched to evaluate this patient. I was a couple of blocks away, so I responded. I asked the subject why he needed to go to the hospital, and he told me he was hungry and cold. He had no medical problem. I cancelled the ladder truck and requested an ambulance. Since the patient had not been "evaluated" by the fire department, they would not send an ambulance. I called the ambulance company directly. The dispatcher told me that an ambulance wouldn't respond until "evaluated by the fire department." I told the dispatcher my name and title and I was requesting an ambulance. "We need fire department authorization," the dispatcher said. I told her for the third time that I was with the fire department. After a five-minute heated conversation, I asked for the dispatcher's name and that I would be following up on this matter with their management. I told the homeless man to get in my car and I drove him up to the emergency room. This was a Friday evening.

The next morning, I got a call at home from the manager of the ambulance company, apologizing for the "miscommunication," and asking what could be done to rectify the situation. I told him that I would like to meet with him and his administrators first thing Monday morning to address the problems we were having with their company. At 0700 hrs. that Monday morning, I met with several management officers and told them what was expected and if things continued, that there was a good possibility that there would be a change in their ability to do business with the Everett Fire Department.

While still the Division Chief of EMS, I was currently drawing up a Request For Proposal, (RFP), to have one ambulance company contractually do business with the city. Currently there was a "verbal" contract with two ambulance companies. At 0800 hrs., the assistant chief of operations came into my office, (the chief was out of town), and I told him what had occurred the previous Friday night and the meeting that morning. I told him that we had "come to an agreement." "Perfect," the assistant chief said as he walked out of my office. My next shift I was back to my assignment on E-6. I decided to send out a memo to all the captains concerning my run in with the two ambulance attendants I had encountered four days earlier. This memo was strictly "For Your Information," and was in no way "taking it upon myself," (as the city charged), to "blackball" the ambulance company from responding on their calls. I simply wrote that these two individuals had committed insubordination to the "Incident Commander" (myself) while on a call and that if they ever responded to another call I was on, that I would send them away. They disobeyed a direct order from me, and very likely would do it to them. That was it. If I had responded to a call where there was a dangerous dog or an unsafe condition, I would have sent out the same memo. I did not circumvent the "chain of command." This memo was sent out laterally.

About a week later, I get a call from the battalion chief to report to headquarters that afternoon. I had no clue what the meeting was about. As we arrived at headquarters, I mentioned to my driver (who was the current union president), "I wonder what this is about." "Oh, I forgot to tell you," he said. "You're under investigation for the ambulance incident." We had worked the past week together and he didn't tell me anything. "Well, thanks for the heads up," I told him as I got out of the engine.

I met with the new assistant chief of operations, who told me that the ambulance company had filed a complaint against me on behalf of the two subjects who couldn't follow a command. A chief with any balls would have told the ambulance company that their employees committed a serious infraction to a company officer of the Everett Fire Department and that they were not allowed to work in the city again. The chief didn't do a fucking thing. A backstabbing, ass-kissing captain (you know who you are) took the memo I had sent out and put it on the chief's desk. I was told the investigation could take weeks, if not months.

About three weeks later, I got a phone call at home from the assistant chief of operations. He advised me that I was being recorded on a conference call with representatives from the department and human resources. I was told I was on "indefinite leave, with pay," pending a further investigation. I was not allowed to contact any fire personnel at work, and I was not allowed in any stations. All station lock combinations had been changed. The charges I was facing were "misrepresentation of the fire department," "unauthorized use and material on my computer," "immoral turpitude," "unprofessional conduct," and a few other bullshit charges. I was looking at "demotion and possible termination." I felt like I had just been kicked in the nuts. The letter that I wrote to the captains "justified" the city to get into my computer. In my computer, the city found the pictures of the hit and run victim we had on the Hewitt trestle and the letter I wrote to the Captains. Also found were a few jokes that had been sent to me, but I had not forwarded.

I was labeled a "racist," a "pervert," and a "pedophile." By Human Resources. I was asked if I wanted a "Loudermill hearing," (a meeting to provide an employee an opportunity to present their side of the story before the employer decides on discipline). I quickly answered yes. During the Loudermill hearing, I had such poor union representation, I requested that the hearing be delayed. Another hearing was scheduled a week later. I was told "because of my exemplary career, distinguished member award, and" blah, blah, blah, I would not be terminated but demoted back to fire-fighter. I could appeal the decision to the Civil Service Commission, but if I lost, I could be terminated. My representatives highly recommended that I not take that route. My only other course of action was to take the disci-pline and fight the decision through arbitration and mediation.

I was assigned two weeks of training to "refresh my firefighting skills." Perhaps the hardest day of my career was when I had to go to a uniform store in Seattle and get "fitted" for new blue uniform shirts that signified firefighter. I was also issued a new black firefighter helmet. I drove down to the Port of Seattle waterfront and spent the next hour staring at the water. I didn't know what to do. I couldn't breathe. For the first time since my dad died almost 40 years earlier, I cried. I was an emotional wreck. I called my wife and told her I couldn't do it anymore. She said, "Come home." All my hard work to get where I was, all the training, all the patients that my team and I had saved, gone.

On the way home, I contemplated suicide. How would I do it? Will it hurt? Will I be successful? What about my family? It was a Friday, and I had all weekend to think about it. I didn't get out of bed all weekend. Monday morning, when I walked through the door at Station 2, instead of walking into my old captain's office, I walked into the sleeping quarters with the other firefighters. I had to clean out an old locker, find a bed and start from scratch. My officer was an acting captain with less than five years on the job. Two months prior, I was his captain. I talked with the acting captain and told him how uncomfortable it was for me, and he felt the same way. I didn't want to put him in that situation so I asked him to call the battalion chief and see if I could switch to an engine that had a more senior captain. The battalion chief said no. The fuck, fuck had begun.

The first month felt like 10 years. I was told by the union to "hold on, we're going to win this. You'll get your job back." The fire administration kept dangling carrots in front of me. "Attend counseling, and in three months, you'll have your job back." "Do this, do that." Six months passed, and still there was no consideration. Every time a mediation meeting was set, the city would postpone it. They knew they could outlast me. By this time, I was so emotionally, mentally, and physically drained that I had had enough.

On my 53rd birthday, March 20, 2011, I retired. In a parting agreement with the city, I retired as a captain if I didn't pursue any legal procedures against the city. No matter the alleged charges against me, as god is my witness, and my right hand on the Bible, I swear every charge was bogus. Everything that was alleged fell within the scope of my duties as a company officer and a chief officer. Even though I may have "colored outside the lines" on a few occasions, I did what was best for my patients, my crew, the department, and especially for the citizens of Everett. I was never a bureaucratic kiss-ass like so many you see today. I had a very respectful career; I worked hard and have no regrets. Yes, I can look myself in the mirror and know that I "did it right."

So here I am today, I suffer from PTSD, can't sleep, have nine stents in my heart, Type II Diabetes, Stage 3 kidney disease, high blood pressure, and depression. Would I do my career all over again? In a heartbeat.......

GLOSSARY

Avulsion-A tearing of skin, rupturing of the tendon from the bone, a protrusion of the eye from the eye socket.

Bag Valve Mask-(BVM)-A hand-held device commonly used to provide positive pressure ventilation to patients who are bot breathing or not breathing properly, Also known as an Ambu Bag.

Blind Alley-Used when a fire is not visible from the street or down a narrow avenue of travel. A water supply line is placed at the entrance of the narrow avenue of travel. A second arriving engine then supplies water to the first arriving engine.

Blitz Line-Usually a pre-connected 2 ½' hose line that is used in a "quick attack" on a fire.

Booster Line-Usually a small diameter rubber hose pre-connected to a "hose reel" that is used for small fires, (dumpster, brush, washdowns). Because it's made of rubber, it does not have to be washed and hung in a hose tower. Popular and convenient choice due to low maintenance. Also known as a "rubbish line."

Bunker Gear-The outfit worn by firefighters during a fire, auto extrication, etc. It consists of a Nomex coat, Nomex pants and Nomex hood, steel-toed rubber boots, Nomex gloves and helmet with eye protection. Also referred to a "safety gear" and "turn-outs."

Burr holes-Small holes that a neurosurgeon makes in the skull. Burr holes are used to are used to help relieve pressure on the brain when fluid, such as blood builds up and compresses brain tissue.

Cheyne Stokes Respiration-Abnormal breathing pattern that involves a period of fast, shallow breathing followed by slow, heavier breathing and moments without breathing at all, (apnea). Usually seen in severe head trauma.

Crepitus-Grinding, creaking, cracking, crunching or popping that occurs when moving a joint or bone that has been fractured.

Cross load-Preconnected hose lines that are loaded near the cab of the engine. Usually, one cross load is shoulder on the right side of the engine and the other on the left.

Deck gun-(Stang), a pre-plumbed device that is mounted to the top of the fire engine. It delivers hundreds of gallons of water per minute, depending on the diameter of the nozzle. Usually used during "quick attacks" and "surround and drown" situations.

Decerebrate posturing-An abnormal body posture that involves the arms and legs being held straight out, the toes being pointed downward, and the head and neck being arched backward. This type of posturing usually means there has been severe damage to the brain. Decerebrate posturing is considered more severe brain damage than decorticate posturing.

Decorticate posturing-An abnormal posturing in which a person is stiff with bent arms, clenched fists, and legs held out straight. The arms are bent toward the body and the wrist and fingers are bent and held on the chest. This type of posturing is a sign of severe damage to the brain.

D.O.A.-Dead on Arrival, either at the scene or at the hospital.

D.R.T.-Dead Right There.

Epidural hematoma-Occurs when blood accumulates between the skull and the dura mater, (the thick membrane covering the brain). This typically occurs when a skull fracture tears an underlying blood vessel. Epidural hematomas are about half as common as a subdural hematoma and usually occur in young adults. Usually, quicker onset than subdural hematomas.

Flail chest-When two or more ribs are broken in two or more places. This can prevent the chest from expanding and contracting in its typical "billow" nature.

Flake of hose-a bended portion of hose that sits on or next to another bent section of hose. When taken off the engine, it is unloaded "one flake" at a time to prevent kinking or the proverbial "pile of spaghetti."

Forward bed-Usually the right side of the hose bed when looking from the rear of an engine. When using house with coupling as a supply line, a male end is loaded first, leaving a female **coupling on top of the hose bed that can be taken off and connected to the hydrant.**

Forward lay-When an engine lays a water supply from the hydrant to the fire. The advantage of a forward lay is that it's a quicker water supply and the engine, along with its equipment is at the fire.

FUBAR-Fucked Up Beyond All Recognition.

Fulminating pulmonary edema-During Congestive Heart Failure, (CHF), blood backs up in the lungs causing pulmonary edema, (fluid). This fluid mixes with air causing "bubbling" of the fluid that, if not treated, can accumulate, then backup in the airway, and out the mouth. If mixed with blood, it can have a pink tinge in color. A very serious condition.

G.O.M.E.R-(Gomer), Get Out of My Emergency Room, "frequent flyer."

Gurney-(Bed, cot), a device with wheels that a patient is put on to ride in the back of a vehicle. Also known as a "stretcher." They can be "one man," "two man," (back breaker), or motorized.

Heel-To hold onto a hose line so it does not get caught up in the hose bed. Usually a supply line.

Incident Command System-(ICS), An organized approach to a large incident that stresses accountability and safety. Also known as **Incident Management System**, (IMS).

Manifold-Usually a three to six port device that is attached at one end to large diameter hose, (supply), and several attack lines connected to the ports. Each port has its own control lever that can be opened or closed with no affect to the other lines.

Monitor-(Deluge), a large device that can deliver several hundred gallons of water depending on the diameter of the nozzle. A monitor is different from a deck gun as it is not pre-plumbed into the engine and can be portable.

P.A.S.S. device-Personal Alarm/Alert Safety System. A device designed to alert rescuers using an audible signal technology. The devise is attached to the firefighters breathing apparatus harness. When turned on, the device will emit a ninety-five decibel "chirp" if the user has been motionless for 20-30 seconds. By touching or moving the device, the "chirp" stops. If the firefighter is incapacitated for more than thirty seconds, the device will "chirp" continuously until the firefighter manually shuts off the device. Most PASS devices are equipped with a flashing strobe light to assist rescuers during their search for the downed firefighter. Also known as **P.A.L.** (Personal Alarm Locator).

Paradoxical respirations-When one side of the chest contracts while the other side expands during respirations. Usually indicative of a flail chest.

Preconnected-A hose that is already connected to the "plumbing" system of a fire engine. The firefighter shoulder loads the hose and advances to the fire without the driver having to connect the hose to a discharge port.

Reverse lay-Usually located on the left side of the engine, when looking from the rear. When coupled hose is used as a supply line. The female, coupling is laid first, ending with the male coupling on top of the hose bed. There is usually a nozzle attached to the male coupling. If a forward lay must be extended, a reverse bed be attached using a double female.

Reverse lay-When the engine lays hose from the first to the hydrant. This evolution is done it it's a large fire and you need to increase the flow of water under pressure from the hydrant. This evolution is also used in defensive fires where there is a possibility of harm to the firefighters. Unless a "short or full strip" of the engine is done, all the equipment is at the hydrant.

S.N.A.F.U.-Situation Normal All Fucked Up.

Subdural hematoma-A pooling or collection of blood between the brain and its outer most lining, (Dura). It's usually caused be a head injury strong enough to burst blood vessels. This can cause the pooled blood to push on the brain causing decerebrate or decorticate posturing. Age, blood-thinning drugs, and alcohol abuse increase risk.

Tag tight-When a hydrant is located next to the fire scene and the engineer can use a short section of hose to connect the engine to the hydrant.

T.I.C-(Thermal Imaging Camera). A hand-held device that can detect heat through a wall or ceiling. Can also be used at night on car accident scenes to detect patients who have been thrown clear of vehicles.

T.M.B.-Too Many Birthdays.

1 ½" & 1 ¾" hose-Attack lines that are used for extinguishing fires. Depending on nozzle selection, they can deliver between 150-250 gallons of water per minute.

2 ½" hose-Hose that can be used for attack or supply. Usually use in large commercial fires. Much more difficult to control and maneuver than smaller attack lines.

4" & 5" hose-Hose used for supplying large amounts of water from hydrant to engine, engine to engine, and engine to a ladder truck with a nozzle, (water tower or snorkel). Also know as **Large Diameter Hose**.